W9-DGJ-015

NO POSTAGE
NECESSARY
IF MAILED
IN THE
UNITED STATES

BUSINESS REPLY CARD
FIRST CLASS   PERMIT NO. 33107   PHILADELPHIA, PA

POSTAGE WILL BE PAID BY ADDRESSEE

HANLEY & BELFUS, INC.
Medical Publishers
P.O. Box 1377
Philadelphia, PA 19105-9990

I..lll.l....lllll....l.l.l.l.l..l.l..l.l.l..ll..l..l..ll

NO POSTAGE
NECESSARY
IF MAILED
IN THE
UNITED STATES

BUSINESS REPLY CARD
FIRST CLASS   PERMIT NO. 33107   PHILADELPHIA, PA

POSTAGE WILL BE PAID BY ADDRESSEE

HANLEY & BELFUS, INC.
Medical Publishers
P.O. Box 1377
Philadelphia, PA 19105-9990

I..lll.l....lllll....l.l.l.l.l..l.l..l.l.l..ll..l..l..ll

STATE OF THE ART REVIEWS (STARs)

SUBJECT	FREQUENCY	PRICE (U.S.)	PRICE (Foreign)	PRICE (Single)
☐ CARDIAC SURGERY	Triannual	$88.00	$98.00	$38.00
☐ NEUROSURGERY	Biannual	$75.00	$84.00	$42.00
☐ OCCUPATIONAL MEDICINE	Quarterly	$68.00	$78.00	$29.00
☐ PHYSICAL MED & REHAB (PM&R)	Quarterly	$66.00	$76.00	$28.00
☐ SPINE	Triannual	$78.00	$88.00	$34.00

☐ 1989 subscription ☐ 1988 subscription   ☐ Single issue
Check subject title above.   Title _____

I enclose payment: ☐ Check ☐ Visa ☐ Master Card   Credit Card # _____ Exp. Date _____
Name _____   Signature _____
Title _____   Street Address _____
Company/Hospital _____   City/State/Zip _____

Send order to:
HANLEY & BELFUS, INC.
210 South 13th Street / Philadelphia, PA 19107 / 215-546-7293

STATE OF THE ART REVIEWS (STARs)

SUBJECT	FREQUENCY	PRICE (U.S.)	PRICE (Foreign)	PRICE (Single)
☐ CARDIAC SURGERY	Triannual	$88.00	$98.00	$38.00
☐ NEUROSURGERY	Biannual	$75.00	$84.00	$42.00
☐ OCCUPATIONAL MEDICINE	Quarterly	$68.00	$78.00	$29.00
☐ PHYSICAL MED & REHAB (PM&R)	Quarterly	$66.00	$76.00	$28.00
☐ SPINE	Triannual	$78.00	$88.00	$34.00

☐ 1989 subscription ☐ 1988 subscription   ☐ Single issue
Check subject title above.   Title _____

I enclose payment: ☐ Check ☐ Visa ☐ Master Card   Credit Card # _____ Exp. Date _____
Name _____   Signature _____
Title _____   Street Address _____
Company/Hospital _____   City/State/Zip _____

Send order to:
HANLEY & BELFUS, INC.
210 South 13th Street / Philadelphia, PA 19107 / 215-546-7293

Cardiac Surgery

Cardiothoracic Transplantation II

Medical Management and Complications

Robert W. Emery, M.D.
Marc R. Pritzker, M.D.
Frazier Eales, M.D.
Guest Editors

Volume 3/Number 3   October 1989
HANLEY & BELFUS, INC.   Philadelphia

STATE OF THE ART REVIEWS

Publisher: HANLEY & BELFUS, INC.
              210 South 13th Street
              Philadelphia, PA 19107

CARDIAC SURGERY: State of the Art Reviews   (ISSN 0887-9850)
October 1989   Volume 3, Number 3   (ISBN 0-932883-90-7)

CARDIAC SURGERY: State of the Art Reviews is published triannually (three times per year) by Hanley & Belfus, Inc., 210 South 13th Street, Philadelphia, Pennsylvania 19107.

POSTMASTER: Send address changes to CARDIAC SURGERY: State of the Art Reviews, Hanley & Belfus, Inc., 210 South 13th Street, Philadelphia, PA 19107.

This issue is Volume 3, Number 3.

The Editor of this publication is Linda C. Belfus.

This volume is dedicated to our children,
who also live with transplantation:

Kate, Liz, Chris, and R. J. Emery
Joshua and Laura Pritzker
Kate, Sarah, Liv, and Marit Eales

PUBLISHED ISSUES, 1986–1989

FUTURE ISSUES

Subscriptions and single issues available from the publisher—Hanley & Belfus, Inc.,
Medical Publishers, 210 South 13th Street, Philadelphia, PA 19107 (215) 546-7293.

CONTENTS

Twenty years have passed since the first attempted use of a total artificial heart as a bridge to cardiac transplantation; however, the first successful use did not occur until 1985. The cooperation of principal investigators from 38 centers worldwide has resulted in the collection of data for the 171 patients who received the total artificial heart as a bridge to cardiac transplantation between 1969 and 1989. This chapter includes the analyzed data with complete patient follow-up, with the exception of the Russian heart.

Although seven different total artificial heart designs have now been implanted in man, the pneumatic Jarvik-7 has gradually become the leading clinical tool for short-term mechanical cardiac replacement. Despite the amazing pumping capabilities of total artificial heart devices, major complications, contraindications to transplantation, and deaths have plagued the trials of all total artificial heart designs. This chapter categorizes the major sequelae following Jarvik-7 implantation and discusses the approaches taken to alleviate or reduce their impact on patient outcome.

When evaluating candidates with pulmonary hypertension for heart-lung transplantation, bilateral lung transplantation, or single lung transplantation, those patients with chronic pulmonary embolism should undergo thromboendarterectomy rather than transplantation. Thromboendarterectomy is currently associated with a lower hospital mortality than heart-lung transplantation, the ravages of immunosuppression are avoided, long-term survival is improved, and precious donor organs are spared.

The ethical fundamentals of transplantation are the same as for other areas of health care: to try to provide appropriate, safe, and effective treatment to whomever needs it. Toward that end, the author addresses three of the major issues that need to be addressed in the formulation of an ethical approach to transplantation: prioritization or allocation of resources, fairness of access and delivery, and safety and credentializing issues.

Protecting the delicate pulmonary structural and functional elements from operative trauma and ischemic damage, facilitating immediate post-transplant function, and allowing distant procurement and maximal utilization of the organ pool are the goals of pulmonary preservation methods. The author presents the lung preservation method used by his institution, which has proved to be simple, reproducible, and adaptable to distant multiple organ procurements.

This chapter reviews the limited literature on double lung transplantation and the pathophysiology of the denervated lung, and concentrates on anesthetic considerations for the recipient operative procedure.

The primary steps in the development of acute cardiac allograft rejection are discussed and the need for effective new immunosuppressive agents with allospecificity is addressed.

Cyclosporine has revolutionized the field of clinical transplantation and has proved useful in the study of cellular immunology. This chapter reviews studies on the mechanism of action of cyclosporine and discusses the effects of cyclosporine on the immune response.

In order to minimize the toxic effects of commonly used antirejection agents, the authors have devised a protocol for multidrug immune suppression in patients who have been mechanically supported prior to human heart transplant. The basis of this support, the use of OKT3, allows other drugs to be administered initially at lower doses to minimize toxic side effects yet enhance immunosuppression.

The authors present a study that confirms prior reports that Doppler echocardiographic indices of cardiac function are useful as a noninvasive method of evaluating patients for myocardial rejection.

This chapter discusses organisms documented to be transmitted by transplantation of the heart and/or lungs—cytomegalovirus, Epstein-Barr virus, human immune deficiency virus (HIV-1), and *Toxoplasma gondii*—and focuses on diagnosis and treatment of primary infection and disease.

The authors review general surgical complications following transplantation and general surgical diseases not directly related to the transplant procedure in their series of 78 cardiac and cardiopulmonary transplants performed in 75 patients at the Minneapolis Heart Institute over a four-year period.

The introduction of cyclosporine, by improving the results of allografting and thus accentuating the need for a markedly increased donor supply, has stimulated surgeons to look anew at the possibilities of xenotransplantation. Clinical experience with xenotransplantation of solid organs and recent experimental data are presented.

CONTRIBUTORS

William Auger, M.D.
Assistant Professor of Medicine, University of California, San Diego, Medical Center, San Diego, California

David K.C. Cooper, M.D., Ph.D., FRCS
Director of Research and Education, Oklahoma Transplantation Institute, Baptist Medical Center, Oklahoma City, Oklahoma

Jack G. Copeland, M.D.
Professor of Surgery, University of Arizona Health Science Center, Tucson, Arizona

Steve Crane, R.N.
Department of Nursing, University of Arizona Health Science Center, Tucson, Arizona

Pat O. Daily, M.D.
Clinical Professor of Surgery, University of California, San Diego, Medical Center; Director, Cardiovascular Surgery, and Codirector, Cardiac Transplant Program, Sharp Memorial Hospital, San Diego, California

Walter P. Dembitsky, M.D.
Clinical Associate Professor, Division of Cardiac Surgery, University of California, San Diego, Medical Center; Codirector, Transplant Program, Sharp Memorial Hospital, San Diego, California

Daniel H. Dunn, M.D.
Clinical Assistant Professor of Surgery, University of Minnesota Medical School; General Surgeon, Abbott Northwestern Hospital, Minneapolis, Minnesota

Frazier Eales, M.D.
Chairman, Department of Cardiovascular Disease, University of Minnesota Medical School, Abbott Northwestern Hospital, Minneapolis, Minnesota

Robert W. Emery, M.D.
Director, Cardiothoracic Transplantation, and Cardiovascular and Thoracic Surgeon, Minneapolis Heart Institute, Abbott Northwestern Hsopital, Minneapolis, Minnesota

John Eugene, M.D.
Assistant Professor of Surgery, University of California, Irvine, Medical Center, Orange, California

James M. Gayes, M.D.
Department of Anesthesiology, Abbott Northwestern Hospital, Minneapolis Heart Institute, Minneapolis, Minnesota

Luis Giron, M.D.
Department of Anesthesiology, Abbott Northwestern Hospital, Minneapolis Heart Institute, Minneapolis, Minnesota

Irvin F. Goldenberg, M.D.
Director of Research, Minneapolis Heart Institute; Clinical Assistant Professor, University of Minnesota Medical School, Minneapolis, Minnesota

Frances M. Hoffman, R.N., M.S.
Transplant Clinic Coordinator, Division of Cardiothoracic Transplantation, Abbott Northwestern Hospital, Minneapolis, Minnesota

Dan R. Holder, Pharm.D.
Research Associate, Cardiothoracic Transplantation, Minneapolis Heart Institute, Minneapolis, Minnesota

Timothy B. Icenogle, M.D.
Assistant Professor of Surgery, University of Arizona Health Science Center, Tucson, Arizona

Kristen E. Johnson, R.N.
Program Director, Mechanical Cardiac Replacement, Minneapolis Heart Institute, Minneapolis, Minnesota

Charles R. Jorgenson, M.D., Ph.D.
Director, Division of Artificial Heart, Cardiovascular and Thoracic Surgeon, Minneapolis Heart Institute; Clinical Associate Professor of Medicine, University of Minnesota Medical School, Minneapolis, Minnesota

Lyle D. Joyce, M.D., Ph.D.
Director, Division of Artificial Heart, and Cardiovascular and Thoracic Surgeon, Minneapolis Heart Institute, Minneapolis, Minnesota

Kathleen D. Lake, Pharm.D.
Program Director, Division of Cardiothoracic Transplant Surgery and Research, Minneapolis Heart Institute, Abbott Northwestern Hospital; Clinical Assistant Professor, College of Pharmacy, University of Minnesota, Minneapolis, Minnesota

Mark M. Levinson, M.D.
Department of Surgery, Section of Cardiothoracic Surgery, Providence Medical Center, Seattle, Washington

Kathryn R. Love, M.D.
Infectious Diseases Consultant and Hospital Epidemiologist, Abbott Northwestern Hospital, Minneapolis, Minnesota

Stephen A. Mikitish
Supervisor, Metal Shop, Department of Physical Resources, University of Arizona Health Science Center, Tucson, Arizona

Timothy C. Mills, Ph.D.
Department of Surgery, University of California, Irvine, Medical Center, Orange, California

Kenneth M. Moser, M.D.
Professor of Medicine, University of California, San Diego, Medical Center, San Diego, California

Robert J. Nelson
Department of Artificial Heart, University of Arizona Health Science Center, Tucson, Arizona

Mark D. Nissen, M.D.
Department of Anesthesiology, Abbott Northwestern Hospital, Minneapolis Heart Institute, Minneapolis, Minnesota

John B. O'Connell, M.D.
Associate Professor of Medicine, Division of Cardiology, and Medical Director, UTAH Cardiac Transplant Program, University of Utah Medical Center, Salt Lake City, Utah

Jeanne D. Olson, R.D.M.S.
Minneapolis Heart Institute, Abbott Northwestern Hospital, Minneapolis, Minnesota

Richard A. Ott, M.D.
Assistant Professor of Surgery, California College of Medicine, University of California, Irvine, Medical Center, Orange, California

D. Glenn Pennington, M.D.
Professor of Surgery, St. Louis University School of Medicine; Director of Replacement Services, The University Hospitals; Director, Cardiac Surgery, Glennon Children's Hospital, St. Louis, Missouri

David A. Plut, M.D.
Department of Anesthesiology, Abbott Northwestern Hospital, Minneapolis Heart Institute, Minneapolis, Minnesota

Marc R. Pritzker, M.D.
Clinical Associate Professor of Medicine, University of Minnesota, Minneapolis Heart Institute, Abbott Northwestern Hospital, Minneapolis, Minnesota

Dale G. Renlund, M.D.
Assistant Professor of Medicine, University of Utah Medical Center; University Hospital, LDS Hospital, VA Hospital, Salt Lake City, Utah

David Sato, MSBE
Department of Artificial Heart, University of Arizona Health Science Center, Tucson, Arizona

Richard G. Smith, MSEE, CCE
Department of Artificial Heart, University of Arizona Health Science Center, Tucson, Arizona

Lynne Warner Stevenson, M.D.
Assistant Professor of Medicine, University of California, Los Angeles; Director, UCLA Cardiomyopathy and Transplant Clinics, Los Angeles, California

David F. Termuhlen, M.S.
Clinical Engineer, St. Louis University School of Medicine, St. Louis, Missouri

Thomas J. Von Rueden, M.D., FACS
Thoracic and Cardiovascular Surgeon, Division of Cardiothoracic Transplantation, Minneapolis Heart Institute, Minneapolis, Minnesota

PREFACE

We are pleased again to edit a volume of **Cardiac Surgery: State of the Art Reviews** on Cardiothoracic Transplantation. This edition, coupled with the one published last year, constitutes a comprehensive survey of the current status of cardiothoracic transplantation and mechanical circulatory assist. The contributors, who represent leading experts in the various disciplines, gave thoughtfully and generously of their time in preparation of their manuscripts. The contents nicely reflect the progress made over the last several years in the refinement of cardiopulmonary transplantation and the role of mechanical bridging. These papers again grew out of the annual Thoracic Organ Transplantation course presented by the Minneapolis Heart Institute and the University of Arizona which was held in February 1989 in Tucson.

We extend our sincere thanks to Cheri Galbraith, Director of Continuing Education at the Minneapolis Heart Institute, for organizing the course; to our transplant coordinators, Frances Hoffman, Michael Oleson, Jan Kilkenny, and Nancy Seimers, whose indispensable clinical assistance permitted the editors the time to assemble this publication; and to our wives, Ann, Linda, and Heidi, who have given graciously of their time and support.

ROBERT W. EMERY, MD
MARC R. PRITZKER, MD
FRAZIER EALES, MD
GUEST EDITORS

MARC R. PRITZKER, MD
CHARLES R. JORGENSON, MD
IRVIN GOLDENBERG, MD

COMPREHENSIVE MANAGEMENT OF CONGESTIVE HEART FAILURE

Marc R. Pritzker, MD
Clinical Associate Professor of
   Medicine
University of Minnesota
Minneapolis Heart Institute
Abbott Northwestern Hospital
Minneapolis, Minnesota

Charles R. Jorgenson, MD
Clinical Associate Professor
   of Medicine
University of Minnesota
Minneapolis Heart Institute
Minneapolis, Minnesota

Irvin Goldenberg, MD
Clinical Assistant Professor
   of Medicine
University of Minnesota
Minneapolis Heart Institute
Minneapolis, Minnesota

Reprint requests to;
Marc R. Pritzker, MD
Minneapolis Heart Institute
920 E. 28th St., Suite 300
Minneapolis, MN 55407

Despite recent developments that have advanced our understanding and treatment of congestive heart failure, epidemiologic and demographic data suggest that congestive heart failure will continue to remain a significant public health problem. Currently, some two million Americans manifest symptoms of congestive heart failure and are thus at risk for significant morbidity and mortality. In view of this high risk, we have recommended a comprehensive diagnostic and therapeutic program for the care of these patients.

DIAGNOSTIC STRATEGIES

In view of the diverse etiologies of disease which may cause congestive heart failure, we have recommended that all patients, except those who are clearly not candidates for interventional strategies, undergo bilateral heart catheterization, coronary arteriography, and endomyocardial biopsy where appropriate.[7] Utilizing nonionic contrast media, biplane fluoroscopy to minimize dye exposure, and newer catheterization equipment, the risk for this procedure should remain well under one half of 1%. Endomyocardial biopsy is recommended in all patients in whom catheterization discloses no obvious cause for the ventricular dysfunction and when the symptoms are of recent onset. This allows the attending physician to exclude, as best as possible, myocarditis as an etiology for the heart failure. When potentially correctable cardiac lesions are found, cardiovascular surgical

CARDIAC SURGERY: State of the Art Reviews—Vol. 3, No. 3, October 1989
   Philadelphia, Hanley & Belfus, Inc.

489

or interventional cardiology consultation is requested. At the time of admission a careful history is obtained and physical examination carried out so as to identify potentially reversible causes such as the cardiomyopathy associated with alcohol ingestion or tachyarrhythmias. Careful questioning and further testing are carried out, where appropriate, to identify patients with symptomatic ventricular arrhythmias who might profit from antiarrhythmic therapy. Unfortunately, the majority of patients seen are not candidates for corrective procedures and are therefore instructed in a comprehensive program of medical management designed to minimize morbidity and mortality.

THERAPEUTICS

Dietary. All patients receive dietary counselling from a registered dietitian regarding a no-added-salt diet. We prefer to use the no-added-salt diet rather than the more restricted diet in the majority of cases and to control symptoms of elevated left ventricular diastolic pressure through diuretic adjustment and afterload reduction. We have found that symptoms of volume overload may be controlled in the majority of patients in this way while maintaining adequate dietary intake.

Activity. All but the most severely debilitated patients are encouraged to maintain a regular walking program. This promotes a feeling of well-being and provides conditioning that allows patients to be maximally active within the confines of their cardiac disease. Patients are instructed to avoid activities that necessitate heavy isometric exertion or otherwise produce symptoms.

Anticoagulation. Congestive heart failure patients with a dilated left ventricle and impaired systolic function, atrial fibrillation, or an enlarged left atrium secondary to functional or structural mitral valve disease are at increased risk for thromboembolic complications. When no strong contraindication exists, we recommend therapeutic anticoagulation with Coumadin in order to maintain the pro-time in the range of 15–16 seconds. Careful surveillance of pro-time determinations are made at regular intervals as well as at any time the patient's clinical status deteriorates. Passive congestion of the liver may impair the metabolism of vitamin K–dependent factors and Coumadin, thereby significantly prolonging the pro-time.

Electrolyte and Renal Surveillance. Because the pharmacologic agents used to treat congestive heart failure may alter electrolyte balance and renal function, we recommend a regular (every 2–4 week) determination of the serum sodium, potassium, magnesium, blood urea nitrogen, and creatinine. The potent loop diuretics that are frequently necessary to control symptoms and findings of fluid excess are intensely potassium- and magnesium-depleting. In addition to the constitutional and musculoskeletal symptoms engendered by electrolyte imbalance, the depletion of intracellular potassium and magnesium may contribute to the genesis of potentially lethal ventricular arrhythmias. As discussed below, approximately 50% of patients with congestive heart failure will die suddenly, presumably from malignant ventricular arrhythmias.[1] Careful supplementation of potassium and magnesium is carried out under serum level monitoring.[2] This is particularly crucial following adjustments of medication dosages. The angiotensin-converting enzyme inhibitors that are frequently prescribed may either impair renal function or increase serum potassium levels to sometimes dangerous levels. Hyponatremia in association with congestive heart failure defines a subgroup with a particularly poor prognosis and a high risk of complications when therapy with angiotensin-converting enzyme inhibitors is initiated. Alterations in renal function not only may affect drug metabolism, thereby contributing to morbidity and mortality, but may also provide an indication of a satisfactory therapeutic response. We like to see a mild elevation of the blood urea nitrogen in the range of 20–40 mg% in a patient with a normal BUN and creatinine as an indication of satisfactory therapeutic volume depletion.

Antiarrhythmic Strategies

Approximately 50% of patients with congestive heart failure will die suddenly.[1,3] However, despite numerous studies designed to identify high-risk patients or reduce morbidity and mortality through the use of prophylactic antiarrhythmic agents, no such study has demonstrated a proven benefit. Strategies investigated have included the identification of patients with nonsustained ventricular tachycardia or complex ventricular ectopy by Holter monitoring, invasive electrophysiologic study, or the prophylactic administration of conventional 1A, 1C or type 3 antiarrhythmic agents. We therefore currently recommend treatment only in patients with symptomatic abnormalities of cardiac rhythm. In these patients, we believe that the use of programmed electrophysiologic stimulation best defines a therapeutic antiarrhythmic program. Because the incidence of pro-arrhythmia is increased in patients with left ventricular dysfunction, initiation of antiarrhythmic therapy should be carried out in the hospital under continuous rhythm monitoring.

Pharmacologic Therapy

Given current pathophysiologic understanding of the host of adaptive and maladaptive adjustments engendered by the poorly functioning heart, it has been possible to design therapeutic regimens that intercede at a variety of key junctures in the disease process.

Contractility.   As contractile dysfunction appears to be a primary descriptive, if not pathophysiologic, event in congestive heart failure, it is not surprising that the oldest of modern pharmacologic interventions has been directed at augmenting contractility. The use of digitalis glycosides for the treatment of dropsy dates back to the late 18th century, and recent research has confirmed their ongoing value in the treatment of symptoms of congestive heart failure. In these recent studies, deterioration of clinical status was noted in patients in whom the drug was withdrawn, whereas in other studies, augmentation of clinical condition was noted with the addition of digitalis preparations. Because of the narrow therapeutic to toxic range of digitalis glycosides, the changing metabolism with the coadministration of other drugs, and the protean manifestations of its toxicity in otherwise ill patients, the utilization of these drugs requires careful patient surveillance.

The search for a non-glycoside pharmacologic agent has become the holy grail of pharmacologic cardiology. As of this day, little in the way of absolutely clear-cut clinical data showing efficacy has been published, although a broad body of anecdotal data suggests that significant developments in this area may be at hand.[8]

Increased Preload.   Many of the incapacitating symptoms and signs of congestive heart failure are a result of an increased preload owing to salt and water retention. Alleviation of these symptoms may do much to enhance the mobility and sense of well-being of patients with congestive heart failure. We believe that aggressive, carefully monitored diuretic therapy is a cornerstone of patient management. Loop diuretics, including furosemide, metolazone or ethacrynic acid, are carefully titrated to eliminate edema, orthopnea, and paroxysmal nocturnal dyspnea and frequently improve dyspnea on exertion as well. Careful supplementation and monitoring of key electrolytes, including sodium, potassium and magnesium, are mandatory. In patients in whom potassium is exceptionally depleted or is recalcitrant to the diuretic effect of loop-acting drug, a postassium-sparing diuretic such as aldactone is added. Elevation of the BUN:creatinine ratio frequently occurs in these patients and moderate elevations serve as a useful marker of the diuretic effect. Once stabilized on a diuretic regimen, the patient's weight is noted and utilized as both a target and a monitoring parameter. We currently ask our patients to weigh themselves daily and report weight gains greater than 1 pound per day. The use of this monitoring frequently allows for additional diuretic administration on an early outpatient basis, forestalling admissions for clinical deterioration.

Use of Afterload Reducing Drugs or Converting Enzyme Inhibitors.   Of all the therapies to emerge from heart failure research, only afterload reducing drugs or angiotensin-converting enzyme inhibitors have been shown to prolong survival in patients with Class III and IV symptoms. To date, several randomized studies utilizing apresoline and isosorbide dinitrate, captopril or enalapril have shown mortality reductions of 20–35% over the length of the trials in treated patients. These drugs are considered to be mandatory in current treatment. Careful titration is necessary, as these drugs may seriously lower blood pressure, although the level of blood pressure per se should not preclude their administration. It is common for pre-treatment blood pressures of 90 systolic to remain unchanged following treatment with maximum doses of these agents. We generally begin with modest doses, titrating every several days to a dosage that consistently produces lightheadedness, suggesting a poorly tolerated decline in blood pressure, and then retreat somewhat on the dosage. Caution should be exercised in initiating therapy with these agents in patients in whom a recent, acute diuresis has been obtained, as precipitous decreases in blood pressure may occur. Careful monitoring of electrolytes and renal function is also recommended. Clinical trials are currently under way to assess the impact of these drugs in patients with lesser degrees of heart failure as well as in asymptomatic patients with reduced ejection fractions.[4–6]

REFERENCES

1. Bigger JT Jr: Why patients with congestive heart failure die: Arrhythmias and sudden cardiac death. Circulation 75(Suppl 4):4–28, 1987.
2. Chadda K: Efficacy of magnesium supplementation in patients with hypomagnemia. Circulation 70(Suppl II):444, 1984.
3. Chandler SL: Clinical determinants of mortality in chronic congestive heart failure secondary to idiopathic dilated or to ischemic cardiomyopathy. Am J Cardiol 59:634–638, 1987.
4. Cleland JGE: Effect of enalapril in heart failure. Br Heart J 54:305–312, 1985.
5. Cohn JN: Effect of vasodilator therapy on mortality in chronic congestive heart failure: Results of a Veterans Administration Cooperative Study. N Engl J Med 314:1547–1552, 1986.
6. Packer M: Physiologic and pharmacologic determinants of vasodilator response. Prog Cardiovasc Dis 25:275, 1982.
7. Srebo J: Congestive heart failure. Curr Probl Cardiol 23:1, 1986.
8. Weber KT: Newer positive inotropic agents in the treatment of chronic cardiac failure: Current status and future directions. Drug 33:503–519, 1987.
9. Wilson JR: Effect of diuresis on the performance of the failing left ventricle in man. Am J Med 70:234, 1981.

LYNNE WARNER STEVENSON, MD

MEDICAL THERAPY TAILORED FOR ADVANCED HEART FAILURE

Assistant Professor of Medicine
UCLA School of Medicine
Los Angeles, California

Reprint requests to:
Lynne Warner Stevenson, MD
Department of Medicine
UCLA School of Medicine
Los Angeles, CA 90024

The success of cardiac transplantation has encouraged the identification and referral of patients with advanced heart failure who previously would have been condemned to a miserable and short existence in their communities. This population has now been concentrated at transplant centers, where the supply of donor hearts will never be adequate for the majority of patients. There are currently over 1000 patients on the UNOS waiting list, to which 50% more patients are added than are transplanted each month. The average waiting time now exceeds 4 months, and many patients wait over a year. Thus the chance of cardiac transplantation has paradoxically forced the design of optimal medical therapy for short-term and in some cases for long-term management of this uniquely compromised population.

Over 90% of patients referred for transplantation have heart failure associated with a dilated left ventricle, in whom the majority have chronic heart failure with either acute or subacute decompensation. This chapter focuses on medical therapy for this population, rather than on patients with acute ventricular failure such as may be seen following cardiopulmonary bypass or acute massive infarction, or on patients with primarily restrictive cardiomyopathies.

While the majority of patients referred for transplantation have ejection fractions below 25%, many patients with low ejection fractions are well-compensated both hemodynamically and functionally, and are able to continue with regular employment and activities. Unless such patients have symptomatic evidence of

CARDIAC SURGERY: State of the Art Reviews—Vol. 3, No. 3, October 1989
Philadelphia, Hanley & Belfus, Inc.

493

life-threatening ventricular arrhythmias or ischemia, transplantation is unlikely to offer major benefit and these patients will rarely be referred for evaluation. Patients referred are generally those with severe symptoms of heart failure (or occasionally of refractory ventricular arrhythmias) despite the standard application of the therapies available in their communities. The clinical and hemodynamic profile of 150 patients with chronic heart failure discharged after evaluation for transplantation in the UCLA Cardiomyopathy Center is shown in Table 1.

The referral of such patients is frequently considered a defeat for medical therapy. But are all these patients really refractory? If the only alternatives were rapid transplantation or crippling congestion, transplant centers would be grim courts for most patients referred. Faced with this large population of patients ineligible for or anticipating long waits prior to transplantation, it became necessary to determine how many had truly "refractory" symptoms and how many could still derive major clinical benefit from more aggressively designed medical therapy.[8]

The new approach to patients referred with severe symptoms of heart failure despite previous use of digitalis, diuretics, and vasodilators has been predicated on the philosophy that therapy must be individually tailored to each patient with heart failure, for whom the hemodynamic status and response to types and doses of various drugs frequently cannot be predicted from empirical evaluation. While previous therapy for these patients has frequently been based upon extrapolation from other populations, specific principles have now been developed for patients with severe heart failure referred for transplantation.

By the time patients have been referred, the clinical picture is usually dominated by symptoms of left- and right-sided congestion. Inability to perform vigorous exercise has usually been long overshadowed by inability to sleep or walk to the bathroom without severe dyspnea. Patients may describe recurrent hospitalizations for intravenous diuretics that improve symptoms for only a few days, due to small fluctuations above and below the pulmonary edema threshold.

Aggressive therapy to minimize rather than merely reduce ventricular filling pressures has previously been limited by concern that cardiac output will be further compromised if congestion is completely relieved, as has been shown for

TABLE 1. Profile of 150 Patients with Ejection Fraction $\leq 20\%$ when Referred for Transplantation

Age (years)	45 ± 13
Ejection fraction	$15 \pm 3\%$
Clinical class (NYHA)	3.6 ± 0.5
Orthopnea (0–4 scale)	3 ± 1
Hospitalization (# previous 6 mos)	2 ± 2
Cardiac index $(L/min/m^2)$	$2.0 \pm .6$
Pulmonary wedge pressure (mm Hg)	28 ± 9
Pulmonary arterial pressure (mm Hg)	55 ± 16
Right atrial pressure (mm Hg)	13 ± 9
Mean arterial pressure (mm Hg)	84 ± 10
Systemic vascular resistance (dynes-sec-cm^{-5})	1700 ± 700
Left ventricular diameter (diastolic, mm)	76 ± 10

some patients with acute myocardial infarction. However acute myocardial infarction is associated with increased stiffness of relatively normal-sized ventricles. Chronic heart failure is usually associated with very large ventricles in which compliance has slowly increased. It has recently been shown that in the chronically dilated ventricle, reduction of filling pressures to normal levels can frequently be achieved simultaneously with maximal cardiac outputs.[10]

Achieving minimal filling pressures is important not only to relieve congestive symptoms, but also to reduce the internal afterload of the failing ventricle. While afterload reduction has generally been employed to improve ventricular ejection by reducing external vascular resistance, the internal afterload is increased by the large ventricular volumes and the secondary mitral regurgitation present in most patients with advanced heart failure.[11] In these patients, total afterload reduction does not significantly increase ejection fraction, but improves stroke volume by reducing the backward flow lost to mitral regurgitation.[6] Because the major determinant of the mitral regurgitation may be the ventricular volume, aggressive reduction of ventricular filling pressures and volumes is actually a key to maximizing cardiac output.

Many patients can maintain good functional capacity on diuretics and vasodilators adjusted empirically in the outpatient setting. However, when severe symptoms of dyspnea and weakness persist despite such efforts, or when symptomatic therapy is limited by declining blood pressure, sodium, or renal function, more exact tailoring of therapy is necessary. Because the physical examination is frequently unreliable for the assessment of filling pressures in chronic heart failure,[9] adjustment of therapy during invasive hemodynamic monitoring may be necessary in order to establish the minimum filling pressure and the oral drug regimen that will effectively maintain it.

These principles have been incorporated into the design of tailored medical therapy (Table 2). Previous data have suggested that the use of hemodynamic parameters for the adjustment of therapy did not predict clinical efficacy.[2,5] However such data pertained to patients with milder heart disease in which the

TABLE 2.   Tailored Therapy for Advanced Heart Failure

1. Measurement of baseline hemodynamics
2. Intravenous nitroprusside and diuretics tailored to hemodynamic goals:
   PCW $\leq$ 15 mm Hg
   SVR $\leq$ 1200 dynes-sec-cm^{-5}
   RA $\leq$ 9 mm Hg
   SBP $\geq$ 80 mm Hg
3. Definition of optimal hemodynamics by 24–48 hours
4. Titration of high-dose oral agents while nitroprusside weaned
5. Ambulation, diuretic adjustment for 24–48 hours
6. Maintain digoxin if no contraindication
7. Detailed patient education
8. Flexible diuretic regimen
9. Progressive walking program
10. Vigilant follow-up

RA = right atrial pressure, PCW = pulmonary capillary wedge pressure, SBP = systolic blood pressure, SVR = systemic vascular pressure major limitation was intolerance to prolonged exercise. Drugs in these studies were frequently studied after only one dosing interval or after a fractional change in filling pressure or cardiac output, and were not adjusted to achieve absolute hemodynamic goals. In addition, the constant diuretic doses required by many trials have limited the benefit observed from vasodilator therapy for advanced heart failure, in which the daily diuretic requirements may change markedly after vasodilator therapy as well as during daily fluctuations in intake and activity. The major reason for apparent failure of an initially effective vasodilator regimen is fluid retention, which can in most patients under 65 without intrinsic renal disease be controlled by loop diuretics and metolazone therapy adjusted to daily weights.

Tailored therapy has been shown to allow discharge and prolonged clinical improvement in patients transferred for urgent transplantation as "refractory" to previous drug therapy.[8] In the overall population of patients with ejection fraction $\leq 20\%$ who were discharged after transplant evaluation, such therapy was associated with a 1-year survival of 63% without transplantation. This is in contrast to an expected survival of $< 50\%$ based on initial ejection fraction, hemodynamic parameters, clinical class, and deteriorating status at the time of referral.[3,4,12]

Following the systematic application of tailored therapy, patients can be reclassified as critical, unstable, or clinically stable (Fig. 1). The critical patients, many of whom have decompensated following a new myocardial infarction or cardiopulmonary bypass, have essentially no predicted survival without transplantation, but have a survival of 70-80% at 1 year with transplantation.[7] While their early postoperative mortality exceeds that of more stable patients, the expected benefit from transplantation is clearly greater, justifying their higher priority status for the limited donor hearts (Fig. 2).

Within the first month of tailored therapy, unstable patients are identified by the presence of increasing fluid retention despite flexible oral diuretics, systolic blood pressure less than 80 mm Hg, serum sodium falling below 130 mEq/dl, creatinine rising above 2.5 mg/dl, blood urea nitrogen rising above 60 mg/dl, frequent angina or symptomatic ventricular arrhythmias, intolerable drug side effects, or declining functional status. These patients frequently require intermittent hospitalization for intravenous diuretics or inotropic infusions, and whether they

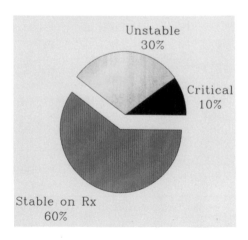

FIGURE 1. Status after medical therapy tailored to hemodynamic goals for advanced heart failure in patients referred for cardiac transplantation.

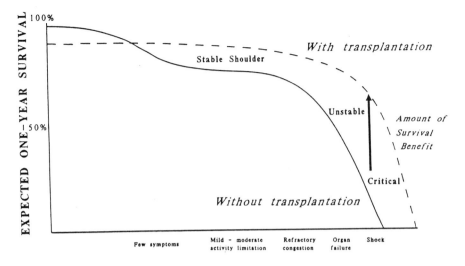

SEVERITY OF HEART FAILURE

FIGURE 2. Shoulder curve of expected survivals with and without transplantation, according to the clinical severity of heart failure.

wait at home or in the hospital for transplantation reflects more the resources of the program than their urgency. These patients have a 60–80% 1-year mortality without transplantation, and thus should deserve higher priority than the patients who appear stable.

Patients with low ejection fractions and a previous history of decompensation who can be stabilized on medical therapy, as defined above, have only a 20–30% 1-year mortality without transplantation. Although their survival is predicted to be improved by transplantation, the expected benefit is proportionately smaller. These patients currently receive the lowest priority for transplantation. As more critical patients are referred for transplantation, the wait for the apparently stable patients may lengthen to the point where they are essentially not true candidates. Unfortunately, for these patients the mode of death is rarely hemodynamic decompensation, which could be recognized during vigilant follow-up. Among patients initially stabilized on tailored medical therapy, over 80% of deaths occur suddenly and cannot be predicted with current methods of risk stratification.

The results of cardiac transplantation have improved greatly over the last 10 years, which have also seen major changes in the efficacy of medical therapy for advanced heart failure. When cardiac transplantation was a novel experiment, few patients were referred and few were transplanted. Now many patients are referred, but transplantation remains a relatively rare event, limited currently by the scarcity of donor hearts[1] rather than by the number of transplant centers offering cardiac transplantation. It is essential that all patients referred with advanced heart failure undergo systematically tailored medical therapy in order to minimize the number of urgent transplants and to improve status while on the waiting list, but more importantly to be able to provide some hope of improved quality and length of life to the majority of patients referred with heart failure, who are ineligible for cardiac transplantation.

REFERENCES

1. Evans RW, Mannihen DL, Garrison LP, Maier AM: Donor availability as the primary determinant of the future of heart transplantation. JAMA 225:1892–1898, 1986.
2. Franciosa JA, Dunkman WB, Leddy CL: Hemodynamic effects of vasodilators and long-term response in heart failure. J Am Coll Cardiol 3:1521–1530, 1984.
3. Franciosa JA, Wilen M, Ziesche S, Cohn JN: Survival in men with severe chronic left ventricular failure due to either coronary heart disease or idiopathic dilated cardiomyopathy. Am J Cardiol 51:831–836, 1983.
4. Likoff MJ, Chandler SL, Kay HR: Clinical determinants of mortality of chronic congestive heart failure secondary to idiopathic dilated or to ischemic cardiomyopathy. Am J Cardiol 59:634–638, 1987.
5. Massie BM, Kramer BL, Topic N: Lack of relationship between the short-term hemodynamic effects of captopril and the subsequent clinical response. Circulation 69:1135–1141, 1984.
6. Stevenson LW, Belil D, Grover-McKay M, et al: Effects of afterload reduction on left ventricular volume and mitral regurgitation in severe congestive heart failure. Am J Cardiol 60:654–658, 1987.
7. Stevenson LW, Donohue BC, Tillisch JH, et al: Urgent priority transplantation: When should it be done? J Heart Transplant 6:267–272, 1987.
8. Stevenson LW, Dracup KA, Tillisch JH: Efficacy of medical therapy for severe congestive heart failure in patients referred for urgent cardiac transplantation. Am J Cardiol 63:461–464, 1989.
9. Stevenson LW, Perloff JK: The limited reliability of physical signs for the estimation of hemodynamics in chronic heart failure. JAMA 261:884–888, 1989.
10. Stevenson LW, Tillisch JH: Maintenance of cardiac output with normal filling pressures in dilated heart failure. Circulation 74:1303–1308, 1989.
11. Strauss RH, Stevenson LW, Dadourian BJ, Child JS: The predictability of mitral regurgitation detected by Doppler echocardiography in patients referred for cardiac transplantation. Am J Cardiol 59:892–898, 1987.
12. Unverferth DV, Magorien RD, Moeschberger ML, et al: Factors influencing the one-year mortality of dilated cardiomyopathy. Am J Cardiol 54:147–152, 1984.

TIMOTHY B. ICENOGLE, MD[1]
RICHARD G. SMITH, MSEE, CCE[2]
DAVE SATO, MSBE[2]
STEVE CRANE, RN[3]
ROBERT NELSON[2]
STEPHEN A. MIKITISH[4]
JACK G. COPELAND, MD[1]

TRANSPORT OF THE CRITICALLY ILL END-STAGE CARDIAC PATIENT

From the University of Arizona
   Health Sciences Center

[1]Section of Cardiovascular and
   Thoracic Surgery
[2]Department of Artificial Heart
[3]Department of Nursing
[4]Department of Physical
   Resources

Reprint requests to:
Timothy B. Icenogle, MD
Assistant Professor of Surgery
Section of Cardiothoracic Surgery
University of Arizona
   Health Science Center
1501 N. Campbell Ave.
Tucson, Arizona 85724

Cardiac care services are widely available in the United States and unstable patients can be rapidly transported by ambulances or aeromedical helicopters for lifesaving therapy. The temporary ambulance environment for these patients is satisfactory; the main goal is rapid transport to a facility offering definitive therapy.

Critically ill end-stage cardiac patients may require transport from a tertiary care facility to a center with cardiac transplantation and pulsatile mechanical assist availability. Approximately 150 heart transplant centers serve the United States but only a few of these centers have pulsatile support devices. These devices are expensive, experimental, and limited to about 20 centers per device. Patients who require these services are not only critically ill but are usually quite unstable and can be very challenging to transport. This chapter explores the present status and the future of long-distance transport of the critically ill end-stage cardiac patient.

THE PRESENT STATUS OF AIR TRANSPORT

A brief review of the present status of the air ambulance industry is necessary to comprehend its limitations. Long-distance transport generally requires fixed-wing aircraft. The rough ride and slow speed of ambulances limit their efficacy for transport of the critically ill. Helicopters have a cramped cabin, high noise levels, and a limited fuel supply that makes them unattractive for transports of over 100 miles. A fixed-wing aircraft offers speed, a smooth ride, and can be medically configured to replicate an intensive care unit.

Fixed-wing air ambulance services are provided by two general groups: hospitals and air-taxi operators. Hospitals frequently use turboprop aircraft in concert with helicopters for shorter transports within their region. The aircraft supports the hospital's referral network but frequently requires significant financial support. The hospital-based services have the benefit of the hospital's oversight in their management, peer review, and quality assurance.

Air-taxi operators provide air ambulance services on a charter basis. State regulations may require that a base hospital be associated with an air ambulance company, but the association is often tenuous. Air-taxi operators perform the majority of interstate transports in the United States. Their aircraft may be configured air ambulances, but many are simply executive aircraft that contain a stretcher and appropriate supplies.

"Brokers" may arrange for transport with the air ambulance operators. The broker's business is to merchandise air ambulance services, contract with the air-taxi operator, and coordinate the logistics. Frequently, glossy full-color pamphlets are sent to social workers describing air ambulance services, complete with pictures of jets with the latest medical technology. Brokering companies often give the impression that they actually perform the transport, have many employees, and have vast resources when in fact they are "paper businesses" that own no aircraft, have no full-time professional personnel, and have little or no medical equipment. There is little margin for error when transporting critically ill patients, yet some "air ambulances" have merely a plywood stretcher jammed between two seats. However, others are flying intensive care units with physicians and nurses on every flight. At the present time, there exists a wide variety in the quality of care from the very best to the dismally inadequate.

Government regulation of the air ambulance industry is sketchy. The Federal Aviation Administration (FAA) has avoided regulation of aeromedical transport. The National Transportation Safety Board (NTSB) investigates aircraft accidents and, after a series of aeromedical helicopter accidents in 1985 and 1986, issued a report with recommendations for the industry.[9] The NTSB is primarily concerned with demonstrated flight safety problems and not with medical concerns. Generally when a patient crosses state lines, there is virtually no regulation. A few states, such as Florida, have enacted laws to regulate interstate transports that originate or end in their state, but this is the exception.

Attempts at self-regulation are arising from industry organizations. The Association of Air Medical Services (AAMS) and the Professional Air Transport Association (PATA) both promote quality health care and their members are encouraged to follow organizational guidelines. The American Society of Testing and Materials subcommittee F30.01 is working to create requirements for rotary and fixed-wing transport. Their recommendations are likely to become adopted as law by many state regulatory agencies.

The busy physician has little time to arrange for patient transport services, and this task is usually delegated to the social worker who, understandably, may be unable to judge the adequacy of the aeromedical provider. To add to the confusion, some poor quality operators have company names strikingly similar to those of reputable organizations in the same area. It is into this chaos that some of the most critically ill patients are cast each year.

INTENSIVE CARE IN THE AIR—A REALITY?

Transport of critically ill patients is difficult for several reasons. The management of intravenous lines, infusion pumps, monitors, and support devices, and the patient's acute clinical condition combine to create a challenging situation during transport. In the short time frame available, an appropriately skilled physician, the necessary personnel, and medical equipment must be assembled. The intra-hospital and inter-hospital transport of critically ill patients has been associated with severe hemodynamic changes, arrhythmias, and occasionally death.[2,12,13] Attempts to improve the safety of transport have included appropriate selection and stabilization of patients, use of portable mechanical ventilators[2] and improved monitoring devices,[11] and utilization of trained ICU personnel and physicians.[4] The inter-hospital transport of acutely ill coronary patients to tertiary care centers for cardiac catheterization and possible revascularization can be safely accomplished, but the condition of this patient population is usually not as severe or life-threatening as that of critically ill end-stage heart patients. In a study of 755 coronary patients, only three were taking inotropic medications.[10] The safe transport of critically ill cardiac patients has been facilitated by use of a special stretcher with a respirator, monitoring equipment, essential cardiac drugs, and a defibrillator.[5] One study reported on the use of this special stretcher in ambulances and helicopters for relatively short distances (mean distance one way was 65 miles), but it did not include an intraaortic balloon pump (IABP) and no mention was made of compliance with FAA regulations. A specialized transport IABP in a stretcher has been safe in a limited number of ground ambulance transports but it has no other ICU devices.[6]

The flying intensive care unit is a notable technologic achievement. The aerospace environment is noisy, moves in three axes and imposes a number of limitations in space, weight, and electrical power. Space is at a premium; the medical equipment used is often a miniaturized or less sophisticated version of that found in the ICU. The patients are secured to small, uncomfortable aluminum stretchers with limited height for cardiopulmonary resuscitation. Federal Aviation Administration regulations require that the medical equipment not interfere with any of the aircraft's systems and that items of mass (i.e., medical equipment) in the cabin of an aircraft be secured to withstand the impact of a survivable crash landing.[1] A ventilator weighing 30 lbs must be secured to withstand a 9g forward force, the equivalent of a 270 lbs static pull (Fig. 1). The hardware used to secure the medical equipment must meet Military Specifications (Milspec) that govern its quality and traceability to the manufacturer.

There are limitations in electrical power. Most medical equipment runs on 120-volt AC power and aircraft generate 28-volt DC power. The aircraft must thus have an inverter to convert DC to AC power. Inverters are heavy, produce heat, and require considerable amperage to create adequate AC power for ICU devices. Careful analysis of power requirements must be considered prior to transport. Multiple layers of circuit breaker protection and redundant systems add safety. Unfortunately the manufacturing standards, reliability, and quality assurance of medical equipment fall far below the standards for products in the aerospace industry. An electrical failure of life support equipment in an aircraft

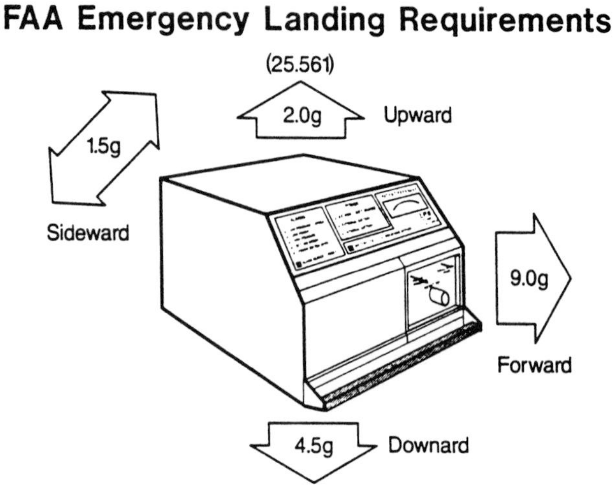

FAA Emergency Landing Requirements

FIGURE 1.   The Emergency Landing Conditions Forces per The Federal Air Regulations (FAR 25.561). Medical devices must be secured to withstand these forces if the device is in the cabin of a fixed-wing aircraft.

places at risk the health care team as well as the patient. Few things are more feared than a fire on board an aircraft.

A "systems analysis" must be performed in order to assure the safety of the ICU configuration in the aircraft. Equipment must not block the aisle or emergency exits. Compressed gases must be in approved containers and have the appropriate Milspec hardware. The electrical equipment must be checked for electromagnetic interference (EMI), so as not to interfere with the aircraft's avionics systems. This analysis is performed by an FAA Designated Engineering Representative (DER), who must file the appropriate documentation with the FAA in order to certify the configuration.

Transport with Mechanical Support Devices

Transport with mechanical support devices has been limited primarily to IABPs and to only a few flight programs.[3] Balloon pump consoles are large and cumbersome to manipulate, and difficult to secure within the aircraft. When balloon pump transports have been carried out, they usually have been done in violation of numerous FAA regulations.

Three balloon pump manufacturers now market devices for air transport. None of the three is ideal or certified by the FAA. All require an assessment by a DER, and some require modification prior to installation into an aircraft. The DER's time and the modification costs necessary to achieve FAA certification can be expensive. Prior to purchase of an air transport IABP, a DER should be retained to act as a liaison between the IABP manufacturer, the aircraft owner, the modification facility, and the local FAA office. FAA regulations are the same throughout the country but their interpretation can vary widely. Installations that are not approved in one region may be approved in another region.

At present, IABPs must be disconnected from the patient in order to load and unload. This process takes more than just a few minutes because of the complex environment of the patient with numerous medical devices. The critically ill patient may not tolerate even momentary interruptions in IABP support.

Some perfusion groups now offer their balloon pump and services to any air ambulance group that happens to have an IABP transport. This practice is mentioned only to be condemned. The safety and legality of the IABP installation are often compromised, and the flight team is working with personnel and equipment whose record is an unknown. The medical-legal exposure for the air ambulance service in these situations is considerable.

Transport with centrifugal force blood pumps has been sporadic. The Centrimed System One (Centrimed Inc. Hopkins, MN) is more easily transported than the BioMedicus (BioMedicus, Inc. Eden Prairie, MN) because of its smaller size. A perfusionist is mandatory and serial blood gas analysis is the only way to document the adequacy of the perfusion. These transports are possible; we have transported a patient 1500 miles on biventricular support with two Centrimed System One pumps, an IABP, a ventilator, three medication infusion pumps, and a pulse oximeter, without any interruptions in support or adverse effects.[7] A miniaturized blood gas/electrolytes analyzer (Gem-6 System, Mallinckrodt Sensor Systems, Ann Arbor, MI) provided serial blood gases.

The MOBI System

The University of Arizona and the Department of Artificial Heart at University Medical Center sought to create a modular mobile ICU to transport critically ill end-stage cardiac patients without interruptions in support devices or monitoring. The system, called MOBI III, now in its third prototype, is designed for use in standard ambulances and chartered Learjet 25 and 35 series aircraft.[8] Chartered aircraft are used to avoid the enormous cost of aircraft leasing or ownership. The conversion time from executive interior to ICU takes about 30 minutes. This system has a volume ventilator, pulse oximeter, IABP, defibrillator, ECG with two pressure channel monitor, and four infusion pumps mounted to a highly modified stretcher frame (Fig. 2). It can run for up to 2 hours on internal power. MOBI is taken to the referring hospital where the patient is transferred onto the stretcher frame, and then is taken by ambulance to the airport. MOBI secures to a honeycomb aluminum pallet mounted to the aircraft seat rails (Fig. 3). A dual inverter module also secures to the pallet and provides over twice the AC power required. There are five layers of circuit breaker protection in the MOBI electrical system, which will operate in engine out, main bus out, and single inverter out failure situations. The main oxygen source is a liquid oxygen convertor (Essex Cryogenics, St. Louis, MO) that carries enough oxygen for any transport in this hemisphere. MOBI has been extensively tested and meets all FAA requirements. We have performed over 20 transports of desperately ill patients by land and air without a death or a complication attributed to the transport process.

CONCLUSION

Patients who require pulsatile mechanical support devices can be found at most hospitals, but only a few centers offer definitive services for these patients. Presently, the air ambulance industry is poorly equipped to manage these critically ill patients. Transport of IABP-dependent patients is especially challenging if compliance with the law and reasonable safety are considered. Safe

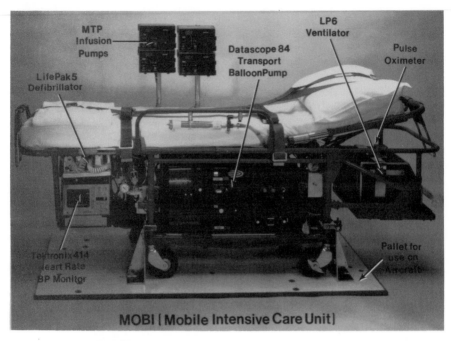

FIGURE 2. The Mobile Intensive Care Unit (MOBI).

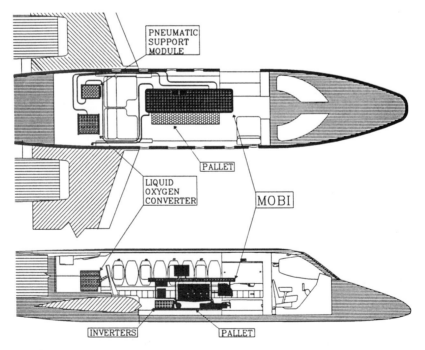

FIGURE 3. The MOBI and its support systems in the Learjet 25 series.

and efficient transport can be accomplished with a well-planned and coordinated effort. Transport of patients on balloon pumps and centrifugal force blood pumps may become increasingly common as the survival data regarding the pulsatile assist devices improve, and when a totally implantable ventricular assist device or total artificial heart becomes available. Transport of the critically ill end-stage cardiac patient may reduce the cost of these "high tech" therapies through regionalization of referrals to select centers. Regionalization would maximize the use of the equipment and experience of the mechanical assist team helping to provide the highest quality care for the lowest possible expense.

REFERENCES

1. Anonymous, Federal Aviation Administration: In Isler ML (ed): The code of Federal Regulations. Washington, D.C., U.S. Government Printing Office, 1987, 14 CFR.
2. Braman SS, Dunn SM, Amico CA, Millman RP: Complications of intrahospital transport in critically ill patients. Ann Intern Med 107:469–473, 1987.
3. Campbell P: Air transport of the intraaortic balloon pump dependent patient. Aero Med J 1:20–21, 1986.
4. Ehrenwerth J, Sorbo S, Hackel A: Transport of critically ill adults. Crit Care Med 14:543–547, 1986.
5. Gore JM, Haffajee CI, Goldberg RL, et al: Evaluation of an emergency cardiac transport system. Ann Emerg Med 12:675–678, 1983.
6. Gotlieb SO, Chew PH, Chandra N, et al: Portable intraaortic balloon counterpulsation: Clinical experience and guidelines for use. Cathet Cardiovasc Diagn 12:18–22, 1968.
7. Icenogle TB, Smith RG: Long distance transport of the asystolic patient. Aviat Space Environ Med 60:479, 1989.
8. Icenogle TB, Smith RG, Nelson R, et al: Long distance transport of cardiac patients *in extremis*: The mobile intensive care (MOBI) concept. Aviat Space Environ Med 59:571–574, 1988.
9. National Transportation Safety Board. Safety Study: Commercial emergency medical service helicopter operations. NTSB/SS-88/01. Springfield, Virginia, National Technical Information Service, 1988.
10. Rubenstein DG, Treister NW, Kapoor AS, Mahrer PR: Transfer of acutely ill cardiac patients for definitive care: Demonstrated safety in 755 cases. JAMA 259:1695–1698, 1988.
11. Taylor JO, Landers CF, Chulay JD, et al: Monitoring high-risk cardiac patients during transportation in hospital. Lancet 2:1205–1208, 1970.
12. Waddell G: Movement of critically ill patients within hospital. Br Med J 2:417–419, 1975.
13. Waddell G, Scott PD, Lees NW, Ledingham IM: Effects of ambulance transport in critically ill patients. Br Med J 1:386–389, 1975.

D. GLENN PENNINGTON, MD
DAVID F. TERMUHLEN, MS

MECHANICAL CIRCULATORY SUPPORT: DEVICE SELECTION

From the Department of Surgery
St. Louis University Medical
  Center
St. Louis, Missouri

Reprint requests to:
D. Glenn Pennington, MD
Department of Surgery
St. Louis University Medical
  Center
3635 Vista Ave. at Grand Blvd.
P.O. Box 15250
St. Louis, Missouri 63110-0250

HISTORICAL PERSPECTIVE

As early as 1928, published reports detailed devices that could substitute for or supplement the heart.[8] The development of cardiopulmonary bypass (CPB) in 1951[9] demonstrated the feasibility of mechanical circulatory support, and subsequently its clinical application grew.[15] Early reports described the application of CPB to patients in cardiogenic shock following myocardial infarction, but there were no survivors.[53] Later, other investigators successfully treated postoperative cardiogenic shock with CPB.[51] In 1968, the intra-aortic balloon pump (IABP) was introduced as an effective tool for treating cardiogenic shock.[25] Progress in the field of circulatory support was accelerated by research with the total artificial heart (TAH) and ventricular assist devices (VADs),[1] and the development of more thromboresistant biomaterials.[5] The first clinical use of a TAH occurred in 1969, when a patient was supported for 64 hours before undergoing cardiac transplantation.[6] Although the patient did not survive, it was the first "bridge-to-transplant" procedure.

Funding from the National Heart, Lung, and Blood Institute (NHLBI) allowed several groups to begin development of new designs for VADs.[3,43] Careful analyses of patients supported with IABPs provided criteria for VAD support.[31,32] By the end of the 1970s, results of the first clinical trials with VADs were being reported.[17,21,28,34,46,56] The first use of a VAD as a bridge to transplantation was reported in 1978,[33] as was the use of the IABP for bridging.[48] An artificial heart was implanted in a human being as a permanent replacement for the first time in 1982, and was followed by four more permanent implantations over the next 3 years.[10] Although all of the patients in this series suffered multiple complications, one patient was supported 21 months, demonstrating the possibility of prolonged mechanical support. Studies in bridging to transplantation with mechanical devices were continued with other devices, particularly centrifugal VADs and extracorporeal membrane oxygenation (ECMO).[36] In 1984, the first two successful bridge-to-transplant procedures were performed within 24 hours. Interestingly, two different types of VAD were used at two different centers within 100 miles of each other.[20,52] Less than a year later, a TAH was successfully used as a bridge to transplantation.[7]

Since that time, there has been increasing interest in the use of mechanical circulatory support devices for a variety of indications. The combined registry of clinical use sponsored by the American Society for Artificial Internal Organs (ASAIO) and the International Society for Heart Transplantation (ISHT) reports over 500 cases. However, this number greatly underestimates the total worldwide use of mechanical support devices, as many cases go unreported. The authors have found 993 instances of mechanical support, excluding ECMO and IABP. Indications for mechanical circulatory support are varied and a diverse selection of devices are available either commercially or with special exemption from the Food and Drug Administration (FDA) for investigational use. Some devices have been designed specifically for a particular circumstance, whereas others are capable of a variety of applications. This review attempts to classify the devices by their best proven clinical use.

PATIENT SELECTION

Regardless of the etiology of cardiac failure, patients with cardiogenic shock should meet uniform criteria to be considered for mechanical circulatory support. Conventional therapy including pharmacologic support and IABP should have been tried and found unsuccessful. Blood gas abnormalities, hypovolemia, cardiac arrhythmias, and hypothermia must be corrected to the greatest extent possible. If the patient's hemodynamic status remains unimproved and the criteria for cardiogenic shock are satisfied, mechanical support should be considered (Table 1). Patients should be excluded from mechanical support if they have any of the following conditions: chronic renal failure, severe peripheral vascular disease, symptomatic cerebrovascular disease, cancer with metastasis, severe hepatic disease, significant blood dyscrasia, severe pulmonary disease with pulmonary arterial hypertension, or severe infections resistant to antibiotic therapy. Inadequate perfusion prior to insertion of the mechanical system resulting in central nervous system damage should also exclude patients. Body size should not be a criterion for exclusion, because systems are available to support individuals of any size.

TABLE 1. Cardiogenic Shock Criteria*

Cardiac output index	< 2.0 L/min/m^2
Systemic vascular resistance	> 2100 dynes sec/cm^5
Left and/or right atrial pressure	> 20 mm Hg
Urine output	< 20 cc/hr

* Adapted from Norman.[32]

There are basically three classifications for patients who are considered for mechanical support: (1) postcardiotomy cardiogenic shock, (2) acute myocardial infarction shock, and (3) bridge to transplantation, although the distinctions between these categories can vary substantially. Patients who have suffered a perioperative myocardial infarction have a greatly decreased chance of survival when compared to patients with stunned myocardia.[37] Because these patients have a poor chance for recovery, cardiac transplantation may be a consideration. Before patients are supported with devices pending cardiac transplantation, they should be evaluated as cardiac transplant recipients, and must meet the criteria for transplantation while being supported on the device before a donor heart is used. Other patients should be evaluated for signs of myocardial recovery while being supported by a device. Through retrospective analysis, criteria have been developed[55] which indicate when a patient may be weaned from a device. Furthermore, careful evaluations prior to implantation of a device are critical so that devices are implanted in a timely fashion and patients do not deteriorate further because of an uncertain first evaluation.[47]

DEVICES AVAILABLE

The available devices can be classified several different ways. Some are investigational and require special approval by the Food and Drug Administration (FDA), whereas others can be purchased commercially. The position of the device can be described as extracorporeal, paracorporeal, heterotopic (internal or external) or orthotopic. Devices can also be classified according to their intended use, i.e., resuscitation or long-term support. Although no universal method of classification has been agreed upon by all investigators, five separate classes are presented herein which include the devices currently being used clinically: resuscitative devices; external centrifugal pumps; external pulsatile assist devices; implantable left ventricular assist systems; and orthotopic biventricular replacement prostheses (or artificial heart).

Resuscitative devices may be applied rapidly in the cardiac catheterization laboratory, intensive care unit, or emergency room for patients suffering acute cardiogenic shock unresponsive to pharmacologic support or IABP. A left atrial–femoral artery system has been developed for use in the cardiac catheterization laboratory.[27] This system requires cannulation of the internal jugular or femoral vein with transseptal puncture for placement of the left atrial catheter. Blood is withdrawn from the left atrium and returned to the femoral artery, so no oxygenator is necessary.

Two different techniques have been developed for the institution of femoro-femoral extracorporeal membrane oxygenation (ECMO): a percutaneous technique[42] and a femoral cutdown method.[39] This type of support utilizes a membrane oxygenator, in line with a heat exchanger and roller pump or centrifugal pump (Fig. 1). These ECMO systems have generally proven ineffective for periods of support longer than 48 hours, but do allow for rapid resuscitation and further patient evaluation.[24] Unfortunately, these systems require continuous heparin anticoagulation and provide incomplete biventricular support.

A new system, the Hemopump, consisting of a small spiral vane rotating at 25,000 rpm is currently undergoing clinical trials (Fig. 2).[57] It is designed to be passed through the femoral artery and across the aortic valve to allow for left ventricular-aortic perfusion.

External centrifugal pumps, including roller pumps, are commercially available and do not require special FDA approval. The combined ASAIO-ISHT

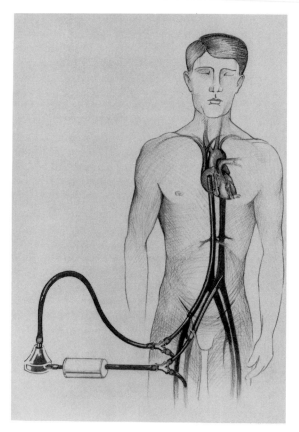

FIGURE 1.   Extracorporeal membrane oxygenation (ECMO).

registry reports 316 uses of centrifugal pumps, both for myocardial recovery and as bridges to transplantation. Several investigators have reported success in both categories.[4,29,40,49] These pumps are positioned extracorporeally, and attach to cannulae that may be placed in any of the cardiac chambers to provide the desired type of support (Fig. 3). Of the devices discussed, external centrifugal pumps are the least expensive. Furthermore, insertion of these devices does not require complicated techniques. Patient mobility is impaired because of the extracorporeal position of these devices, although greater mobility may be possible with newer designs. These pumps are well suited to short durations of support (less than 1 week), but at least one case of support of greater than 30 days before cardiac transplantation has been reported.[16]

External pulsatile assist devices have had extensive worldwide use. The Pierce-Donachy VAD developed at Pennsylvania State University[13] has been used in 205 patients. Investigators have reported successful use of this device in both bridge-to-transplantation and postcardiotomy cardiogenic shock applications.[14,38] The device is positioned paracorporeally so that it causes less impairment of patient mobility (Fig. 4). It can be used to support either the right or left side, or both if biventricular support is needed. The power source is compressed air.

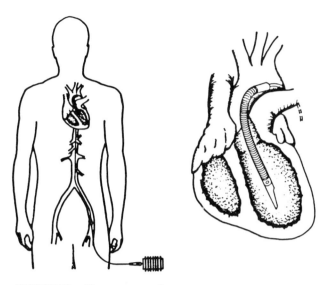

FIGURE 2.   Hemopump (Nimbus, Rancho Cordova, CA).

This device has proved to be effective for intermediate-term support. Several bridge-to-transplant patients were supported more than 30 days, and one patient was successfully transplanted after 81 days on this VAD.

The Symbion device, known as the AVAD (acute ventricular assist device), is similar to one ventricle of the artificial heart, which will be discussed later. The power source is also compressed air. Both right and left support can be provided.

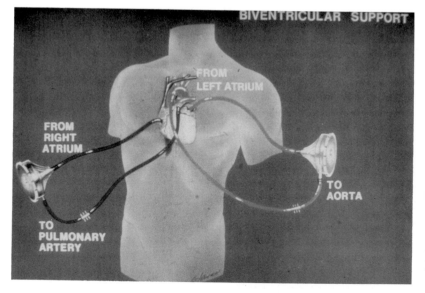

FIGURE 3.   Centrifugal pump (Biomedicus, Eden Prairie, MN).

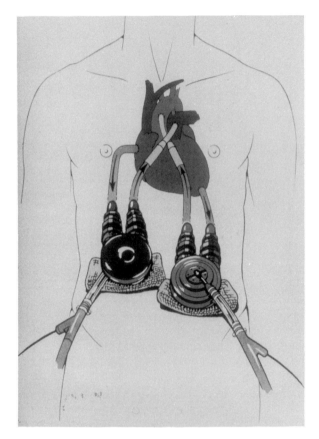

FIGURE 4.   Pierce-Donachy ventricular assist devices (Thoratec, Berkeley, CA).

There have been 79 cases, both in the postcardiotomy cardiogenic shock application and for bridge to transplantation.

The Abiomed device (the BVS 5000 or Biventricular Support System) is different in configuration from the other devices discussed in this section. It is located extracorporeally, and significantly impairs patient mobility. It has only atrial cannulae, and can provide right, left, or biventricular support. Filling of the device is accomplished by gravity, so there is no need for diastolic vacuum, which may result in less trauma to the blood. Forty-three patients have been supported with this device, both as a bridge to transplantation and pending recovery of the native myocardium.

Implantable left ventricular assist systems are of particular significance because these devices are prototypes of permanent non-tethered systems which will provide an alternative for patients with end-stage heart disease who are not suitable heart transplant candidates.[44] With the support of NHLBI contracts, several investigators are developing permanent implantable systems. Two devices (Novacor LVAS and Thermedics) are currently in clinical studies in tethered configurations. Both devices have been used in postcardiotomy and bridge-to-transplant patients.

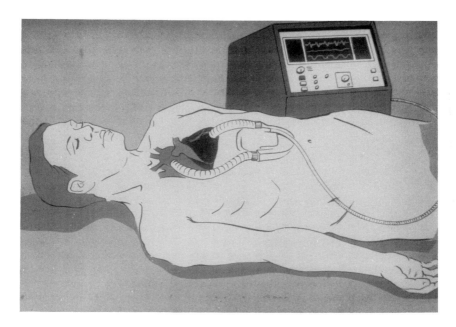

FIGURE 5. Left ventricular assist system (Novacor, Division of Baxter Healthcare Corp., Oakland, CA)

These devices are not well suited for postcardiotomy use, as they are designed for left ventricular cannulation only and require removal of a portion of myocardium at insertion. Only left-sided support can be provided with these devices, and biventricular failure has been shown to be more prevalent than previously thought.[45] Novacor has reported use of its system in 44 patients (Fig. 5), including postcardiotomy and bridge-to-transplantation applications. This device is currently the only electrical system available. An external power cable is the only element traversing the skin, allowing for excellent patient mobility. Patients have been successfully transplanted after 90 days of support with this device.

The Thermedics system is similar, except that it presently uses compressed air as its power source. A unique feature of this system is that it utilizes a textured rather than smooth blood contacting surface, so that a layer of endothelium develops. A total of 14 patients have been supported with the Thermedics device.

Orthotopic biventricular replacement prostheses (or artificial hearts, as they are commonly called) are perhaps the most publicized devices available. The Jarvik-7 TAH, manufactured by Symbion, has been used in 142 cases worldwide. Powered pneumatically, it requires removal of the patient's ventricles, and can be used only for bridge-to-transplantation applications. Two drivelines exit the abdomen, so patient mobility is not severely restricted. Twenty-seven other artificial heart implantations with seven different TAHs have been performed worldwide, but no survivors with these other devices have been reported.[23,50]

SELECTION OF THE APPROPRIATE DEVICE

Proper device selection necessitates a careful analysis of the circumstances leading to the patient's state of cardiogenic shock. Few, if any, investigative centers are fortunate to have all the previously mentioned devices at their disposal. However, it is critical to have the proper device for a given application. For the purpose of discussion, it is assumed that an investigator will have a representative of each of the five classes mentioned. In actual practice, however, the investigator's decisions are often limited by device availability. Possible scenarios for cardiogenic shock are presented below, and appropriate device choices suggested. Although it is not possible to describe every possible situation, perhaps these representative clinical circumstances will provide helpful guidelines to selecting the appropriate device. These guidelines are summarized in Table 2.

When a patient suffers an acute cardiac arrest, perhaps in the cardiac catheterization laboratory or in the emergency room, the immediate concern of the investigator is to restore perfusion to the vital organs. Rapid access to the circulatory system is therefore of paramount importance in this application. All of the systems mentioned in the section on Resuscitative Devices have this advantage, and would therefore be appropriate choices. Although these devices are generally not effective for support longer than 24 hours, they do allow a period of stabilization for further evaluation. Cardiac surgery may be an effective intervention at this point, especially for those patients having undergone unsuccessful percutaneous transluminal coronary angioplasty. If a patient is determined to be inoperable, cardiac transplantation may be considered for the patient meeting transplant criteria. Unless a donor organ is immediately available, some other system should be considered for long-term support.

TABLE 2. Guidelines for Appropriate Selection of Mechanical Circulatory Support Devices

Device	Investigational*	Position	Support	Anticoagulation Required	Preferred Application	Duration
Abiomed BVS	yes	extracorporeal	Rt, L, B	moderate	P,B-Tx	short-intermediate term
Biomedicus	no	extracorporeal	Rt, L, B	moderate	P,B-Tx	short-intermediate term
ECMO	no	extracorporeal	B	full	R	short-term
Elecath	yes	extracorporeal	L	full	R,P	short-term
Hemopump	yes	internal	L	moderate	R,P	short-term
Novacor LVAS	yes	internal	L	low	B-Tx	intermediate-long term
Pierce-Donachy VAD	yes	paracorporeal	Rt, L, B	low	P, B-Tx	intermediate-long term
Sarns/Centrimed	no	extracorporeal	Rt, L, B	moderate	P, B-Tx	short-intermediate term
Symbion AVAD	yes	paracorporeal	Rt, L, B	moderate	P, B-Tx	short-intermediate term
Symbion TAH	yes	internal	B	moderate	B-Tx	intermediate-long term
Thermedics VAD	yes	internal	L	low	B-Tx	intermediate-long term

* Investigational device exemption required from Food and Drug Administration.
BVAS = biventricular support system; ECMO = extracorporeal membrane oxygenation; LVAS = left ventricular assist system; VAD = ventricular assist device; AVAD = acute ventricular assist device; TAH = total artificial heart; Rt = right; L = left; B = biventricular; R = resuscitative; P = postcardiotomy; B-Tx = bridge-to-transplantation.

Prolonged support with ECMO may lead to bleeding and infectious complications.

Postcardiotomy ventricular failure has traditionally been the application for which mechanical support has been used, with well over 500 cases reported worldwide. Survival rates vary between 15 and 40%. Several factors figure prominently in the decision as to which device would best fit the patient's needs, but perhaps the most important is the probability of cardiac recovery. If the patient has not suffered a large perioperative myocardial infarction[37] or had previous extensive myocardial damage, the possibility for recovery should be assumed. For this reason, an artificial heart would not be an appropriate choice. The resuscitative systems may have little, if any, positive effect on myocardial recovery,[2] so these devices will not be effective for postcardiotomy cardiogenic shock. External centrifugal pumps or external pulsatile assist devices would be appropriate for this application. A second major consideration in choosing a device for postcardiotomy use is whether right, left, or biventricular failure is present. In the past, support of the left ventricle was thought to be the most crucial aspect of mechanical support. However, right ventricular support has been found to be necessary in certain circumstances.[35] A good indicator of the type of assistance needed is the associated atrial pressure of the ventricle suspected of failure. Support of the left side may "unmask" right-sided failure, or vice versa.[41] For that reason, careful evaluation of both ventricles should be made preoperatively as well as intraoperatively. When myocardial damage is severe and is believed to preclude recovery, transplantation may be considered. However, it is important to underscore the requirement that the patient be thoroughly evaluated for transplant candidacy before a firm decision is made to attempt to bridge the patient. Factors such as psychological stability, compliance, family support, and past medical history are very important considerations. Fortunately, the external pulsatile assist devices are effective for use as bridges to transplantation as well as for postcardiotomy recovery. Centrifugal pumps may not be desirable if the wait for a donor organ is extended beyond a few days.

Another circumstance that may lead to the institution of mechanical support involves the patient who has previously been evaluated for cardiac transplantation but deteriorates suddenly. Because such patients have already been selected for transplantation, devices allowing myocardial recovery need not be considered. Because the waiting time for donor organs lengthens annually, it is important to support transplant candidates on devices that may be effective for periods of more than 30 days. Minimal monitoring and adjustments and reduced impairment of patient mobility are other desirable attributes for devices intended for intermediate and long-term support. Several patients have been supported for intermediate periods (21–90 days) with the Thoratec, Novacor, and Symbion TAH, so all of these devices would be possible options for bridge-to-transplantation support. The Novacor and Thermedics VADs are implanted heterotopically and may not fit easily in all potential patients. If severe biventricular failure is present, we believe TAH or biventricular paracorporeal devices are preferable. In cases of acute rejection of a previously transplanted heart, or when a large amount of intraventricular thrombus is present, a TAH is preferred. A major consideration in the use of a TAH is that once it is implanted, the only option is transplantation, which is not possible if the patient develops a complication precluding transplantation, if a suitable donor heart cannot be located, or if a positive cytotoxic antibody screen develops..

COMPLICATIONS

Because of their inherent structure, mechanical circulatory support devices create a large surface area for blood/biomaterial interface, which is a potential site for thromboembolism and infection. Platelet activation with subsequent thrombus formation may result from contact with an artificial surface.[22] These materials also allow infectious organisms the opportunity to seed themselves.[19] Regardless of the choice of device, there will be a potentially high risk of both these complications.

To date, there has not been a large enough patient sample to compare complication rates by device. Even if it could be done, the wide variability in protocols between centers would cast doubt on the results. However, there have been retrospective analyses of results with a variety of devices at a single institution.[54] Of almost 150 patients in that study who had either ECMO, centrifugal VADs, external pulsatile VADs, or implantable devices, the complication rates with the different devices were essentially the same.

Other multicenter studies have examined the interrelation between infection and thromboembolism.[12] Among the conclusions drawn were that both these complications were persistent and serious, particularly in patients undergoing long-term support, and that these events occur regardless of the various therapies attempted. These complications are probably inevitable, so consistent patient protocols stressing preventive measures, rather than choice of device, become the primary determinant of complications.

Because patients requiring mechanical circulatory support are critically ill, they may have multiple transfusions, several invasive monitoring lines, extended durations of ventilator support, re-explorations for bleeding, and a depressed nutritional state. All of these factors may contribute to an added risk of infection. Infectious complications occur regardless of the device chosen, and no differences in the infection rates between devices have been documented. Implantable devices, such as the TAH, were thought to have a lower risk of infection, but recent studies indicate that the large amount of bioprosthetic material in the mediastinum may actually pose a higher risk for infection.[18,26] In an unpublished report, one investigator used an omental wrap around the TAH to lessen this risk, and at the time of this writing the patient had been supported 270 days without mediastinal infection.[30]

Thromboembolic complications have not been as prevalent with these devices as was once feared. However, unlike infection, which seems to afflict patients supported with any of these devices indiscriminately, thrombus formation occurs more readily with some devices than others. Both the Novacor and Thoratec devices have been used for intermediate-term support (21–90 days) without the use of prolonged heparinization. Oral dosages of warfarin (to maintain the prothrombin time approximately 1.5 times control) and dipyridamole have proved to be adequate, with little or no fibrin deposition found at the time of device explantation. The Jarvik-7 TAH does not require continuous heparinization either, although a more anticoagulated state is desirable for this device. Centrifugal pumps generally require limited heparinization, and ECMO requires full anticoagulation.

CONCLUSION

In the past 40 years, there has been significant progress in the application of mechanical circulatory support. Clinical and technologic advances have brought the dream of permanent cardiac replacement to the doorstep of reality. However, the final steps will certainly come no easier than the preceding ones. Only through cooperative efforts among investigators, manufacturers, and the government can the threshold be crossed. Before meaningful comparisons can be made between devices, several current problems with data accumulation and dissemination must be corrected. The ASAIO-ISHT registry mentioned in the text is voluntary, and unfortunately not well publicized. To further confuse matters, individual investigators maintain unofficial registries. Uniform criteria for classifying patient complications, indications, and even survival do not exist, so the data that are reported are non-uniform. Objective criteria must be established which can be applied to every investigative center and sponsor. Uniform minimal standards for data collection should be adopted. Although all investigators cannot be expected to follow identical protocols for every case with every device, more cooperative efforts are essential for progress to be made in this field.

REFERENCES

1. Akutsu T, Kolff WJ: Permanent substitutes for valves and hearts. Trans Am Soc Intern Organs 4:230–234, 1958.
2. Bavaria JE, Ratcliffe MB, Gupta KB, et al: Changes in left ventricular systolic wall stress during biventricular circulatory assistance. Ann Thorac Surg 45:526–532, 1988.
3. Bernhard WF, Poirier V, LaFarge CG, Carr JG: A new method for temporary left ventricular bypass: Preclinical appraisal. J Thorac Cardiovasc Surg 70:880–895, 1975.
4. Bolman RM, Cox JL, Marshall W, et al: Circulatory support with a centrifugal pump as a bridge to cardiac transplantation. Ann Thorac Surg 47:108–112, 1989.
5. Boretos JW, Pierce WS: Segmented polyurethane: A new elastomer for biomedical applications. Science 158:1481–1482, 1967.
6. Cooley DA, Liotta D, Hallman GL, et al: Orthotopic cardiac prosthesis for two-staged cardiac replacement. Am J Cardiol 24:723–730, 1969.
7. Copeland JG, Levinson MM, Smith R, et al: The total artificial heart as a bridge to transplantation: A report of two cases. JAMA 256:2991–2995, 1986.
8. Dale HH, Schuster EHJ: A double perfusion pump. J Physiol 64:356–364, 1928.
9. Dennis C, Spreng DS, Nelson GE, et al: Development of a pump-oxygenator to replace the heart and lungs; an apparatus applicable to human patients, and application to one case. Ann Surg 134:709–721, 1951.
10. DeVries WC: The permanent artificial heart—four case reports. JAMA 259:849–859, 1988.
11. DeVries WC, Anderson JL, Joyce LD, et al: Clinical use of the total artificial heart. N Engl J Med 310:273–278, 1984.
12. Didisheim P, Olsen DB, Farrar DJ, et al: Infections and thromboembolism with implantable cardiovascular devices. Trans Am Soc Artif Intern Organs 35:54–70, 1989.
13. Donachy JH, Landis DL, Rosenberg G, et al: Design and evaluation of a left ventricular assist device: The angle port pump. In Unger F (ed): Assisted Circulation. Berlin, Springer-Verlag, 1978, pp 138–146.
14. Farrar DJ, Hill JD, Gray LA, et al: Heterotopic prosthetic ventricles as a bridge to transplantation: A multicenter study in twenty-nine patients. N Engl J Med 318:333–340, 1988.
15. Gibbon JH Jr: Application of a mechanical heart and lung apparatus to cardiac surgery. Minn Med 37:171, 1954.
16. Golding LAR, Stewart RW, Sinkewich M, et al: Nonpulsatile ventricular assist bridging to transplantation. Trans Am Soc Artif Intern Organs 34:476–479, 1988.
17. Golding LR, Groves LK, Peter M, et al: Initial clinical experience with a new temporary left ventricular assist device. Ann Thorac Surg 29:66–69, 1980.
18. Griffith BP, Kormos RL, Hardesty RL, et al: The artificial heart: Infection related morbidity and its effect on transplantation. Ann Thorac Surg 45:409–414, 1988.
19. Gristina AG, Dobbins JJ, Giammara B, et al: Biomaterial-centered sepsis and the total artificial heart. JAMA 259:870–874, 1988.
20. Hill JD, Farrar DJ, Hershon JJ, et al: Use of prosthetic ventricle as a bridge to cardiac transplantation for postinfarction cardiogenic shock. N Engl J Med 314:626–628, 1986.

21. Holub DA, Hibbs CW, Sturm JT, et al: Clinical trials of the abdominal left ventricular assist device (ALVAD): Progress report. Cardiovascular Diseases, Bulletin of the Texas Heart Institute 6:359–372, 1979.
22. Joist JH, Pennington DG: Platelet reactions with artificial surfaces. Trans Am Soc Artif Intern Organs 33:341–344, 1987.
23. Joyce LD, Johnson KE, Cabrol C, et al: Nine year experience with the clinical use of total artificial heart as cardiac support devices. Trans Am Soc Artif Intern Organs 34:703–707, 1988.
24. Kanter KR, Pennington DG, Vandermael M, et al: Emergency resuscitation with extracorporeal membrane oxygenation for failed angioplasty (abstract). J Am Coll Cardiol 11:149A, 1988.
25. Kantrowitz A, Tjonneland S, Freed PS, et al: Initial clinical experience with intra-aortic balloon pumping in cardiogenic shock. JAMA 203:135–140, 1968.
26. Kunin CM, Dobbins JJ, Melo JC, et al: Infectious complications in four long-term recipients of the Jarvik-7 artificial heart. JAMA 259:860–864, 1988.
27. Laschinger JC, Cunningham JN, Catinella FP, et al: "Pulsatile" left atrial femoral artery bypass: A new method of preventing extension of myocardial infarction. Arch Surg 118:965–969, 1983.
28. Litwak RS, Koffsky RM, Jurado RA, et al: Use of a left heart assist device after intracardiac surgery: Technique and clinical experience. Ann Thorac Surg 21:191–202, 1976.
29. Magovern GJ, Park SB, Maher TD: Use of a centrifugal pump without anticoagulants for postoperative left ventricular assist. World J Surg 9:25–36, 1985.
30. McBride LR: Personal communication, 1989.
31. McEnany MT, Kay HR, Buckley MJ, et al: Clinical experience with intra-aortic balloon pump support in 728 patients. Circulation 58(Suppl I):124–132, 1978.
32. Norman JC, Cooley DA, Igo SR, et al: Prognostic indices for survival during postcardiotomy intra-aortic balloon pumping. J Thorac Cardiovasc Surg 74:709–720, 1977.
33. Norman JC, Cooley DA, Kahan BD, et al: Total support of the circulation of a patient with postcardiotomy stone heart syndrome by a partial artificial heart (ALVAD) for 5 days followed by heart and kidney transplantation. Lancet 1:1125–1127, 1978.
34. Olsen EK, Pierce WS, Donachy JH, et al: A two and one-half year clinical experience with a mechanical left ventricular assist pump in the treatment of profound postoperative heart failure. Int J Artif Organs 2:197, 1979.
35. Parr GVS, Pierce WS, Rosenberg G, Waldhausen JA: Right ventricular failure after repair of left ventricular aneurysm. J Thorac Cardiovasc Surg 80:79–84, 1980.
36. Pennington DG, Codd JE, Merjavy JP, et al: The expanded use of ventricular bypass systems for severe cardiac failure and as a bridge to cardiac transplantation. J Heart Transplant 3:170–175, 1984.
37. Pennington DG, McBridge LR, Kanter KR, et al: The effect of perioperative myocardial infarction on survival of postcardiotomy patients supported with ventricular assist devices. Circulation 78(Suppl III):110–115, 1988.
38. Pennington DG, McBridge LR, Swartz MT, et al: Use of the Pierce-Donachy ventricular assist device in patients with cardiogenic shock after cardiac operations. Ann Thorac Surg 47:130–135, 1989.
39. Pennington DG, Merjavy JP, Codd JE, et al: Extracorporeal membrane oxygenation for patients with cardiogenic shock. Circulation 70(Suppl I):130–137, 1984.
40. Pennington DG, Merjavy JP, Swartz MT, Willman VL: Clinical experience with a centrifugal pump ventricular assist device. Trans Am Soc Artif Intern Organs 28:93–99, 1982.
41. Pennington DG, Merjavy JP, Swartz MT, et al: The importance of biventricular failure in patients with postoperative cardiogenic shock. Ann Thorac Surg 39:16–26, 1985.
42. Phillips SJ, Zeff RH, Kongtahworn C, et al: Percutaneous cardiopulmonary bypass: Application and indication for use. Ann Thorac Surg 47:121–123, 1989.
43. Pierce WS, Brighton JA, O'Bannon W, et al: Complete left ventricular bypass with paracorporeal pump: Design and evaluation. Ann Surg 180:418–426, 1974.
44. Portner PM, Oyer PE, Jassawalla JS, et al: An alternative in end-stage heart disease: Long-term ventricular assistance. J Heart Transplant 3:47–59, 1983.
45. Portner PM, Oyer PE, Pennington DG, et al: Implantable electrical ventricular assist system: Bridge to transplantation and the future. Ann Thorac Surg 47:142–150, 1989.
46. Radvany P, Pine M, Weintraub R, et al: Mechanical circulatory support in postoperative cardiogenic shock. J Thorac Cardiovasc Surg 75:97–103, 1978.
47. Reedy JE, Swartz MT, Pennington DG, et al: Bridge to cardiac transplantation—importance of patient selection (abstract). J Heart Transplant 8:87, 1989.

48. Reemstsma K, Drusin R, Edie R, et al: Cardiac transplantation for patients requiring mechanical circulatory support. N Engl J Med 298:670–671, 1978.
49. Rose DM, Connolly M, Cunningham JN Jr, Spencer FC: Technique and results with a roller pump left and right heart assist device. Ann Thorac Surg 47:124–129, 1989.
50. Shumakov V, Zimin N, Religa Z: Clinical application of total artificial heart (TAH) by living rates (abstract). Am Soc Artif Intern Organs 18:2, 1989.
51. Spencer FC, Eiseman B, Trinkle JK, Rossi NP: Assisted circulation for cardiac failure following intracardiac surgery with cardiopulmonary bypass. J Thorac Cardiovasc Surg 49:56–73, 1965.
52. Starnes VA, Oyer PE, Portner PM, et al: Isolated left ventricular assist as a bridge to cardiac transplantation. J Thorac Cardiovasc Surg 96:62–71, 1988.
53. Stuckey JH, Newman MM, Dennis C, et al: The use of the heart lung machine in selected cases of acute myocardial infarction. Surg Forum 8:342–344, 1957.
54. Swartz MT, Pennington DG, McBridge LR, et al: Temporary mechanical circulatory support: Clinical experience with 148 patients. In Unger F (ed): Assisted Circulation. Berlin, Springer-Verlag, 1989, pp 132–151.
55. Termuhlen DF, Swartz MT, Pennington DG, et al: Predictors for weaning patients from ventricular assist devices. Trans Am Soc Artif Intern Organs 34:131–139, 1988.
56. Turina M, Bosio R, Sennig A: Clinical application of paracorporeal uni- and biventricular artificial heart. Trans Am Soc Artif Intern Organs 24:625–631, 1978.
57. Wampler RK, Moise JC, Frazier OH, Olsen DB: In "vivo" evaluation of a peripheral vascular access axial flow blood pump. Trans Am Soc Artif Intern Organs 34:450–454, 1988.

RICHARD A. OTT, MD
TIMOTHY C. MILLS, PhD
JOHN EUGENE, MD

CURRENT CONCEPTS IN THE USE OF VENTRICULAR ASSIST DEVICES

Reprint requests to:
Richard A. Ott, MD
Assistant Professor of Surgery
California College of Medicine
University of California Irvine
  Medical Center
101 The City Drive
Orange, CA 92668

Nearly 20% of patients accepted for cardiac transplantation die while waiting for a donor heart.[4] As the number of cardiac transplants increases each year, so will the fatalities of those waiting on transplant lists. In addition, approximately 1.0% of open heart surgery patients become unweanable from cardiac bypass during the surgical procedure. Mechanical ventricular assist devices (VADs) provide a realistic solution to these dilemmas.

Successful use of both heterotopic and orthotopic mechanical assist support has been reported. Clinically the heterotopic approach has the advantage of leaving the native heart in place, providing additional pre-transplant options. This approach allows the native heart a resting period during which reversible injuries may resolve. This chapter describes the technical considerations and indications for the use of several heterotopic VADs.

CENTRIFUGAL VENTRICULAR ASSIST DEVICES

By far the simplest and least expensive VADs are the centrifugal nonpulsatile assist systems. These nonocclusive pumps provide a constant flow of blood, do not require inflow or outflow valves, and may be used for right, left, or biventricular support. The cannulation can be accomplished using standard tubing for cardiopulmonary bypass. The flow rate is controlled by a small tabletop drive unit, which drives an impeller type of pump.

CARDIAC SURGERY: State of the Art Reviews—Vol. 3, No. 3, October 1989
Philadelphia, Hanley & Belfus, Inc.

521

FIGURE 1.   Centrifugal blood pump head showing internal components.

The nonpulsatile pumps may not be able to maintain end-organ perfusion adequately over long periods of time, possibly due to nonpulsatile pressure effects. A much greater concern, however, is the damage to the formed blood elements that these devices inflict. This damage, in the form of hemolysis, platelet destruction, and complement activation, limits utility of these devices to a 5–7 day period.

The most commonly used centrifugal VADs are those manufactured by Centrimed, Inc. (Hopkins, MN) and by Bio-Medicus, Inc. (Minneapolis, MN). Both devices are similar in design and function, using an acrylic cone-shaped pump head impeller mounted on a circular magnetic plate (Fig. 1). The drive motors of the blood pump spin a magnet that is isolated from the pump head magnet by a clear plastic cover. Because of the close proximity of the two magnets, their interaction locks the angular velocity of the pump head to that of the drive motor.

Inflow and outflow cannulae are usually implanted so that the VAD pumps in parallel with the affected ventricle. The cannulae are then brought through the chest wall and attached to the pump head. As the impeller rotates, the blood within the pump is centrifugally forced through the outlet and back into the circulation. The rate of blood flow is set by choosing a rotational speed for the drive motor. Changes in the patient's preload and afterload, as detected by the pump, ultimately dictate the blood flow rate for a given drive motor rpm setting. Typical flow rates achieved with these devices range from 2 to 6 L/min. The manufacturers recommend that the pump heads be changed every 24 hours to reduce the risk of thromboembolic complications.

The CardioPulmonary Support System (CPS) (Bard, Inc., Billerica, MA) consists of a Bio-Medicus, Inc. centrifugal blood pump, Normotherm blood heater system, battery pack, oxygen sources, and disposable blood bypass circuit integrated on a transport cart (Fig. 2). The disposable blood bypass circuit

FIGURE 2. Bard Cardiopulmonary Bypass System (CPS) which includes Normotherm blood heater, Bio-Medicus blood pump, and membrane oxygenator.

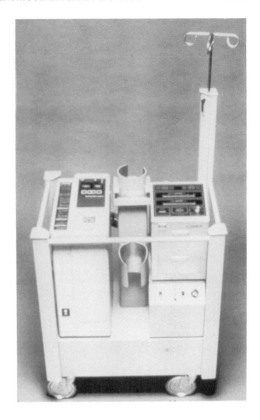

consists of the Bio-Medicus blood pump head, heat exchanger, oxygenator, flow and pressure transducers, and connecting lines.

The CPS system is intended for use as an extracorporeal blood oxygenation system for patients needing cardiac and/or pulmonary support. The cannulation is accomplished by a femoral-femoral veno-arterial percutaneous insertion of either 20, 18, or 16 French cannulae. The maximum blood flow rate is limited by cannulae size, with typical flow rates of 6, 5, 3.5 L/min for the 20, 18, and 16 French sizes, respectively. The total bypass time should be limited to a maximum of 6 hours to avoid hematologic problems.

PULSATILE VENTRICULAR ASSIST DEVICES

Novacor

The Novacor, Inc. left ventricular assist system (LVAS) is an electromechanical device. About the size of a large man's fist, weighing 1.5 pounds, the Novacor LVAS is positioned with an experimental power source (Fig. 3). The inflow and outflow cannulae are brought through the diaphragm and sutured to the left ventricular apex and ascending or descending thoracic aorta, respectively. The pump is surgically implanted preperitoneally within the left upper quadrant of the abdomen. The clinical version of the Novacor system requires an electrical connection as well as a vent tube that exits the skin and is connected to a bedside console that provides power and control signals for the LVAS.

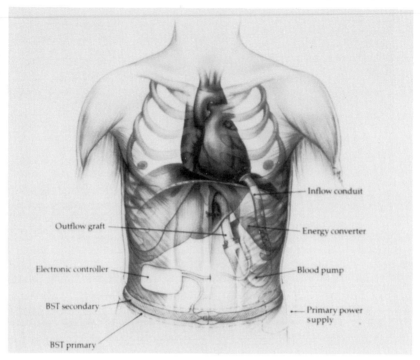

FIGURE 3.   Novacor LVAS showing implantation with experimental power source.

The device uses a pulsed-solenoid energy converter. This energy converter resembles a magnetically activated clam shell armature. Pulsed electrical energy is translated into mechanical energy that closes the armature. Two parallel pusher plates are attached to the armature and, when activated, displace the blood from a blood-contacting bladder located between the two circular pusher plates. This dual pusher plate–bladder type blood pump is made of a one-piece seamless, smooth polyurethane bladder of Biomer (Ethicon, Inc.) blood contacting surface. The bladder is boned to the pusher plates to ensure symmetric deformation. The cylindrical pumping chamber has tangential inflow and outflow valve placement with 25 mm or 21 mm porcine pericardial tissue valves, respectively (Edwards CVS, Baxter Healthcare Corporation, Oakland, CA). The tangential placement provides optimal flow characteristics without areas of stasis. The outer shell of the device is fabricated using epoxy-impregnated Kevlar fabric.

The Novacor LVAS does not pump blood in parallel with the native heart as do other VADs. Instead, the ventricular apex cannulation allows blood in the left ventricle to be ejected into the empty LVAS during systole. This arrangement greatly reduces the afterload seen by the left ventricle and can provide cardiac outputs in excess of 9 L/min. Normally the Novacor LVAS is triggered to pump using the fill-rate mode, in which the LVAS is triggered to pump when the rate of blood ejected by the native heart into the LVAS approaches zero. By triggering in this mode the LVAS beats at the same rate as the native heart without having to be synchronized to the ECG signal. The LVAS can also be triggered to pump in a fixed rate mode that is set by the operator on the bedside console or can be triggered by the native heart rate by using the ECG signal obtained with external electrodes. Position sensors within the pump device are used to measure the fill volumes of each beat. The fill volume information and the device pump rate are used by the console to compute the LVAS cardiac output.

The current clinical system that requires the external control console is an intermediate step to an overall goal of providing a self-contained ventricular assist system. By using the same blood pump and energy converter, Novacor, Inc. has miniaturized the controller and power supply so that it too can be implanted (Fig. 3). This totally implantable ventricular assist system is currently being evaluated in animals, has shown great promise in testing to date, and may be available for clinical use by mid-1990.

Thermedics

The Thermedics device (Woburn, MA) is a pneumatically driven left ventricular assist device (LVAD). The Heartmate LVAD is implantable and has only a single pneumatic drive line exiting the skin (Fig. 4). This blood pump is implanted in the abdomen just below the diaphragm in a position similar to that of the Novacor LVAS. Inflow cannulation penetrates the diaphragm and connects to the left ventricular apex. The outflow cannulae enters the thoracic cavity and is sewn to the ascending aorta. The pneumatic drive line connects to a relatively small bedside controller that provides the pulsed compressed air that powers the pumping device.

The Heartmate blood pump is approximately 6 inches in diameter with a stroke volume of 80 ml. The pump is based on a single pusher plate design, using

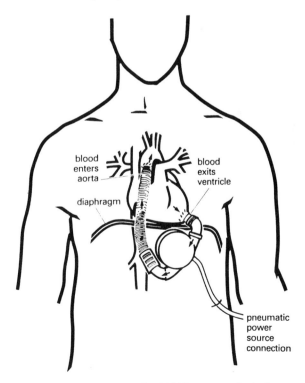

FIGURE 4. Thermedics LVAD pneumatic device.

a Biomer diaphragm to separate the blood chamber from the pneumatically driven actuator. Except for the unidirectional inflow and outflow valves, all blood-contacting surfaces utilize textured blood contacting surfaces that are designed to help reduce the potential for embolic episodes. The titanium surfaces are sintered with titanium microspheres approximately 75–100 μm in diameter. This process forms a continuous layer of microspheres 3 to 4 microspheres thick. The textured polyurethane Biomer diaphragm is cast on a flocked mandrel, which results in a fibril textured surface with fibril diameters of approximately 15 μm. This "rough" surface provides the blood a framework on which a pseudoneointimal lining can form. This lining then functions as the biocompatible blood-contacting surface.

The rigid pump housing is fabricated from medical-grade titanium with the inflow and outflow ports located posteriorly from the drive line connection site. Porcine xenograft tissue valves (25 mm) are located in the inflow and outflow ports to provide unidirectional blood flow.

The pump is actuated by a portable bedside console. The console does not require any additional compressed air tanks or compressors. The console contains an electric motor that drives a diaphragm-type air pump, and the air pump is connected directly to the blood pump through a pneumatic driveline. Each stroke of the console air pump corresponds to one beat of the blood pump. From the drive console the operator can select one of three rate-triggering modes. The **fixed rate mode** sets the pumping rate to a value selected on the console's front panel; **automatic mode** triggers the device to pump after a predefined volume of blood has filled the device, thus providing a constant stroke volume at a varying pump rate; or **external mode** synchronizes the pump rate to an external trigger such as the R-wave of an ECG signal. A position transducer in the pump device provides pusher plate position information from which the console can calculate and display stroke volume, flow rates, and blood pump diaphragm position. The console also displays pump rates and mode control settings. The system includes an internal battery pack that provides power for patient transfer and for temporary loss of AC power.

The Heartmate does not pump blood in parallel with the native heart; instead, it functions as a low afterload/high output buffer for the left ventricle, similar in function to the Novacor LVAS previously described. This device can provide a cardiac output in excess of 9 L/min.

Additional development work is under way to use the Heartmate blood pump in a totally implantable electric LVAD system. The system uses the Heartmate blood pump powered by an internal electric motor and battery pack/controller that is completely implantable (Fig. 5). Electrical energy is transmitted into the body by a pair of nested coils, one implanted just under the skin and the second positioned just outside the body. Energy from the external battery pack is inductively transmitted across the skin to charge the internal battery and power the blood pump driver. The implanted battery pack can power the pump for short periods of time to free up the recipient for bathing or to provide power support in the event of misalignment of the external coil. The electrically powered device is currently undergoing endurance testing in the laboratory to determine the reliability of the system.

Thoratec

The Thoratec, Inc. ventricular assist device (Berkeley, CA) is a pneumatically driven paracorporeal device that can be used for left, right or biventricular

FIGURE 5. Totally implantable Thermedics LVAD system with experimental power source.

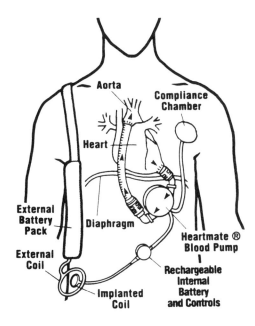

support. The VADs rest on the anterior abdominal wall and are connected to the heart and great vessels using cannulae that penetrate the chest wall. Thoratec, Inc. recommends that cannulation for left heart support be achieved from either the left atrium or left ventricle with return to the aorta. Cannulation for right heart support uses right atrial cannulation with return to the pulmonary artery. The VAD(s) are connected to the control console by a pneumatic drive line, which provides positive and negative pressure pulses that drive the blood pumps.

The VAD blood pump consists of a rigid polysulfone case with pneumatic and blood pumping chambers separated by a polyurethane diaphragm (Fig. 6). The blood pumping chamber consists of a smooth, seamless 80 ml volume

FIGURE 6. Thoratec pneumatic VAD.

bladder made of Thoratec's proprietary polyurethane multipolymer. Two Bjork-Shiley monostrut Delrin (inflow and outflow) valves are used to obtain unidirectional flow and are located in the respective cannulation ports.

During VAD diastole, air is either vented or evacuated from the pneumatic chamber causing the diaphragm to move away from the blood-pumping bladder, allowing it to fill. Systole begins when the amplitude of the pulse of compressed air delivered to the device overcomes the arterial pressure and the blood bladder can be compressed by displacing the blood out of the device.

The contacting surface between the diaphragm and the blood-contacting bladder is lubricated with silicone oil to prevent bladder abrasion. Movement of the diaphragm is monitored by a Hall effect sensor built into the rigid case of the VAD. A small magnet mounted on the diaphragm generates the signal received by the Hall effect device. The Hall effect device is connected to electrical leads that are bundled with the pneumatic drive line that exits the case of the VAD.

The pneumatic drive console supplies the air pressure pulses that cause the VAD to pump blood. The console operates for pumping rates from 20 to 150 bpm. In practice an effective stroke volume of 65 ml can be achieved at any pumping rate from 20 to 100 bpm, which results in a device output up to 6.5 L/min. The drive console consists of two independent drive modules and associated displays and alarms. Each console was designed for single VAD use with primary and backup drivers. Bi-VAD support from a single console is possible as long as a second driver console is available for backup, in the event of a drive module failure.

Each drive console consists of four air compressors, two for each driver. Each drive module has both a positive and negative (vacuum) compressor which generates the characteristic pressure pulses corresponding to the operator settings on the console. These settings include: driver pressure pulse amplitudes, both positive and negative; device pumping rate; percent systole or eject time; and the triggering mode of the device. Each driver is equipped with two E-sized compressed air cylinders and internal battery backup to be used during patient transport or as short-term emergency backup sources.

The Thoratec, Inc. VAD has four different modes of triggering. The **manual mode** is a single-step mode of operation that permits the operator to change the VAD from either eject or fill status by a touch of a button. This mode of operation is often used during de-airing of the pump or for certain diagnostic procedures. **Asynchronous mode** lets the operator choose the pumping rate and ejection period (systolic duration) of the pumping cycle. This mode results in a fixed rate, variable stroke volume mode of operation. The **volume mode** provides a variable rate, fixed stroke volume operation and is commonly referred to as the "full-to-empty" mode. In this mode the VAD begins ejecting blood when the Hall effect sensor signals that the VAD is full of blood. The pumping rate varies with changes in the device preload which affect its filling rate. For example, as the device preload increases, so does its filling rate, which results in earlier ejection and thus an increase in the pumping rate. **External synchronous mode** uses an external electrical signal to trigger the drive console to eject. Usually the trigger signal is the R-wave of the electrocardiogram. In this mode a programmable delay setting allows the operator to fine-tune the trigger point to provide a counterpulsation effect in order to further reduce the afterload as seen by the native heart. This mode can be set to provide one beat of the VAD for every one, two, three, or four beats of the native heart.

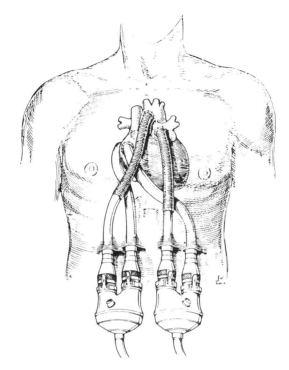

FIGURE 7.   Symbion AVAD bi-VAD configuration.

Symbion

The Symbion Corporation (Salt Lake City, UT) currently has two pneumatically driven pulsatile blood pump systems. Both systems, the Total Artificial Heart (Jarvik-7) and the Acute Ventricular Assist Device (AVAD), are the direct descendants of the original pneumatic device developed by Willem Kolff, M.D., Ph.D. The AVAD, a recently developed pneumatically driven ventricle, is an extracorporeal pump connected to the circulatory system via percutaneous cannulae (Fig. 7). The AVAD can be used for left, right, or biventricular support. Cannulation for left heart support involves left atrium inflow cannulation with AVAD outflow return to the aorta. Cannulation for right heart support uses right atrial inflow cannulation with outflow into the pulmonary artery. The device(s) pumps blood in parallel with the native heart. Symbion recommends that the AVAD pump during physiologic diastole to provide both cardiac augmentation and increased cardiac output.

The AVAD has a pelethane injection molded housing with a 70-ml stroke volume (Fig. 8). The blood and compressed air chambers are separated by a four-layer polyurethane diaphragm. Each layer of the diaphragm is separated and lubricated from the adjacent layer by graphite powder. All blood-contacting surfaces are coated with a smooth Biomer coating to reduce blood/device interaction.

The pumping action of the AVAD results from the inflation and evacuation of the air chamber of the ventricles. During systole, pulses of compressed air are delivered to the air chamber, causing movement of the diaphragm which displaces

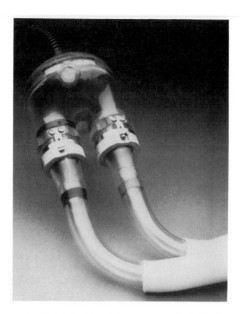

FIGURE 8.   Symbion pneumatic AVAD.

the blood from the ventricle. Unidirectional inflow and outflow is achieved by the use of two 25-mm Medtronic-Hall (Medtronic Inc., Minneapolis, MN) clinical grade valves in each ventricle. The AVAD(s) connects to the Symbion System III E bedside pneumatic Heart/VAD controller, which provides positive and negative air pressure pulses to power the devices.

The System III E Heart/VAD Controller Console is a self-contained, semi-portable drive system that provides continuous, pulsed, pneumatic drive support for the blood pumps. Each controller console consists of two dual-output Heart/VAD controller drivers, a vacuum pump, alarm panel, two high-pressure air tanks, battery backup electrical power, Cardiac Monitor Computer (COMDU), and printer (Fig. 9). Only one of the two heart/VAD controllers is needed to drive either a Total Artificial Heart or Bi-AVAD configuration. The second controller is available as a backup unit that can be used if the primary controller fails or if it becomes necessary to drive each ventricle independently. Each controller has five adjustments; right and left drive pressure, heart rate, systolic duration and trigger delay. The vacuum control, located on the front panel of the console, controls the vacuum setting for both controllers in the console. The vacuum encourages diastolic filling of the blood pumps by reducing the pressure required to collapse the diaphragm.

The System III E console provides three trigger modes of operation. **Asynchronous mode** allows the pump rate and % systole to be controlled by the settings on the front panel of the Heart/VAD controller. **ECG synchronous mode** utilizes the R-wave of the ECG signal to trigger the controller. The ECG signal can be obtained from an external source or directly from patient leads. The blood pump can be made to pump synchronously with every first, second, or third beat of the native heart. **Fill volume mode** triggers systole when the AVAD has filled to a preset volume.

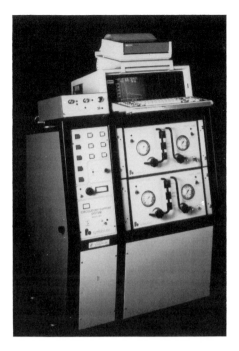

FIGURE 9. Symbion Heart/VAD controller console.

In addition to the console controller settings, the System III E has a dedicated computer, COMDU, to monitor and record system functions. The COMDU computer monitors and stores data concerning system alarm status, backup battery voltage, device cardiac output, drive pressure, and returned airflow wave forms for each ventricle. COMDU analyzes the diastolic portion of the returned air flow wave form and calculates the corresponding fill volume. Calculated fill volumes and device cardiac outputs are continuously displayed on the systems CRT, along with device cardiac output, pump rate, and percent systole. Pseudo–real-time wave forms of either drive pressure or air flow wave forms can be displayed as well as battery voltage and device(s) output trends. The COMDU is equipped with a 1200 band modem and communication software that permit remote access of the COMDU system. This feature makes possible the monitoring of multiple systems from a central location or patient management from a remote sight.

Abiomed

The Abiomed device currently available for clinical trial is the BVS System 5000. This pneumatically powered, pulsatile assist pump can be used for right, left, or biventricular assist. The extracorporeal blood pump chamber mounts on an IV pole and is connected to the heart via medical-grade PVC tubing connected to inflow and outflow cannulae. The transthoracic inflow and outflow cannulae are made from wire-reinforced PVC. The atrial inflow cannula incorporates a standard lighthouse tip, with the outflow cannula having a woven Dacron graft for anastomosis to either the aorta or pulmonary artery.

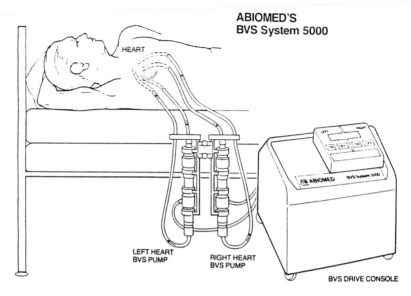

FIGURE 10.   Abiomed BVS system 5000.

The blood pump device consists of two chambers configured vertically and mounted alongside the patient's bed at a level below the heart (Fig. 10). The inflow chamber, which acts as a compliant reservoir or artificial atrium, empties into the main pumping chamber. The main pumping chamber has both inflow and outflow trileaflet Abiomed prosthetic valves with an effective stroke volume of 80 ml. The pumping chambers consist of an elastomeric bladder, which like the valves, are made from a smooth-surfaced Angioflex polyurethane. The inflow chamber fills continuously from the native atrium by gravity alone. The main pumping chamber is collapsed by a pulse of positive pressure air from the control console (Fig. 11).

The pneumatic control console derives all necessary information to run and control the device by monitoring the returned air through the pneumatic driveline. The drive console is a microprocessor-controlled pneumatic drive system that operates one or two blood pumps. Pump rate and systolic intervals are determined automatically and do not need operator intervention. The pumps are triggered to run in a fill-to-empty mode. In the bi-VAD mode the two devices are controlled completely independently to achieve maximum device assist. The front panel of the console continuously displays pump rate and device output. The console provides battery power backup, audible and visible alarms, and a foot-operated mechanical pump that allows continued support for even the most unlikely events.

For long-term support Abiomed is developing a permanently implantable untethered device called the VAS. The device can be used for either single or bi-ventricular support with only a slight modification to the device cannulation ports. This added flexibility is possible because the same energy converter and pumping chambers are used in either configuration. The only similarity of Abiomed's permanent system to the temporary assist systems of Novacor and Thermedics are the trileaflet valves and blood-contacting material Angioflex, both proprietary to Abiomed.

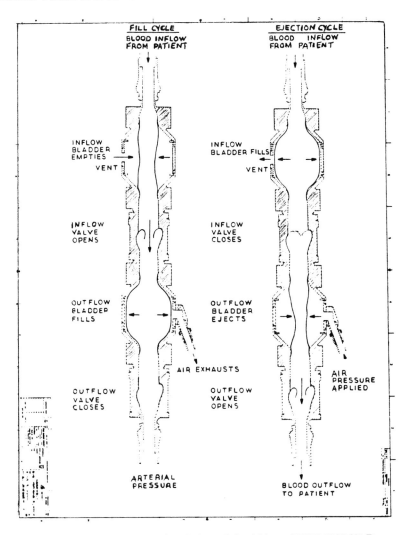

FIGURE 11. Cross-sectional view of the Abiomed BVS 5000 VAD.

The VAS LVAD system consists of an electrohydraulic energy converter, hydraulic flow controller, a trileaflet valve leading into two pumping chambers in series separated by a second trileaflet valve, an internal battery pack, and hybridized electronic controller. In the LVAD configuration the device is implanted in the abdominal region (Fig. 12). The proximal blood chamber is cannulated to the left ventricular apex and the distal blood chamber outflow is cannulated to the abdominal aorta proximally to the iliac bifurcation. This configuration provides afterload reduction for the left ventricle while increasing aortic pressure.

The blood is displaced from the device by the movement of flexible diaphragms. The diaphragms are moved by hydraulic fluid that is pumped from one VAD to the other, thus completing the pumping cycle. In vitro testing has

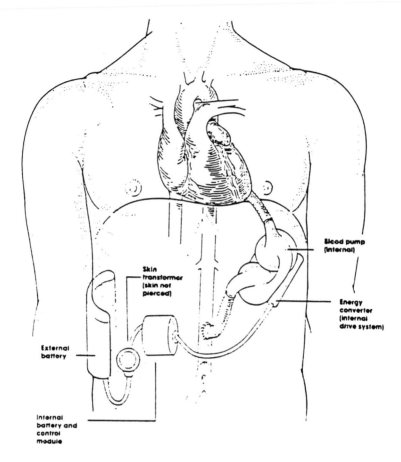

Blood pump
(internal)

Skin
transformer
(skin not
pierced)

Energy
converter
(internal
drive system)

External
battery

Internal
battery and
control
module

FIGURE 12.   Totally implantable Abiomed VAS LVAD system.

demonstrated a device output capability of 10 L/min, developing an aortic pressure of 120 torr with a filling pressure of 15 torr. Each of the two chambers serves as the compliance for the other, obviating the need for an additional gas compliance chamber as used in other systems.

The system is triggered to pump by sensing the R-wave of the native heart. The preferred mode of operation is synchronous copulsation. Copulsation results in the native and assist systems arterial pressure pulses being in phase. During ventricular systole, hydraulic fluid is withdrawn from the proximal blood chamber and pumped into the distal chamber. This transfer of hydraulic fluid provides the native ventricle with nearly zero afterload when pumping blood into the proximal chamber. At the same time that the proximal chamber is filling with blood, the distal chamber is filling with hydraulic fluid and ejecting its blood into the aorta. All control adjustments for optimal assist are determined by sensing the hydraulic pressure gradients of the devices.

The VAS permanently implantable device is still undergoing long-term reliability studies and has not been used clinically to date.

CLINICAL REVIEW

Since the introduction of mechanical circulatory assist in the early 1960s and subsequent successful application,[6,31] much information has been gained concerning the use of various devices and factors associated with successful application. A variety of systems have been used during this time, including roller pumps,[6,29,31] centrifugal pumps,[1] sac-type pneumatic pumps,[8,11,19] and more recently an electrically driven device,[28] with the principal focus directed at post cardiotomy cardiogenic shock. However, with increased experience, two other important patient groups have emerged: patients with cardiogenic shock following acute myocardial infarction and patients whose condition deteriorates before or after cardiac transplantation.

With the introduction of centrifugal pumps (Biomedicus, Centrimed), these devices became the most popular systems used because of their availability, easy application, and ability to generate high-volume flow rates. While success using centrifugal VADs in postcardiotomy patients is well known,[1,17] the effectiveness of these systems is limited by hemolysis, which often develops with extended use. In addition, patients must be immobilized because of current cannulation techniques, which may adversely affect survival.[19] The greatest disadvantage, however, is probably the nonphysiologic nature of nonpulsatile flow that effects end-organ function during prolonged perfusion.[17]

To counter these limitations, several types of pulsatile VADs have now been developed and are pneumatically (Thoratec, Symbion AVAD, Abiomed, Thermedics) or electrically driven (Novacor). These devices can be used for extended periods and can be applied to patients with reversible injury as well as to those requiring a "bridge" to transplantation.

Broad experience with several VADs has now been gained. Although survival, particularly in postcardiotomy patients, is not as high as desired, it should be noted that the overall results have improved substantially with increased experience. Information obtained through these efforts have identified several important areas that affect survival. These include patient selection, appropriate device selection, and postoperative management.

Patient Selection

The single most important determinant for survival with the use of VADs is patient selection.[10,19] Central to establishing criteria for the application of such devices is the definition of cardiogenic shock. Table 1 outlines hemodynamic criteria that suggest the need for circulatory assistance. The presence of elevated left or right atrial filling pressures coupled with reduced cardiac index and elevated systemic vascular resistance (> 2100 dyne-s/cm^5) typifies this setting and carries an extremely high mortality.[19]

In selecting patients for circulatory assistance, age is an important factor as data from the combined registry (ASAIO-ISHT) for postcardiotomy cardiogenic

TABLE 1.   Hemodynamic Criteria for VAD Use

Left Ventricular Failure	Right Ventricular Failure
LAP > 25 mm Hg	CVP > 22 mm Hg
Systolic pressure < 90 mm Hg	C.I. < 1.8 L/min/m^2
C.I. < 1.8 L/min/m^2	Normal pulmonary artery pressures

shock has shown that patients beyond the age of 65 have a survival of 12%, whereas those 66–70 years old have a survival of only 6%. This contrasts markedly with the 21–31% survival of patients less than 65 years of age.[18] Other exclusion criteria, although often difficult to define, include previous neurologic event with residual deficit, significant cerebral vascular disease, severe chronic pulmonary disease, hepatic failure, sepsis, and multi-organ failure. Of particular significance in the group of non-survivors is the presence of a recent myocardial infarction and acute renal failure.[19] Perioperative myocardial infarction was present in 75% of the non-survivors and suggests non-recoverability; however, this should not exclude patients from ventricular assistance who are otherwise candidates for cardiac transplantation.[19]

Several factors contribute to the improved results with the use of VADs as a bridge to transplantation. Acceptance of a cardiac transplant candidate implies the absence of exclusion criteria in patients who are otherwise less than 60 years old. Renal insufficiency when present generally reflects the consequences of a chronic low-output state and usually reverses with the improved hemodynamics of ventricular assistance. However, frank renal failure (BUN > 100 mg% creatinine > 5 mg/dl) in the presence of cardiogenic shock requiring circulatory support indicates a poor prognosis and should be grounds for exclusion.[19]

SELECTION OF THE APPROPRIATE CIRCULATORY SUPPORT SYSTEM

With the development of various support systems occurring somewhat simultaneously, the data from these experiences suggest that no single system has universal application.[10,21] Rather, the individual patient must be matched to the most suitable system specific to the clinical situation. Device selection remains largely based on systems availability, the type of failure encountered, and the potential for reversibility.[10] The selection of an assist device is discussed in more detail in the chapter by Pennington and Termuhlen in this text.

External centrifugal ventricular assist devices are effective in the treatment of cardiogenic shock following cardiac surgery[17] and as a bridge to transplantation.[1,17] While virtually supplanting roller pump systems, convenience and easy application remain the greatest attributes. Technical problems associated with extended use of these systems frequently limit success and are related to the consequences of mechanical deterioration, fibrin deposition, hemolysis, and end-organ dysfunction. Another point to consider with the use of external VAD systems is the limitation to patient mobilization, a factor critical to minimizing complications. Centrifugal pump VADs are most useful in conditions responsive to short-term assistance (right ventricular infarction, "stunned" myocardium) as a bridge to transplantation (< 7 days) or bridge to more effective long-term support (pulsatile VADs, TAH).

Another form of circulatory assistance based on centrifugal pump technology is extracorporeal membrane oxygenation (ECMO). The Bard Corporation has developed a commercially available portable ECMO system (CPS). This system requires immediate and constant heparinization and is therefore unsuitable for postcardiotomy patients.[21] However, this unit is highly effective in providing acute resuscitation and can be applied either with a cutdown[17] or by percutaneous cannulation.[25] Use of this device, however, should be limited to patients in acute myocardial infarction cardiogenic shock or patients with cardiomyopathy awaiting transplantation who acutely deteriorate.[17] If a patient demonstrates potential for long-term survival after initial stabilization, the ECMO system should be changed for a more long-term support system.

Pulsatile systems represent the newest and most advanced form of VADs currently available. While the type of energy source used to drive systems differ, functionally they can be divided into two groups, paracorporeal (Thoratec, Symbion AVAD, Abiomed) and implantable (Novacor, Thermedics). All systems currently require an externalized energy source and therefore are for temporary use and not fully implantable in their current application. Three of these devices (Novacor, Thermedics, and Abiomed) are being developed as permanent, totally implantable, non-tethered systems. Pulsatile VADs represent a significant improvement over external assist devices principally due to the blood contact surfaces, which allow for extended use with minimal hemolysis.[19,28]

The utility of paracorporeal assist devices include several options for inflow cannulation. Atrial cannulation is most applicable to postcardiotomy patients and can be achieved through the left atrial appendage, the dome of the left atrium, or the left atrium beyond the interatrial groove. The advantage of the latter site is the capability of insertion without the use of cardiopulmonary bypass,[2] while avoiding previously placed coronary bypass grafts. Although atrial drainage is technically easier and avoids additional injury to the myocardium, the resistance of the long inflow cannula occasionally limits filling and can affect device output. This problem can be overcome by the application of vacuum within the system; however, it requires closure of the chest and may not aid in improving flow volumes interoperatively. To counter this, there is an option of direct left ventricular apical cannulation, which improves filling and offers distinct advantages to bridge patients when myocardial injury is of little concern.[9]

When biventricular assistance is necessary, the right atrium is readily cannulated through the appendage or the freewall. In utilizing atrial cannulation sites, two rows of pledgetted sutures are generally placed and snared. The snares are left in the chest at closure for easy accessibility when the device is removed.

For outflow cannulation a partially occluding clamp is placed on the ascending aorta or the main pulmonary artery and a longitudinal arteriotomy performed. A previously measured and beveled graft is sewn in end-to-side fashion using 4-0 polypropylene sutures. Outflow cannulae should be prepared by soaking in 25% albumin and autoclaving for three minutes to greatly reduce subsequent bleeding from the dacron graft.[24]

Placement of the outflow cannulae is critical and for patients bridged to transplantation the aortic outflow should be placed on the greater curve of the ascending aorta at the lowest possible site near the aortic valve. Similarly, the pulmonary artery outflow should be placed just beyond the pulmonary valve. Utilization of these sites allows for excision of all foreign material at the time of explantation, leaving sufficient length of great vessel for transplantation. In postcardiotomy patients, the site of the aortic anastomosis is largely dictated by the presence of proximal vein grafts and, at the time of explantation, removal of all the prosthetic material is not mandatory.

Of special concern for outflow cannulation is that the caliber of the great vessels must be of adequate dimension to accommodate the grafts; in this regard adolescents and small adults less than 40 kg may not be suitable candidates. The position of inflow cannula can also present technical problems in nondilated hearts, because the large (51 French) cannula can be difficult to position in the normal-sized left atrium. When confronted with these circumstances, paracorporeal devices may not be applicable and external VADs should be considered.

Of the implantable devices, the Novacor LVAS has been used most extensively. Common features of the Novacor LVAS and Thermedic Heartmate devices include left ventricular apical cannulation and aortic perfusion either through the ascending aorta or the superceliac aorta. Total implantation of these devices is realized with the device positioned in a subcutaneous pocket in the left upper quadrant. The drive line source then exits through a single port transcutaneously. The Novacor LVAS is electrically activated, whereas the Thermedics is currently a pneumatic device. Both Novacor and Thermedic require an external control console. Totally implantable models of these systems are being evaluated experimentally with the promise that a clinical device will be available in the near future.[27]

The major advantage of these systems is increased cardiac output capability (> 9 L/min). Unlike the paracorporeal devices, neither system pumps blood in parallel with the native heart but rather fills transapically as the left ventricle empties into the system during systole. This results in greatly reduced afterload with subsequent left ventricular decompression and maximal reduction in myocardial oxygen consumption.[7,23] While theoretically of benefit in reducing infarct size,[13,30] the necessary trauma that results from direct left ventricular cannulation may be undesirable in the patient with potential reversible injury.

The Novacor and Thermedic systems are specifically suited for isolated left ventricular failure, and, in the presence of severe right ventricular dysfunction, a second mechanical assist device may be required.[20] Experience with these systems demonstrates that both provide extraordinary unloading for the left heart. As a consequence, in the absence of elevated pulmonary vascular resistance, the development of significant right heart failure becomes more theoretical than practical and seldom requires mechanical support.[27] Both the Novacor and Thermedic systems do require continuous anticoagulation and there have been instances of thrombus formation around the porcine valves despite the absence of thromboembolism.

The advantages of the implantable device is that they generally perform well and are capable of greater flows than the paracorporeal systems. The single drive line exit site may also offer the prospect of reduced device-related infections, especially during long periods of implantation. The disadvantages are that they are large and somewhat bulky to implant. They also require dissection of the diaphragm from the chest wall for apical cannulation and rather extensive dissection of the anterior abdominal wall for implantation. As a result, the potential for bleeding and wound complications must be taken into account, particularly for postcardiotomy patients.

POSTOPERATIVE MANAGEMENT

Severe postoperative bleeding requiring re-exploration is the most common complication following implantation of heterotopic prosthetic ventricles[15] and remains one of the most important factors associated with device-related mortality.[16] Patients at greatest risk are those requiring ventricular assistance following cardiac surgery as a result of thrombocytopenia and platelet dysfunction related to the duration of cardiopulmonary bypass.[16] Thus VAD implantation occurs in a setting in which severe bleeding and prolonged hemostatic alterations were already present. VAD placement then further compounds the preexisting hemostatic derangement, with abnormal flow conditions introduced by the device and by biomaterial surfaces that interact with blood.[12] It is therefore important to achieve hemostasis rapidly with early and vigorous infusions of platelet concentrates and fresh frozen plasma before prolonged bleeding results in uncontrollable coagulopathy.[5] Of equal magnitude in the control of intraoperative bleeding is the assurance that all surgical reasons have been eliminated. Following a thoroughly determined effort to correct all bleeding, the sternum should be closed whenever possible to mechanically aid hemostasis and allow the possibility of early extubation.

When to begin anticoagulation following transfer to the intensive care unit then becomes problematic. Although anticoagulation protocols with pulsatile VADs differ among institutions, it is generally believed that heparin should be started only after several hours following closure or when the outflow from the chest tubes is less than 100 ml/hour for 2 to 3 hours. At this time intravenous heparin is started with the goal of maintaining the activated clotting time between 150–200 seconds. Another approach for short-term anticoagulation has been the use of 5% dextran. For periods less than 7 days, dextran at 25 ml/hour has not resulted in thrombus formation in the pump, valves, or tubing of the devices.[5] Beyond this period, heparin or Coumadin therapy is recommended.

Other points to consider in postoperative management is the development of multi-organ failure and infectious complications. Often, the central element in the development of multi-organ failure is the time elapsed with the patient in cardiogenic shock prior to the institution of ventricular assistance. It is important to decide for early intervention, as prolonged hypotension beyond 12 hours is associated with poor recovery despite assistance.[19] Not to be overlooked is the importance of early hemostasis, as massive transfusion of blood and blood products promotes end-organ dysfunction and multi-organ failure.[26]

To counter the potential for infection complications, all patients should be placed in strict reverse isolation. Short-term, broad-spectrum antibiotic coverage (cephalosporin) should be given with the goal of early extubation and mobilization. Infections related to drive line and cannulation sites, although uncommon, should be treated aggressively with local debridement and appropriate antibiotic therapy. Of particular importance is prophylactic care of the exit sites with frequent dressing changes (every 4 hours), using Betadine or Dakin's preparations.

WEANING AND BRIDGING WITH VENTRICULAR ASSIST DEVICES

After support with mechanical circulatory assist, the patient will be weaned or transplanted, or support will be discontinued. To optimize the chance of successful mechanical assistance, VAD implantation should occur early to avoid deterioration of heart and other vital organs. Regardless of the type of device used, once inserted, it should be left in place for at least 24 hours. Although quite often the heart appears to recover remarkably during the early postoperative period, most attempts to wean and remove devices within 24 hours have met with calamity.[14] Determining when to wean from VAD assistance is based almost exclusively on hemodynamic evidence that recovery is present and sustained. Reducing pump flows and noting the ability of the native heart to assume increased work load, without significant elevation of left atrial or pulmonary pressures, is critical to successful weaning.

When centrifugal pump devices are used, patients will most often have an interaortic balloon in place. To determine myocardial recovery, the interaortic balloon can be stopped for short periods while the objective data is obtained during reduced pump flows. When the native heart is capable of generating a cardiac index of at least 2.2 L/minute/m^2, in the absence of interaortic balloon pumping, it is likely that successful explantation of the VAD is possible. In reducing pump flows with centrifugal devices, the process should be notably deliberate to allow the heart to accommodate the altered dynamics. Flows should never be reduced below 0.5 L/min during weaning, and heparin should be increased to minimize the increased potential for thrombus or fibrin deposition. At the time of removal of a centrifugal VAD, the IABP should remain in place and the patient maintained on mild inotropic support. Support with the IABP should continue for at least 24 hours to ensure stability. Criteria associated with successful outcome using centrifugal pumps include assistance less than 75 hours, mild or absent left ventricular failure, some left ventricular function recovered within 24 hours, and no electrocardiographic evidence of myocardial infarction.[14]

With the use of pneumatic VADs, the basic principles outlined for centrifugal type pumps also apply. Deciding when to begin the weaning process is again based on hemodynamic criteria after at least 24 hours of assistance. When weaning has begun, it is of little concern whether left ventricular or biventricular support is present. Pump flows are gradually reduced over the course of 24 hours to achieve approximately 50% output of the maximum support previously required. With the pneumatic devices, however, pump flows should not be reduced below 2 L/min at any time because of the increased likelihood of thromboembolism.

As with the centrifugal devices, it is important to increase anticoagulation while the flows are serially decreased. While this process is undertaken, hemodynamics are closely monitored to determine that cardiac output is maintained. Of equal importance is repeated measurements of pulmonary artery and left atrial pressures to determine if any degree of left ventricular decompensation occurs with weaning. Unlike centrifugal pumps, when a patient is weaned from pneumatic ventricular assistance, IABP has no role in subsequent management following explantation.[14] However, patients are often placed on small doses of dopamine for renal perfusion but not for cardiotonic effect.

Bridging to Transplantation

Regardless of the circumstances leading to transplantation, all patients bridged on heterotopic prosthetic ventricles should achieve stable clinical status with organ system recovery prior to surgery. One of the early lessons learned with bridging patients on mechanical assistance was not to transplant too early.[3] Logically, patients to be bridged must be transplant candidates prior to VAD implantation. Often it is difficult to completely ascertain the suitability of a patient for transplantation when insertion of the VAD is considered. However, age, evidence of preserved end-organ function, absence of infection, and some knowledge of the patient's psycho-social profile are critical to the ultimate success of the two-stage procedure. Once implantation has occurred, however, it is important that reversal of end-organ dysfunction be achieved, bleeding be controlled, no neurologic deficit be present, nutrition be adequately supported, and that the presence of pre-formed antibodies does not preclude successful transplantation. It is only when these criteria have been met that cardiac transplantation can be undertaken with a reasonable likelihood of success.

CONCLUSION

Ventricular assist devices have and will continue to play a very important role in the regimen of total cardiac care. The overall success statistics, while modest (approximately 25% of patients discharged after cardiotomy and 45% of patients discharged after bridge to transplant procedures), represents considerable triumph over certain death. In addition these statistics are burdened with the unavoidable learning curve and device development difficulties encountered with any new medical therapy. With the use of the newer pulsatile devices by centers that have developed experience with such devices, the statistics for VAD intervention will greatly improve.

This evolutionary process that has continued since the early 1970s is now approaching another major milestone. The implantation of a completely self-contained mechanical ventricular assist system is now on the horizon. Such a system will improve the quality of life for individuals who are not candidates for heart transplantation as well as serve as an ambulatory bridge to transplantation alternative for patients who might have died waiting for a donor heart.

In the near future specialized cardiac care centers will need to provide an array of ventricular assist systems to support the variability of patient requirements. Such an investment both monetarily and intellectually will require a dedicated and talented staff of individuals. Such centers will become a focal point in their respective regions for cardiac care and related services. The inevitable challenges of such intervention can best be handled by those who have the technical resources to support the clinical intervention. It is these challenges and their outcome that will indelibly color the next decade of cardiac care.

REFERENCES

1. Bolman RM, Cox JL, Marshall W, et al: Circulatory support with a centrifugal pump as a bridge to cardiac transplantation. Ann Thorac Surg 47:108–112, 1989.
2. Brugger JP, Bonandi L, Meli M, et al: Swat team approach to ventricular assistance. Ann Thorac Surg 47:136–141, 1989.
3. Copelant JG: Personal communication.
4. Copeland JG, Emery RW, Levinson MM, et al: The role of mechanical support and transplantation in treatment of patients with end stage cardiomyopathy. Circulation 72(Suppl):II-7, 1985.
5. Copeland JG, Harker LA, Joist JH, DeVries WC: Bleeding and anticoagulation. Ann Thorac Surg 47:88–95, 1989.
6. Debakey ME: Left ventricular bypass for cardiac assistance: Clinical experience. Am J Cardiol 27:3, 1971.
7. Eugene J, Ott RA, Moore-Jeffries EW, et al: Left atrial-to-aortic assistance: Effect of in-line venting on myocardial oxygen consumption. Heart Transplant 3:329–335, 1984.
8. Farrar DJ, Hill JD, Gray LA, et al: Heterotopic prosthetic ventricles as a bridge to cardiac transplantation: A multicenter study in 29 patients. N Engl J Med 318:333–340, 1988.
9. Ganzel BL, Gray LA, Slater AD, et al: Surgical techniques for the implantation of heterotopic prosthetic ventricles. Ann Thorac Surg 47:113–120, 1989.
10. Hill JD: Bridging to cardiac transplantation. Ann Thorac Surg 47:167–171, 1989.
11. Hill JD, Farrar DJ, Herskoon JJ, et al: Use of a prosthetic ventricle as a bridge to cardiac transplantation for postinfarction cardiogenic shock. N Engl J Med 314:626–628, 1986.
12. Joist JH, Pennington DG: Platelet reaction with artificial surfaces. Trans Am Soc Artif Intern Organs 10:341, 1987.
13. Laks H, Ott RA, Standever J, et al: Servo-controlled cardiac assistance: Effect of left ventricular-to-aortic and left atrial-to-aortic assistance on infarct size. Am J Cardiol 42:244–250, 1978.
14. Magovern GJ, Golding LAR, Oyer PE, Cabrol C: Weaning and bridging: Circulatory support—1988. Ann Thorac Surg 47:102–107, 1989.
15. Pae WE, Pierce WS: Combined registry for the clinical use of mechanical ventricular assist pumps and the total artificial heart: Second official report—1987. Heart Transplant 1:1–4, 1989.

16. Pennington DG: Personal communication.
17. Pennington DG, Codd JE, Merjavy JP, et al: The expanded use of ventricular bypass sytem for severe cardiac failure and as a bridge to cardiac transplantation. J Heart Transplant 3:38–46, 1983.
18. Pennington DG, Joyce LD, Pae WE, Burkholder JA: Circulatory support—1988: Patient selection. Ann Thorac Surg 47:77–81, 1989.
19. Pennington DG, McBride LR, Swartz MT: Use of the Pierce-Donachy ventricular assist device in patients with cardiogenic shock after cardiac operations. Ann Thorac Surg 47:130–135, 1989.
20. Pennington DG, Merjavy JP, Swartz MT, et al: The importance of biventricular failure in patients with postoperative cardiogenic shock. Ann Thorac Surg 39:16–26, 1985.
21. Pennington DG, Swartz MT, McBride LR, et al: Selection of circulatory support devices. Bull Minn Heart Inst VI:1:5–10.
22. Pennington DG, Termuhlen DF: Mechanical circulatory support: Device selection. In Emery RW, et al (eds): Cardiothoracic Transplantation. II. Cardiac Surgery: State of the Art Reviews, vol. 3, no. 3. Philadelphia, Hanley & Belfus, Inc., 1989.
23. Pennock JL, Pierce WS, Prophet A, et al: Myocardial oxygen utilization during left heart bypass: Effect of various percentage of bypass flow rate. Arch Surg 109:635–641, 1974.
24. Phillips SJ, Kongtahworn C, Zeff RH, et al: Intravenous balloon pumping for acute right ventricular failure. Artif Organs 7:368–369, 1983.
25. Phillips SJ, Zeff RH, Kongtahworn C, et al: Percutaneous cardiopulmonary bypass: Application and indication for use. Ann Thorac Surg 47:121–123, 1989.
26. Pierce WS, Gray LA, McBride LR, Frazier OH: Other postoperative complications: Circulatory support—1988. Ann Thorac Surg 47:96–101, 1989.
27. Portner P: Personal communication.
28. Portner PM, Oyer PE, Pennington DG, et al: Implantable electrical left ventricular assist system: Bridge to transplantation and the future. Ann Thorac Surg 47:142–150, 1989.
29. Rose DM, Connolly M, Cunningham JN, et al: Technique and results with a roller pump left and right assist device. Ann Thorac Surg 47:124–129, 1989.
30. Ruf W, Smith GT, Geary G, et al: Effects of left ventricular-to-aortic bypass on infarct size in infarct microcirculation in baboons. J Thorac Cardiovasc Surg 81:408–418, 1981.
31. Spencer FC, Eiseman UG, Trinkle JK, et al: Assisted circulation for cardiac failure following intracardiac surgery with cardiopulmonary bypass. J Thorac Cardiovasc Surg 45:56, 1965.

LYLE D. JOYCE, MD, PhD
KRISTEN E. JOHNSON, RN

TOTAL ARTIFICIAL HEART AS A BRIDGE TO TRANSPLANT: WORLD RESULTS 1989

Lyle D. Joyce, MD
Director, Division of Artificial
  Heart
Cardiovascular and Thoracic
  Surgeon
Minneapolis Heart Institute
Minneapolis, Minnesota

Kristen E. Johnson, RN
Program Director, Mechanical
  Cardiac Replacement
Minneapolis Heart Institute
Minneapolis, Minnesota

Reprint requests to:
Lyle D. Joyce, MD
Minneapolis Heart Institute
920 East 28th Street
Minneapolis, MN 55407

Twenty years have passed since the first attempted use of a total artificial heart as a bridge to cardiac transplantation in 1969.[1] However, the first successful use of the total artificial heart as a bridge did not occur until 1985.[3] Since that time a worldwide total of 174 total artificial hearts have been implanted as temporary devices to bridge to cardiac transplantation. The following is an update as of January 1, 1989. The five patients who received an artificial heart as a permanent device will not be discussed here.

The cooperation of principal investigators from 38 centers worldwide has resulted in the collection of data for the 171 patients who received the total artificial heart as a bridge to cardiac transplantation. (Three patients received a second total artificial heart after the failure of a donor organ.) This report includes the analyzed data with complete patient follow-up with the exception of the Russian (POISK) heart.

RESULTS

A total of 174 total artificial hearts were implanted in 171 patients between April 4, 1969 and January 1, 1989. Three patients received a second total artificial heart after a donor heart failure. Thirty-eight centers worldwide participated in the collection of data (Table 1).

Ten types of total artificial hearts have been implanted. Thirty-one implants were of the Symbion J7-100 type and 111 implants were J7-70 hearts. Thirty-two patients received non-Symbion devices (Table 2).

TABLE 1. The 38 Centers that Participated in Collection of Data from 174 Implantations of a Total Artificial Heart as a Bridge to Transplantation

Center	No. of Implants
Hopital La Pitie (Paris, France)	38
University of Pittsburgh (Pittsburgh, PA)	19
Loyola University (Maywood, IL)	14
Ottawa Heart Institute (Ottawa, Canada)	10
Minneapolis Heart Institute (Minneapolis, MN)	8
Midwest Heart Surgical Institute (Milwaukee, WI)	8
University of Arizona (Tucson, AZ)	7
Moscow, Russia	7
University of Vienna (Austria)	5
Warsaw, Poland	4
Texas Heart Institute (Houston, TX)	4
Henri Mondor Hopital (Paris, France)	4
Methodist/Baylor College of Medicine (Houston, TX)	4
Free University of Berlin (Berlin, W. Germany)	3
Karolinska Institute (Stockholm, Sweden)	3
Sharp Memorial Hospital (San Diego, CA)	3
Brno, Czechoslovakia	2
Humana Heart Institute (Louisville, KY)	2
Pennsylvania State University (Hershey, PA)	2
Mercy Medical Center (Des Moines, IA)	2
Methodist Hospital of Indiana (Indianapolis, IN)	2
German Heart Center (Berlin, W. Germany)	2
St. Louis University (St. Louis, MO)	2
CV Centre (Zabrze, Poland)	2
Northern Indiana Heart Institute (Fort Wayne, IN)	2
Montreal Heart Institute (Montreal, Canada)	2
Hopital de la Santa Creu (Barcelona, Spain)	2
St. Joseph's Hospital of Atlanta (Atlanta, GA)	2
Herzchirurgie, Salzburg (Austria)	1
Papworth Everard Hospital (Cambridge, England)	1
University of Florida (Gainsville, FL)	1
University of Ankara (Ankara, Turkey)	1
Clinica Puerto de Hierro (Madrid, Spain)	1
Ohio State University (Columbus, OH)	1
University of Michigan (Ann Arbor, MI)	1
Hopital de Nantes (Nantes, France)	1
Katowice, Poland	1
Prague Institute for Clinical and Experimental Medicine (Prague, Czechoslovakia)	1
	174

TABLE 2. Use of Non-Symbion Devices

Non-Symbion Devices	No. of Implants
Liotta	1
Akutsu	1
Phoenix	1
Penn State	2
Ellipsoid (Unger)	4
Berlin	7
Czechoslovakian	5
POISK	11

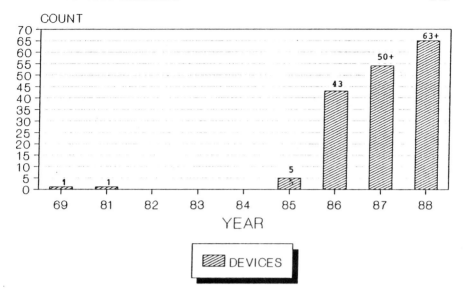

FIGURE 1. Number of total artificial hearts implanted per year: worldwide results as of January 1, 1989.

The number of implantations each year (Fig. 1) has progressively increased since 1985. Early implantation was sporadic, with a 12-year gap separating the first two implantations. In 1985, 5 patients received total artificial heart implantation as bridges. Growth continued at a moderate pace, with 43 implants done in 1986, 50+ in 1987, and 63+ in 1988.

A majority of the patients were in the fourth to sixth decades of life at the time of implant (Fig. 2), with the youngest patient being 15 and the oldest 64.

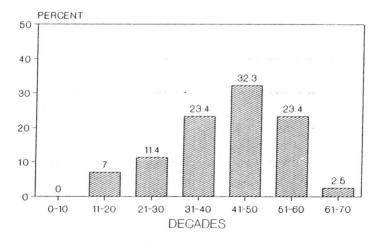

FIGURE 2. Percent of patients receiving a total artificial heart implant according to decade of age: worldwide results as of January 1, 1989.

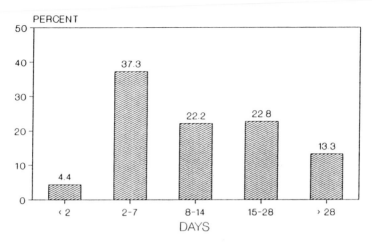

FIGURE 3. Number of days spent on the total artificial heart: worldwide results as of January 1, 1989.

There were 142 males and 20 females. (The sex of nine of the Russian patients is unknown.) The number of days spent on the device ranged from less than 1 to 243 days (Fig. 3), with the majority of patients supported for less than 2 weeks.

The etiology of underlying heart disease (Fig. 4) fell into six categories: ischemic heart disease (52%), idiopathic cardiomyopathy (35%), acute viral cardiomyopathy (6%), valvular heart disease (3%), congenital heart disease (2%), and postpartum cardiomyopathy (2%).

Indications for implantation of the total artificial heart as a bridge to cardiac transplantation are shown in Figure 5. The largest group of patients consisted of individuals who were already on the transplant waiting list but deteriorated prior to the location of a donor heart (34%); 30% of the patients received implants because of acute cardiogenic shock; 16% were unweanable from cardiopulmonary bypass following a surgical procedure, and 15% were transplant patients who had

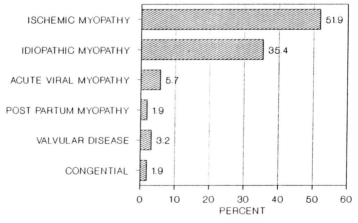

FIGURE 4. Etiology of underlying heart disease of patients requiring a total artificial heart: worldwide results as of January 1, 1989.

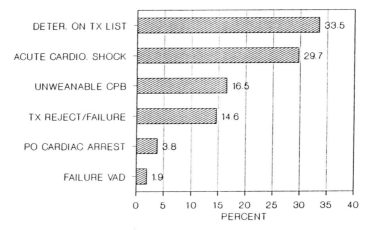

FIGURE 5. Indications for the implantation of the total artificial heart for mechanical support to bridge patients to cardiac transplantation: worldwide results as of January 1, 1989 (DETER = deterioration, TX = transplant, CARDIO = cardiogenic, CPB = cardiopulmonary bypass, PO = postoperative, and VAD = ventricular assist device).

immediate graft failure or acute rejection. Postoperative cardiac arrest in the recovery room occurred with 4% of patients; 2% had initially been supported by a ventricular assist device but needed conversion to the total artificial heart because of inadequate cardiac support or because long-term support was expected.

Not all patients supported on the total artificial heart as a bridge received a donor organ (Table 3). There were 111 Symbion J7-70 devices implanted, with 84 (76%) receiving a transplant. Of these, 59 had a 30-day or longer survival. Forty-five were alive as of January 1, 1989, with the longest survival being 967 days. Thirty-one patients received the Symbion J7-100, and 21 (68%) of these patients were transplanted, 14 with a 30-day or longer survival and 10 alive as of January 1989. The longest survivor is at 1,210 days. The POISK device has been implanted in 11 patients, 1 of whom received a transplant. There were no survivors as of January 1989. None of the patients survived at least 30 days. The Berlin total artificial heart was implanted 7 times, with 3 (43%) patients receiving a transplanted organ. Two of these patients survived at least 30 days; however, none was alive as of January 1989. The Czechoslovakian total artificial heart was

TABLE 3.   Results

Device Type	No. of Implants	No. of Transplants	30-Day Survival	Alive as of Jan. 1, 1989
Symbion J7–70	111	84	59	45
Symbion J7–100	31	21	14	10
POISK	11	1	0	0
Berlin	7	3	2	0
Czechoslovakia	5	0	0	0
Ellipsoid	4	3	1	0
Penn State	2	2	0	0
Phoenix	1	1	0	0
Akutsu	1	1	0	0
Liotta	1	1	0	0

placed in 5 patients, with none receiving a transplant. The Ellipsoid (Unger) device was used in 4 patients, with 3 (75%) receiving a transplant; one had a 30-day survival after transplant, but was not alive as of January 1989. The Penn State total artificial heart was implanted in 2 patients; both received a transplant but neither survived for 30 days. The Akutsu and Liotta devices each were implanted in one patient. Both patients were transplanted but neither survived for 30 days. The Phoenix total artificial heart was implanted in one patient, who did not survive transplantation.

The most frequent cause of death in both transplanted and non-transplanted patients was multiple organ failure due to sepsis (Fig. 6). The "other" category includes deaths from a wide variety of causes such as noncompliance, bleeding complications, pulmonary infarction, brain death prior to implant, neurologic complications after transplant, post-transplant malignancies, graft failure not due to rejection, post-transplant infections, and hepatitis.

DISCUSSION

The increase in the number of yearly implants of the total artificial heart throughout the world over the past four years is primarily a reflection of the number of patients who are in need of some type of long-term cardiac support for end-stage myocardial disease. During the same period there has been a rapid growth in the number of transplantation centers throughout the world, thus placing an increased demand on the already inadequate donor supply. As cardiac assist devices become more successful in providing intermediate-term life support, one can only assume that more devices will be used in desperation to keep patients alive long enough for a donor organ to become available. Improvements in organization and education have and will increase the donor supply slightly. However, a more certain solution to this problem will most likely occur only when a totally implantable permanent cardiac support device becomes available.

Although the vast majority of the world experience is comprised of data from use of the Symbion total artificial heart, many other devices are being

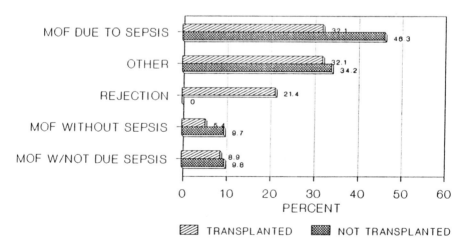

FIGURE 6. The cause of death in individuals who received the total artificial heart as a bridge to cardiac transplantation: worldwide results as of January 1, 1989 (MOF = multiple organ failure).

investigated and will be undergoing clinical trials in the near future. The success or failure of the devices presently used appears to be a reflection of patient selection rather than of characteristics of the device itself.

The clinical statistics reported here reveal few unexpected findings. Patients who received the total artificial heart were limited to individuals who fell within the accepted age categories for human cardiac transplantation. By definition, the patient was presumed to be a transplant candidate before the use of the total artificial heart as a bridge was even considered. Clinical experience would also predict that individuals in the younger age categories would recover from multiple organ failure more easily than older individuals. Thus, a majority of this population falls under the age of 50.

Early in the experience of the use of the total artificial heart, surgeons felt pressured to explant the device as quickly as possible. However, as the devices have proved to be reliable, there has been a shift toward waiting for cardiac transplantation until the patient showed signs of clinical improvement from the acute deterioration that led to the need for the device. On the other hand, long-term implants ($\geq$ 3 weeks) have demonstrated increased problems of infection and thromboembolism. Consequently, our data show that most patients have been placed back on the transplant waiting list, and the attempt made to transplant the patient after the first 2 days, but at least within the first 2 weeks, of support. The increased donor shortage problem is the major reason for extending support beyond 1 week to 10 days after implant.

The etiologies of the underlying heart disease in the individuals who underwent implantation of the total artificial hearts are similar to the reasons for cardiac transplantation. The immediate availability of a total artificial heart has allowed more frequent treatment of two disease processes: acute viral cardiomyopathy and postpartum cardiomyopathy.

The total artificial heart has been used most frequently for patients who are already on cardiac transplantation waiting lists and are acutely deteriorating. However, two thirds of the patients fell into other categories where previously there was little chance for cardiac transplantation. In the past, some patients have been fortunate enough to receive donor organs for indications such as inability to wean from cardiopulmonary bypass, acute donor organ failure or rejection, failure of ventricular assist devices, postoperative cardiac arrest, or onset of acute cardiogenic shock. Most of these patients died before they were ever able to be considered as potential transplant recipients. As more of these patients are salvaged with the use of assist devices, there will be a further growth in the pool of potential transplant recipients.

Perhaps the greatest lesson to be learned from the use of total artificial hearts as a bridging device over the past 10 years stems from an evaluation of the cause of death in the individuals who either died on the device or died following transplantation. A major cause of death in either category was multiple organ failure caused by or occurring with or without sepsis. Patient selection is a primary determinant of success. As the device becomes internalized, the septic complications should become less significant. However, identification of the point at which multiple organ failure becomes irreversible continues to be crucial.

As previously reported,[2] detailed analysis of the first 100 Symbion total artificial hearts used as bridge devices did not show a statistical difference in survival when comparing age, sex, etiology, indications for the use of the device, or days on the device. There was a 9% incidence of thromboembolic events related to the use of the total artificial heart. The presence of anuria in the 12 hours prior to implant was not a determinant of transplantability or survival; however, the need for hemodialysis resulted in a grave prognosis. The inability to provide statistical significance in these areas is perhaps partially due to the fact that multiple centers[2] were involved and thus many centers had a very limited experience. The trends do reveal that patients with the fewest organ system failures pre-implant had the greatest chance of survival.

There are several potential advantages of a total artificial heart. The device provides immediate biventricular support and allows the physician to have complete cardiac control. If the device could be used permanently, the donor shortage problem would be avoided and the device could be an "on the shelf" item readily available for immediate use. There would be no threat of rejection; therefore, immunosuppression would be unnecessary. Thus, risk for infection might be less than what is currently seen.

Disadvantages of the total artificial heart in its present state of development include the requirement for an external power source, and thus the need for percutaneous leads, resulting in an increased risk of infection. The device also requires continuous anticoagulation therapy. Additionally, because implantation of the device requires the excision of both ventricles, one has to assume irreversible myocardial damage before considering its use. Ongoing investigation of new devices is costly; only further development of this technology will determine whether it can truly be cost effective.

The use of the total artificial heart specifically as a bridge to cardiac transplantation will merely compound the shortage of donor organs. The true benefits of the above reported studies will be achieved only if the positive findings serve to influence the development of a totally implantable permanent device that will alleviate donor shortage problems. The results of the first 10 years of experience with the total artificial heart would appear to justify further scientific investigation into the development of a totally implantable device.

REFERENCES

1. Cooley DA, Akutsu T, Norman JC, et al: Total artificial heart in two-staged cardiac transplantation. Cardiovasc Dis 8:305–319, 1981.
2. Joyce LD, Johnson KE, et al: Results of the first one hundred patients who received Symbion total artificial hearts as a bridge to cardiac transplantation. Circulation (in press).
3. Levinson MM, Smith RG, Cork RC, et al: Three recent cases of the total artificial heart prior to transplantation. Heart Transplant 5:215–228, 1986.

MARK M. LEVINSON, MD

THE SPECTRUM OF PATHOPHYSIOLOGY AND COMPLICATIONS IN HUMAN RECIPIENTS OF THE JARVIK-7 ARTIFICIAL HEART

Department of Surgery
Section of Cardiothoracic
  Surgery
Providence Medical Center
Seattle, Washington

Reprint requests to:
Mark M. Levinson, MD
1600 E. Jefferson St.
Suite 101
Seattle, WA 98122

Only within the past 8 years has cardiac transplantation transformed from a morbid experimental technique into a safe and successful modality for the treatment of endstage heart disease. Over 2,000 cases are now being performed annually worldwide.[23] Unfortunately, the utility of transplantation is limited by critical donor shortages. A recent expert panel[2] has estimated that between 15,000 and 35,000 U.S. heart failure patients per year are suitable candidates for cardiac replacement. However, despite our best efforts, the maximum potential donor pool will probably never be greater than 2,500 to 3,000 per year.[22] In addition, present immunosuppressive regimens are not specific enough, nor powerful enough to permit organ donation across the interspecies barrier (i.e., xenotransplantation). This persistent donor shortage has created a therapeutic gap, gradually being filled by mechanical assist or replacement devices.

Ingenious research by engineers and physicians over the past several decades has led to the development of various pumps specifically for replacement or assistance of the diseased human heart. Conceptual proposals for an "artificial heart"[24] eventually progressed to an initial attempt in 1937 by Demikhov[14] to circulate the left ventricular return using a crankshaft-driven hydraulic pump. Actual replacement of the heart with a mechanical pump was first

CARDIAC SURGERY: State of the Art Reviews—Vol. 3, No. 3, October 1989
Philadelphia, Hanley & Belfus, Inc.

551

achieved experimentally in 1957 by Akutsu and Kolff.[1] Wilhelm Kolff continued his developmental research on the artificial heart addressing such problems as anatomical fit, thrombogenesis, infection, pannus formation, and mechanical reliability, which remained as major barriers. Under Kolff's direction, Robert Jarvik modified previous designs of pneumatically powered prosthetic ventricles, improving fatigue resistance, reducing areas of stasis, and making the new models more suitable for implantation into the human mediastinum.

The first human total artificial heart (TAH) implant was performed in 1969,[10] using the pneumatic Liotta heart to salvage a patient who failed to separate from cardiopulmonary bypass. This patient subsequently underwent orthotopic heart transplantation and the device was removed, establishing a monumental principle later known as "bridge-to-transplantation" (BTT). A second patient implanted by Cooley in 1981 (with the Akutsu III TAH) also died from infectious complications.[8,9] Four years later, the team from the University of Arizona achieved the first survivor of interim TAH implantation using the Jarvik-7. This 26-year-old patient is still alive 46 months following cardiac transplant.[11,48] Although 7 different TAH designs have now been implanted in man,[39] the pneumatic Jarvik-7 has gradually become the leading clinical tool for short-term mechanical cardiac replacement.[38]

Despite the amazing pumping capabilities of these devices, major complications, contraindications to transplantation, and deaths have plagued the trials of all TAH designs. This article categorizes the major sequelae following Jarvik-7 implantation and discusses the approaches taken to alleviate or reduce their impact on patient outcome. The selection criteria and indications for implantation for various mechanical assist devices are summarized elsewhere.[44,54] Because of the broad nature of the problem, infectious complications are not included.

THROMBOEMBOLISM AND ANTICOAGULATION

Early efforts at pump development were troubled by mechanical inefficiency, inadequate output, sizing difficulties, and extensive hemolysis. Implant experiments usually failed within hours, making assessment of the thrombotic potential of each design fairly limited. However, pumps removed from animals surviving more than a few days demonstrated thrombus accumulation at characteristic sites, particularly along surface defects or near areas of flow disturbance.[3,4,7,52]

Olsen et al.[52] initially reported that the thrombi in early Jarvik designs accumulated primarily at the junction between the flexing diaphragm and the semi-rigid housing (the DH junction). In addition, crevices between the valves and the housing often contained small thrombi, especially near the bases of the valve struts.[52] Subsequent redesigns and improvements have rendered the DH junction nearly thrombus-free.[60] However, the valve mounting seams and crevices between the quick-connector components are still areas with a propensity for thrombus formation in the current Jarvik-7.[3,4,49,60]

Despite aggressive anticoagulation, most centers are reporting characteristic thrombotic attachments at similar locations within the explanted pumps.[26,49] Taylor et al.[60] reported the appearance of 33 explanted Jarvik-7 hearts following temporary human implantation. Utilizing a semiquantitative analysis, small thrombi were always seen scattered around the valve seats, connectors, and the atrial-cuff junctions in a similar distribution as seen in animals (Fig. 1). Using a modified anticoagulation protocol, Cabrol et al.[5,51] and Semb[25] reported thrombi primarily at the atrial-cuff suture line.

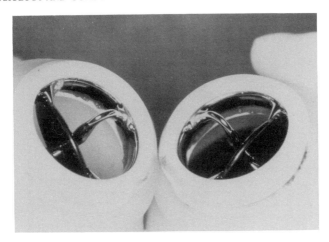

FIGURE 1. Thrombotic deposits surrounding the valve rings and the crevices created for seating the valves within the Jarvik-7 housing.

Cooley's pioneering recipients of the Liotta TAH[10] and Akutsu TAH[9] in 1969 and 1981, respectively, were free of recognizable embolic complications.[8] In 1981, Dr. Barney Clark became the celebrated recipient of the first permanent mechanical heart.[18] On warfarin anticoagulation alone, no cerebral embolic events were proven in 112 days on the Jarvik-7. However, the second permanent recipient suffered a major dysphasic and hemiparetic episode on the 13th post-implant day despite heparin and dipyridamole. In addition, 3 of the original 5 permanent patients implanted from 1982 to 1985 suffered neurologic events.[16,39] Four of the first seven Jarvik recipients (57%) developed focal neurologic findings.[11,49] The first "bridge" Jarvik-7 recipient suffered transient neurologic symptoms.[17] Shortly thereafter, the device was removed for cardiac transplantation and the interior inspected. Thrombotic accumulation at the aortic quick-connector was most likely responsible for the clinical embolus in this case (Fig. 2).[49] Subsequent patients have shown variable propensities for major and minor neurologic events.

Between 1985 and 1987, over 45 short-term Jarvik-7 implants were performed, with proven cerebral embolic events occurring in only 6 patients (13%). All but two recovered with minimal or no residual deficits. These improvements can be attributed to more diligent monitoring of the anticoagulation, more consistent addition of antiplatelet therapy to the regimens, and the shorter duration of implantation in the "bridge" population than in the original permanent TAH program.

Risk factors for developing thromboembolism in individual Jarvik-7 patients have not been clarified. The duration of implant is certainly one factor. Patients implanted for only a few days are at low risk. Toward the end of the first implant week, hypercoagulability tends to develop. Platelet count and serum concentrations of coagulation factors such as fibrinogen[42,47,49] reach a peak at this time, favoring the formation of thrombus. Several patients were definitely hypercoagulable just prior to the onset of neurologic symptoms.[16,42,47,49] After several weeks, the role of infection in stimulating thrombosis becomes more prominent. The incidence of device infection appears to increase with time of implantation, particularly beyond 30 days. DeVries[16,62] has elegantly demonstrated

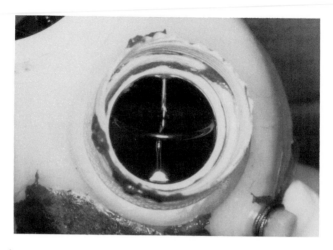

FIGURE 2. Explanted Jarvik-7 examined 36 hours following a transient neurologic deficit. Loose thrombotic debris in the quick-connector junction most likely constituted the source of embolization in this patient.

in permanent recipients that clinical emboli appear to be timed in association with bacteremic episodes. Infection may, in some way, affect the blood-material interaction, predisposing to thrombosis. The exact mechanism of thrombogenesis following periods of sepsis is not currently known.

Short half-life, reversible, and titratable drugs are better suited than warfarin-based regimens for anticoagulation in temporary situations. The "bridge" programs have thus relied primarily on heparin.[39] Its 30 minute half-life and ease of adjustment are desirable properties for "bridge" applications.[47] However, even with continuous heparin infusions, embolization has occurred. Control, monitoring, and standardization of heparin remains a clinical problem. In addition, this drug has little fundamental activity against platelets, which are probably more crucial to the interaction of blood with artificial surfaces than is the fibrin mechanism.[25] Instantaneously after contact with circulating blood, any artificial surface becomes coated with plasma proteins, notably fibrin, fibronectin, and von Willebrand's factor. These proteins are recognized by platelet surface receptors.

Although platelet numbers and function are subnormal following cardiopulmonary bypass and exposure of the blood to the oxygenator surfaces,[30] sufficient platelet activity remains to begin the process of surface deposition on a circulatory assist pump. It would be ideal to impair such responses from the moment of implantation, but this risks complete paralysis of coagulation and severe hemorrhage. Attempts by DeVries to pretreat with antiplatelet agents and continue both antifibrin and antiplatelet therapy throughout the early hours after implantation have been associated with marked postoperative bleeding. Copeland first proposed a delay in the initiation of anticoagulant therapy to permit surgical hemostasis, followed by heparin with or without antiplatelet therapy (personal communication). Copeland, Joyce, DeVries, and others have championed heparin/dipyridamole combinations,[39] which have gradually become the standard for BTT anticoagulation. Munretto and Cabrol[51] have extensive experience with a similar heparin/dipyridamole regimen but with reduced heparin dosage (1,000 to 5,000 IU/day). The Kunitz inhibitor aprotinin (Trasylol) is used when increased fibrin degradation is evident.[5] With this multi-drug approach, Cabrol reported no thromboembolic events in 28 consecutive Jarvik-7 recipients implanted for an average of 15 days and a maximum of 42 days.[5,51]

Because the specter of neurologic injury outweighs concerns over bleeding, aggressive anticoagulation is still the cornerstone of current therapy. Ideally, close monitoring of the therapeutic effect can achieve a narrow but safe "window," allowing antithrombotic effects without major bleeding complications. Heparin monitoring is familiar to most physicians and the activated clotting time (ACT) or activated partial thromboplastin (aPTT) times are the current standards of measurement for heparin effect. Standard thrombin time assays may be too sensitive to low levels of heparin to follow therapeutic doses of the drug. However, the group at the Minneapolis Heart Institute has been successful in monitoring continuous IV heparin using a diluted thrombin time assay. Most centers are currently following the ACT and/or aPTT but there is no accepted standard range of therapeutic values. Bleeding complications have been more common when the aPTT is greater than 60 seconds and nearly absent when the target aPTT is 45 seconds. Bleeding that begins with an aPTT of 45 seconds or less has always proved to be a surgical source unmasked by low levels of anticoagulant. The ACT has been a useful supplemental test to help confirm the aPTT and 200 seconds seems to be the optimal range. Thromboelastography, which is independently sensitive (and specific) for both fibrin and platelet mechanisms, is still being evaluated by one implant center as a tool for monitoring drug effects.[51]

Aspirin has the unique disadvantage of nonreversibility and its effects do not wane until new platelets are produced by the bone marrow during an aspirin-free period. In this regard, cardiopulmonary bypass for cardiac transplantation after a course of aspirin will carry a greater risk of severe intraoperative bleeding. The mediastinum is penetrated by vascularized granulation tissue within days of implanting the Jarvik device. Functionless, aspirin-treated platelets, in combination with these raw, inflamed surfaces, create the perfect setting for severe bleeding after implanting the donor heart. For these reasons, routine use of aspirin is discouraged in the "bridge" setting.

Various release products from the coagulation system have been studied in BTT recipients with the intent of developing a reliable assay of ongoing thrombogenesis.[25,55] Green et al. have reported steady elevations of fibrinopeptide A (FPA), beta-thromboglobulin (BTG), and urinary metabolites of thromboxane A2 in a long-term recipient. They concluded that the synthetic surfaces of the TAH continuously stimulate low-grade intravascular coagulation throughout the implant.[25] Platelet granular products, particularly thromboxane, appear to be central to the production of several other biochemical markers of thrombogenesis. Treatment with aspirin and reduction in thromboxane synthesis correlated with marked reductions in markers of fibrin metabolism and clinical heparin requirements.[25]

Newly described subunits broken off during fibrin degradation may offer additional sensitivity to such events (Fig. 3). In a pilot study by Ring et al.,[55] comparing Jarvik-7 patients against relative controls (i.e., primary heart transplant recipients), cross-linked fibrin degradation products (XDPs) and B-beta subunits (as well as FPA and BTG) increased consistently in TAH recipients after the first few implant days despite aggressive heparin anticoagulation (Table 1).

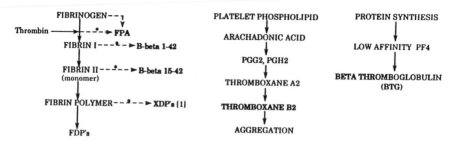

FIGURE 3. A simplified schema accounting for measurable circulating products of thrombotic activity. * = plasmin-mediated enzymatic hydrolysis; [1] XDP = cross-linked degradation products.

This observation and others[25] indicate that activation of both the platelet and fibrin arms of the coagulation mechanism is ongoing throughout implantation. In addition, BTG levels in Jarvik-7 patients were higher than in heart transplant recipients even on the first postoperative day, implying that the extensive artificial surfaces do indeed react strongly with circulating platelets early after initial blood contact.

While most values stabilized or decreased by the end of the first week in transplant recipients, the FPA, XDP, and BTG continued to rise in TAH patients. In one patient, BTG levels increased three-fold just prior to a transient ischemic attack.[55] XDP markers rose sharply in another patient in the days preceding his stroke. Preliminary data on two patients showed elevations of XDPs and B-beta subunits of fibrin degeneration just prior to clinical emboli.[55] In another patient, severe pump thrombosis occurred secondary to inflow obstruction.[12] The markers in this patient progressively elevated to very high levels, correlating with the evolution of the thrombotic process. Autopsy revealed multiple cerebral and visceral emboli. The magnitude of these biochemical changes indicates that TAH implantation is followed by marked stimulation of platelet function, fibrin formation, and fibrin degradation which occurs independently and well after the effects of the implant operation. There is some suggestion from the curves that maximum stimulation of the platelet and fibrin mechanisms occurs at days 5 through 7, but more data will be needed for confirmation. These ELISA assays may eventually prove to measure active thrombus formation with enough sensitivity to detect early pump thrombosis and encourage treatment with more powerful agents (such as fibrinolytic drugs) prior to the onset of a clinical embolus.

TABLE 1. Markers of Thrombotic Activity in Jarvik-7 "Bridge" Recipients Versus Primary Transplant Recipients

	NL	POD 1		POD 7	
		Txn	TAH	Txn	TAH
Beta-thrombo globulin (ng/ml)	23	88	286.5	44	220.7
Fibrinopeptide A (ng/ml)	2.3	18.2	22.15	8.5	31.1
XDP subunits (ng/ml)	56	623	667.5	555	2150

POD = postoperative day; NL = normal; Txn = transplantation; TAH = total artificial heart; XDP = cross-linked fibrin degradation products.

Semb, DeVries, Levinson,[16,48,49] and others have also noted a sudden rise in circulating platelet counts just preceding clinical neurologic events in different Jarvik recipients under different circumstances. The cause is unknown, but may simply reflect a nonspecific stimulation of platelet release in response to stress or infection. In at least two of the permanent patients studied by DeVries, thrombocytosis coincided with positive blood cultures and embolic events.[16] In another patient,[12,47] secondary hypercoagulability brought on by rapid clinical recovery from preexisting cardiogenic shock was associated with rebound thrombocytosis, hyperfibrinogenemia, and finally embolization. The timing of these neurologic events and the observed rise in platelet counts suggest a mechanistic action, but the link is not clear.

Griffith[26] and Kormos[42] have noted alterations in blood rheology in their Jarvik-7 recipients characterized by elevated whole blood viscosity, elevated serum fibrinogen, and increased red cell rigidity. These authors suggest that the TAH somehow alters RBC membrane rigidity through direct, mechanical forces. Such rheologic effects may decrease capillary flow within the cerebral microcirculation, resulting in a predisposition to neurologic events. These changes were associated with decreased cerebral blood flow (as measured by xenon washout) despite high cardiac outputs when compared with a cohort of transplant recipients. However, despite these measured effects, the incidence of cerebral events in their studied population remained low (6%).[26]

BLEEDING

Serious hemorrhagic complications followed 75% of the initial human Jarvik-7 implantations, with 24–33% requiring early surgical reexploration.[26] Many factors are responsible: (1) patient age, (2) prior cardiac surgical procedures, (3) chronic CHF and elevated intracardiac pressures leaving thinned-out cardiac tissues, (4) atherosclerotic degeneration of the ascending aorta, and (5) longer periods on cardiopulmonary bypass (mean = 3.2 hours). In addition, the great vessels of human subjects are of variable sizes, requiring accurate suturing to construct the anastomosis with a semi-rigid conduit of fixed size without folds or pleats.

Attempts to re-start heparin early after surgery have been associated with postoperative bleeding.[16] Continuous heparin ($\pm$ dipyridamole) does appear to have an acceptable risk/benefit ratio if delayed for 6 to 12 hours until surgical hemostasis is secured. However, this regimen is still far from ideal. The difficulties in controlling heparin effect are well known. In vitro aPTT analysis can occasionally be misleading, resulting in over or under heparinization.

Most serious bleeding has originated at or near the aortic graft suture line. In older patients, the diseased, atherosclerotic aorta may be friable[17] and difficult to join onto a stiff Dacron graft in a totally water-tight fashion. Once off bypass, the posterior aortic suture line is nearly impossible to visualize. Lifting the aorta to inspect for bleeding can stress the suture line, further aggravating bleeding. Should the connectors need to be unsnapped to reposition the heart, the mechanical stresses during this maneuver can disrupt previously constructed suture lines. Any undue tension created while positioning the heart more leftward in the chest further aggravates suture line and needle hole bleeding. In addition, the elevated dP/dT of the Jarvik/Utah drive system imparts considerable kinetic energy to the blood. The aortic graft pulsates vigorously and there is considerable systolic tension on the suture line.

Techniques found to reduce suture line bleeding include (1) incorporating felt strips into the suture lines,[17] (2) external wrapping of the completed suture line with strips of felt, (3) application of fibrin glue[56] over the suture line, and (4) application of gelatin-resorcine-formal topical sealant.[51] Once completed, suture line integrity can be assessed using specially fabricated injectors[45] to temporarily pressurize the conduits, unmasking folds or tears that are prone to bleed.

Before placing the right ventricle, it is essential to de-air and start pumping the left ventricle. This not only decompresses the pulmonary venous return, but applies partially pulsatile pressure to the aortic suture line, assisting in the detection of leaks. Once the right pump is in place, exposure to the posterior aorta or left atrium is poor. DeVries[16] found it necessary to reexplore one patient through a left posterior lateral thoracotomy for bleeding, because exposure of these critical sites is so difficult from the median sternotomy approach after the device is completely in place and functioning.

Despite impressive hemorrhagic complications early on, surgical expertise is improving and bleeding complications are fewer. Meticulous attention to critical portions of the implant operation and delay of anticoagulation for several hours have made a major impact in postoperative bleeding rates.

TAMPONADE

Cardiac tamponade is characterized by (1) low cardiac output and clinical shock, (2) decreased cardiac filling, (3) normal (or unchanged) systolic ventricular function, and (4) elevation of intrapericardial pressures at or above the corresponding venous filling pressures. The condition is life-threatening unless quickly corrected and normal cardiac output restored. The most common cause is intrapericardial bleeding. Compression of the ventricles was once thought to explain the low cardiac output state. However, with rigid prosthetic ventricles it would seem impossible to "tamponade" a patient with an artificial heart. However, cases of tamponade are well documented in such patients. Clinically they present as inflow obstruction. The Jarvik-7 drive console is equipped with a diagnostic unit that displays graphic representations of the airflow waveforms in both systole and diastole (Fig. 4).[59,66] Diagnosis of inflow obstruction on either side of the mechanical heart is possible (Fig. 5). In the face of mediastinal hemorrhage, low TAH output and impaired inflow portend tamponade physiology. Nine cases have been documented with this device. The onset of shock

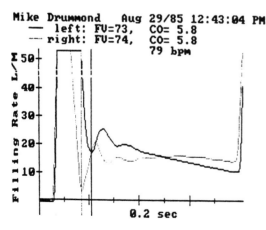

FIGURE 4. Normal diastolic waveforms as viewed from the computer on the Utah II drive console. Area under the curve reflects the volume of blood entering the ventricles during diastole. The downward slope toward the end of diastole is a physiologic tapering of inflow as the atrial-ventricular pressure gradient equilibrates just before systole.

FIGURE 5. Sudden reduction of inflow in mid-diastole with flat persistent low filling rates in the second half of diastole. Filling curves such as these are characteristic of inflow obstruction from either tamponde or malfit.

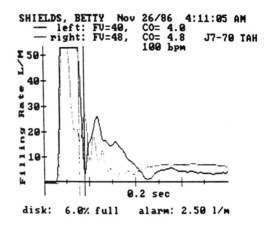

from atrial tamponade occurs quickly with few clinical warning signs,[16,17] although dropping cardiac output trends may be seen early on the monitoring console. Relief through decompression of the mediastinum is associated with return of TAH filling, normalization of the filling curves, and return of stable blood pressure (Fig. 6). These observations confirm the physiology of cardiac tamponade as limited atrial inflow, because the prosthetic ventricles themselves cannot be compressed or distorted. Once intrapericardial pressure exceeds venous pressure, this device will fail to fill and the physiology of tamponade occurs. Mechanical compression of the atrial suture cuffs is another possible explanation, although unlikely.

CYTOTOXIC ANTIBODY FORMATION

Presensitization is hazardous to "bridge" TAH recipients. TAH recipients are in competition with other qualified recipients for a limited pool of donors, and a positive PRA greatly limits their access to quality donor hearts. Following TAH implantation, blood transfusions and the use of components such as platelets and cryoprecipitate provide sufficient antigen challenge to sensitize the recipient against transfused HLA antigens. In renal transplantation, presensitization does provide a meaningful survival advantage.[53] However, the TAH "bridge" patient is complication-prone and cannot continue to wait indefinitely

FIGURE 6. A patient with mediastinal bleeding and tamponade physiology. This continuous 2-hour cardiac output record demonstrates a sudden increase in right heart output when the tamponade is decompressed. (Recent events are recorded beginning on the left hand side of the abscissa.)

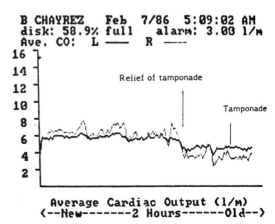

for a crossmatch-negative or HLA-compatible donor organ. Several patients have developed a marked PRA (50–100%), making donor location and screening nearly impossible. The long wait for a crossmatch-negative donor and the logistical problem of performing so many crossmatches greatly impaired the resolution of these patients' problems and contributed to their deaths.[48,50] Minimization of bleeding and conservative use of all blood and coagulation products are essential in preventing sensitization prior to transplant. It remains uncertain why some patients become hypersensitized to transfused antigens during TAH implantation despite the known T-helper cell and B-cell lymphopenia observed in this patient population.[58]

SURGICAL IMPLANTATION, POSITIONING, AND FIT

Anatomical Considerations

Initial attempts at designing an artificial heart were frustrated by the inability to implant a workable device within the limited mediastinal space. Early experiments demonstrated that the geometry and size of TAH devices were critical design features. Compression of the surrounding anatomy became crucial limitations.[37] When redesigning early versions of diaphragm-style blood pumps, Jarvik engineered his models to fit anticipated dimensions of the human mediastinum and confirmed this with cadaver fit trials.[37] Other characteristics, such as a smooth, low-turbulence blood pathway, and support of adequate stroke volumes needed to be considered in the final design as well.[36] This led to the semi-conical shape of the current Jarvik-7 100 cc and 70 cc devices. These features were confirmed with a unique set of cadaver implants:[41] Jarvik-7 TAHs were implanted into brain-dead accident victims and normal circulatory hemodynamics were maintained for up to 72 hours. This study confirmed that physiologic pumping was possible, but anatomic fit without compression of surrounding structures still remained crucial to successful implantation.[41]

The human mediastinum is wider than it is deep. It is also bounded anteriorly by the inner table of the closed sternum and posteriorly by the anterior border of the vertebral column. Both of these are unyielding, bony structures in between which the device must fit and function properly (Fig. 7). In addition, the esophagus sits on the anterior border of the vertebral column, somewhat shortening the free space distance as compared with radiographic measurements. In contrast, the lateral extent of the mediastinum is delineated by the borders of the pericardium. This membrane is compliant and will adapt to the enlarging dimensions of the failing heart. In many victims of endstage cardiac disease, impressive ventricular dilatation occurs, enlarging the pericardial space toward the left pleural cavity and displacing the overlying phrenic nerves secondarily. Although cardiomegaly raises the total volume of the pericardial space, the bony structures maintain a fixed anterior-posterior dimension.

The retrosternal anterior-posterior distance is the most critical dimension for successful fit of a prosthetic heart.[37] CT scanning of the chest provides the most accurate assessment of anterior-posterior distance without significant distortion or magnification error.[17,37] However, it is not always possible to obtain CT scans in near-terminal cardiac patients. Individuals under consideration for emergency TAH implantation are too ill to move safely to the CT scan suite unless very carefully monitored and managed. Lateral upright chest x-rays can measure the anteroposterior distance but are prone to magnification errors in the range of 10–15%.[37]

FIGURE 7. Lateral radiograph of a patient following Jarvik-7 implantation. The right ventricular air diaphragm is evidenced by the retrosternal air bubble. The prosthetic right ventricle lies directly beneath the inner table of the sternum. The narrow distance between the sternum and spine restricts the ability to fit this device in humans.

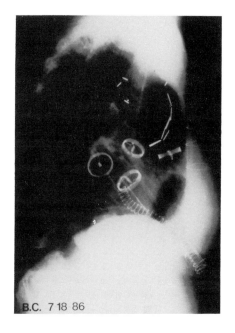

B.C. 7 18 86

Patient Selection and Positioning

The ultimate goal of surgical positioning is to implant the device free of: (1) arterial, venous, atrial, phrenic nerve, or pulmonary compression, (2) undue tension on the suture lines, and (3) bleeding. Jarvik et al.[37] analyzed the earliest patients receiving either the 100 cc or 70 cc devices. Thoracic measurements, body size, surgical positioning, and physiologic results were compared between patient groups. This study included twelve 100 cc and seven 70 cc implants and remains the only scientific analysis of fit characteristics in human subjects with this device. The authors concluded that two primary factors needed to be considered preoperatively: (1) *size* (i.e., body surface area and thoracic dimensions), and (2) *positioning* (i.e., medial or lateral placement). The most accurate measurement of size was the distance between the anterior T-10 vertebral body and the inner table of the sternum as measured by CT (the "DT-10" value). Clinical results were categorized physiologically and anatomically according to criteria developed from both animal and human experience. Using these criteria, 68% of all implants were classified as excellent[37] and another 10% as good. Poor anatomic fit was obtained in only 10% of implants.

These authors developed recommendations for selecting the pump size and surgical positioning which favor optimal TAH fit and function. The 100 cc device will usually fit satisfactorily in patients with a body surface area (BSA) of more than 2 square meters (m^2) and a DT-10 diameter of more than 12.5 cm. In addition, larger patients (> 2 m^2) will require more cardiac output, and thus the larger stroke volume available with this device. Smaller individuals (BSA < 2 m^2) will receive adequate hemodynamic support from the smaller, 70 cc model. If such patients also have a DT-10 < 12 cm, the pump should be displaced laterally into the left pleural space to make room for the right heart prosthesis under the

Sizing and Positioning of the Jarvik-7 Artificial
Heart According to Patient Anatomy

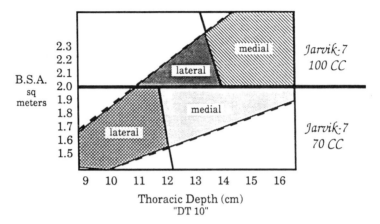

FIGURE 8. Schematic diagram comparing body surface area (B.S.A.) to thoracic depth at the tenth vertebral body. The choices of pump size and positioning for proper implantation of the two models of Jarvik-7 artificial heart are illustrated.[37]

sternum (Fig. 8). The same positioning recommendations apply in large patients if the DT-10 is less than 13.5 cm.[37]

There are two primary choices for positioning—medial and lateral.[37] Medial positioning is defined as placement within the intact pericardial space without opening the left pleural space. Medial placement is desirable, but does not take precedence over physiologic performance of the pump or freedom from vascular compromise. In many patients the enlarged pericardium is of suitable size to contain the entire TAH without subsequent vascular compression. However, when prior cardiac surgery has taken place, pericardial thickening and adhesions may limit the ability of this membrane to dilate. Many such patients have a small pericardial space and medial placement is nearly impossible. The shape of the pericardium (boot-shaped or pointed) also makes a difference when considering medial positioning.[37]

With lateral positioning, the prosthesis lays directly on the left lower lobe of the lung, creating compression atelectasis. Continuing atelectasis in the postoperative period interferes with pulmonary function, and the affected lobe may scar in so densely as to require decortication during the subsequent transplant operation.[12,40] In one notable case,[12] pressure necrosis led to "sterile abscess" formation, gross destruction of lung parenchyma, and fatal intraoperative hemorrhage during attempted decortication. In addition, lateral placement may make the pleural space more vulnerable to infection, because blood and fluid invariably collect while transthoracic drains and drive tubes enter in from the environment.

Because of these concerns, many surgeons[5,12,26,51] have migrated toward implanting only the 70 cc device in all patients, regardless of body size or dimensions. This approach eliminates confusion about which patients are candidates for the small or large device. Cabrol has placed all such devices in the

TABLE 2.   Surgical Maneuvers to Improve Leftward Positioning of the Jarvik-7 Device

Excise native ventricles just below the AV groove (leaving maximum atrial tissue)
Complete mobilization of the ascending aorta to the innominate artery and separation from both the MPA and the RMPA
Complete restriction of the left parietal pericardium and mediastinal pleura down to the phrenic nerve
Mobilization of both cavae from their pericardial attachments
Relatively long aortic (5–7 cm) and pulmonary (9–10 cm) conduits
Extreme posterior placement of the left ventricle with as much posterior rotation of the aortic outflow as possible
Oblong atrial cuffs with the leftward side trimmed close to the connector[45]
Longitudinal relaxing incision posterior to the phrenic nerve, with deep placement of the left ventricle
Umbilical tape sling (around inflow of right ventricle) anchored to a convenient rib to pull the RV to the left[12]
Extreme lateral placement of the drive lines (mid-axillary line)
Crossed drive lines (left-medial; right-extreme lateral)
Extreme leftward and cephalad placement of the LV within the pleural space to allow the RV room to sit deeper in the chest

medial position, and to date only one of 33 patients has suffered from caval or pulmonary venous obstruction.[5,51] The smaller device is still capable of 6 L/min cardiac output (with diastolic vacuum applied), and these investigators have not yet needed the larger pump for any "bridge" patients solely for hemodynamic performance.[5,51]

Table 2 summarizes the surgical maneuvers that assist in positioning the device lateral to the pericardial membranes. Essentially, this means resecting the left parietal pericardium down to the phrenic nerve. After the pleural space has been entered, the left ventricle can be positioned more posteriorly. In addition, the pericardium posterior to the phrenic may be opened longitudinally in a relaxing-type incision and the left ventricle slipped underneath the phrenic nerve. The ascending aorta should be well mobilized from its attachments to allow leftward displacement without tension.

Appropriate sizing of the aortic and pulmonary grafts is also critical.[16,17,37,45] Through experience, a length of 5 to 7 cm for the aortic conduit is most often correct,[16,45] whereas 10 to 12 cm suffices for the pulmonary graft. However, it is preferable to measure the distances directly during implantation to be more precise.[17] This can be done by temporarily placing the empty prosthetic ventricles into the mediastinum in their respective positions and directly measuring the gap between the cut end of the great vessels and the connection points on the TAH.[17] Alternatively, a set of "dummy" Jarvik ventricles (devoid of drive tubing) can be sterilized and temporarily positioned within the mediastinum to facilitate this measurement. Should the conduits prove to be too short, excessive suture line tension and bleeding result from attempts to forcibly position the device laterally in the pleural space.[16,37]

Diagnosis of Malfit

Most clinical episodes of malfit are manifested by obstruction or kinking of one or more of the vascular structures in the mediastinum adjacent to the device. Sternal closure is the critical moment for assessing the adequacy of fit. The right

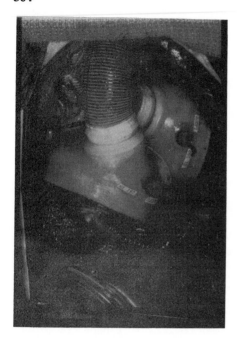

FIGURE 9. The Jarvik-7 100 cc total artificial heart *in situ*. The semi-conical blood pumps are overlapped, with the right pump straddling over the left pump.

ventricular prosthesis straddles over the body of the left ventricle and usually ends up just underneath the sternum (Fig. 9). Anteroposterior compressive forces are exerted on the base plate of the right ventricle as the sternal halves are drawn together. In this manner compression of normal vascular anatomy by the prosthetic right ventricle, the underlying left ventricle, or both may occur.

Right-sided venous compression usually occurs in the setting of medial positioning or the placement of the larger device into a small patient. The right atrial cuff is driven posteriorly into the body of the right atrium and may invaginate into this structure.[12] In addition, the cuff or the ventricular housing may compress the inferior or superior vena cava, or both. A sudden drop in cardiac output follows immediately after drawing the sternum closed (Fig. 10). In

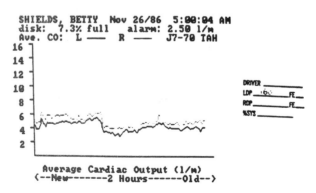

FIGURE 10. Low cardiac output after sternal closure in a patient with medial positioning and malfit. Immediate increase in cardiac output when the sternum is reopened. (Recent events are recorded beginning on the left hand side of the abscissa.)

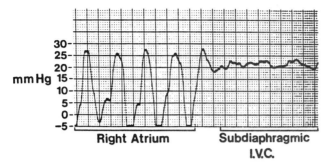

FIGURE 11. Transfemoral venous pullback pressure tracing, confirming a pressure gradient at the diaphragm level in a Jarvik-7 recipient with malfit and inferior vena caval obstruction.

addition, filling traces show continuous slow filling throughout the second half of diastole (Fig. 5) and filling volumes remain low despite systemic volume loading. Corresponding atrial pressures measured by central venous catheters rise above expected values (> 15 mm Hg). The addition of diastolic vacuum compensates to some degree by improving diastolic right ventricular filling, but does not restore pump outputs to normal. Releasing the sternal wires allows the right ventricle to rise off the cavae and restores hemodynamics and filling pressures to baseline levels. If right-sided inflow obstruction is suspected after the chest has been closed, a transfemoral venous pullback tracing may demonstrate a discreet pressure gradient at the level of the diaphragm (Fig. 11). Symptoms of caval compression mimic those of pericardial constriction with a predominance of right-sided "failure" on clinical examination. Findings may include anasarca, ascites, jugular venous distention, periorbital edema, hepatomegaly, and renal failure.

Pulmonary venous return is also vulnerable to compression posteriorly behind the left ventricular prosthesis. Anterior-posterior compression by the straddling right ventricle as the sternum is closed can displace the left ventricular device posteriorly into the left (or both) pulmonary veins. Cardiac output may drop during sternal closure, and partial fill tracings persist on the left side despite appropriate volume loading (see Fig. 5). Pulmonary gas exchange deteriorates quickly and frothy pulmonary edema appears in the endotracheal tube. Once again, short-term relief can be gained by reopening the sternotomy. Early radiographs often demonstrate asymmetric pulmonary edema (Fig. 12).

Treatment of Malfit

Treatment of malfit begins by recognizing its existence. After a long and difficult operation under emergency conditions, it is not always easy to recognize the physiologic subtleties involved. During the implant, device positioning has usually been difficult with the bulk of the right ventricle (particularly the base plate near the drive line entrance) coming to lie directly beneath the sternotomy. If pressing the device downward into the mediastinum becomes necessary to reapproximate the edges of the sternum, malfit is likely to be present. Further attempts to close the sternum while the patient is dependent on the device are associated with loss in pump output (see Fig. 10).

If malfit occurs with the 100 cc unit, substituting the smaller unit might seem to be an attractive solution at first. However, the 100 cc device and 70 cc

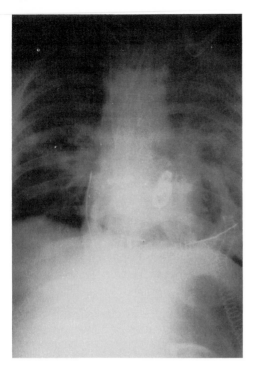

FIGURE 12. Asymmetric (left-sided) acute pulmonary edema developing within an hour of sternal closure in a patient with malfit. Pulmonary venous compression, pulmonary venous hypertension, interstitial edema, and eventually hemoptysis complicated this implant.

device do not currently share a common sized connector, and thus an entirely new set of conduits would need to be resutured.

The principle of treatment is to reposition the ventricles more leftward within the patient's chest. This is sometimes difficult because the position of the device becomes fixed by the tethering effects of the great vessel conduits, atrial connectors, and the transthoracic drive lines. However, only a few centimeters of displacement will often allow the right ventricular device to move out from under the sternum and/or drop more deeply into the chest. The left ventricular device can be pulled more to the patient's left by traction on the drive lines. It is important to place the drive lines laterally if fit is a major concern. Other maneuvers such as those listed in Table 2 have been shown to improve leftward displacement. Although it seems simple just to leave the sternum open in such circumstances, most surgeons believe this invites unacceptable hazards such as infection, pulmonary insufficiency, persistent wound drainage, and sepsis. Failure to close the sternum has been associated with fatalities after TAH implantation (although all were complex cases with many other morbid features).

PULMONARY EDEMA

Virtually all patients currently implanted with Jarvik-7 hearts for either short-term or long-term use arrive in the operating room near death. Progressive deterioration in pulmonary function, tachypnea, clinical or radiographic pulmonary edema, and deteriorating gas exchange typically occur in the days or hours preceding the decision to implant an artificial heart. Moderately severe transudative interstitial or alveolar pulmonary edema is quite common postoperatively despite normal or high cardiac outputs and normal to low filling pressures. Ventilatory support is usually needed for several days and extubation should not be hurried unduly. Although positive end-expiratory pressure (PEEP) does decrease pump filling slightly, the effects of PEEP may be easily overcome by adding diastolic vacuum.[47] This maneuver improves the efficiency of pump filling, increases cardiac output, and lowers left atrial filling pressures. Diastolic vacuum has become a valuable adjunct to standard therapy with diuretics, fluid restriction, and ventilatory support in such cases.

If the pulmonary edema is unilateral (especially left-sided), the surgeon must suspect pulmonary venous compression by the device (see Fig. 12). Diastolic vacuum in this situation actually impairs filling even further and pulmonary edema worsens steadily. Nothing short of repositioning the heart will relieve this form of pulmonary edema. Progressive development of pulmonary infarction and hemoptysis (aggravated by obligatory anticoagulation) is destined to occur if venous compression is not relieved.

HEMOLYSIS

Hemolysis is occasionally seen with prosthetic heart valves and may be related to the design or the mechanics of valve closure. Since the Jarvik-7 contains four mechanical valves, there was initial concern among investigators about the potential for cell trauma. Indeed, early Jarvik-7 patients were reported to have plasma free hemoglobin (PFH) levels of 30 to 90 mg/ml[18,46] (normal < 10) and serum LDH values persistently in the range of 500 to 1,000 IU/L (normal < 220 IU/L).

Early Jarvik-7 models were equipped with Delrin disc Bjork-Shiley valves. However, there were occasional mechanical failures during animal trials,[20] mostly at the left inflow ("mitral") position.[7] Dr. Barney Clark, the first human TAH recipient, suffered from a fractured Bjork-Shiley mitral strut on the second week of implantation and required emergency replacement of the left-sided prosthesis. Subsequently, a stronger, more durable valve was sought. The Medtronic-Hall tilting disc valve was chosen for its durability and proven resistance to mechanical breakage, despite markedly elevated closing forces generated by the pneumatic drive system.[34] Clinically, this valve is not known for excessive hemolysis. However, when utilized within the Jarvik-7, significant increases in PFH and serum LDH were noted with the Medtronic-Hall valve when compared with the Bjork-Shiley prosthesis.[34] These elevations were independent of the animal species, heart rate, and other parameters. These drawbacks were considered an acceptable trade-off for achieving superior mechanical reliability during human implantation.[34]

The Medtronic-Hall valve was incorporated into the clinical Jarvik-7 just prior to the second permanent implant. The next several permanent Jarvik-7 recipients were noted to have elevated LDH and PFH levels,[19,34,46] again raising the specter of persistent hemolysis with this TAH design. Long-term survivors required frequent transfusions to compensate for persistent hemolytic anemia.[16,19]

Cavitation effects surrounding the disc seats were pinpointed as the most likely source of localized physical forces sufficient to cause cell membrane injury. Cavitation itself (local hydraulic pressure gradients) proved to be a function of the dP/dT of valve leaflet closure. The original (Utah I) pneumatic drive system delivered pressurized impulses to the TAH diaphragm at 6,000–8,000 mm Hg/sec, almost four times that of a normal left ventricle. The driver was subsequently modified to deliver impulses with a dP/dT of $< 4,500$ mm Hg/sec, and hemolytic indices in all subsequent patients dropped sharply despite the continued use of the Medtronic-Hall prosthesis.[19,46]

Levinson et al.[46] reported the hemolytic parameters recorded in 15 of the earliest Jarvik-7 recipients and found that no patient developed clinically significant hemolysis following the drive unit modification including patients with the smaller, 70 cc Jarvik heart, which characteristically is driven at higher rates and driving pressures than its 100 cc predecessor. Mean PFH levels prior to drive unit modification were 35.8 mg/dl and serum LDH 1,383 IU/L, whereas the same parameters fell to 10.1 and 680, respectively, following dP/dT reduction.[46] This improvement was seen in all patient groups and was independent of age, sex, weight, cardiac output, heart rate, drive pressures, or rate pressure products (RPP) used clinically.[46] In fact, the clinically reported RPPs actually went up considerably (2.5 fold), whereas the LDH and PFH dropped markedly following drive unit modification. Thus, the dP/dT of valve closure appears to be the key element in the degree of hemolysis seen clinically.

Henker et al.[31] demonstrated that the dP/dT generated by the Utah II pneumatic drive system was essentially independent of any of the adjustable settings (rate, pressure, or percent systole). Instead, the pressure/time derivative is intrinsic to the solenoid-activated valves within the drive unit and reflects a critical design characteristic of such drivers. In this respect, modifications of heart rate, drive pressure, or systolic duration have little effect in modulating dP/dT during clinical use of this TAH system. Thus, driver adjustments may be made independent of concerns about undue red cell trauma. In this respect, the substitution of a slightly more hemolytic valve[34] has been negated by important salutary modifications in the pneumatic heart drive mechanism.[19]

SERUM COMPLEMENT ACTIVITY

The complement system is a series of enzymatic plasma proteins that defend against invading pathogens, particularly bacteria. However, complement has many other functions, particularly as a chemical mediator and amplifier of inflammatory reactions. Activated moieties of complement are responsible for chemotaxis, stimulation of phagocytosis, and anaphylactoid reactions. Complement-stimulated neutrophils have increased adhesiveness and will sequester in the microcapillary circulation, releasing granular contents and creating local injury. The complement system can be activated through either the classic or alternative pathway.

Exposure of blood to artificial surfaces activates the complement cascade, primarily through the alternate pathway. This phenomenon is a well-recognized side effect of membrane lungs, bubble oxygenators, and hemodialysis membranes.[6,33] Because the TAH is a large surface of foreign material, exposure to the blood is expected to activate complement in a similar fashion. Stelzer et al.[58] and Wellhausen[63] found normal C5a levels but dramatic increases in circulating C3a (up to 3 μg/ml) in Jarvik-7 patients surviving more than several months. After introduction of the Utah II driver, plasma C3a (and PFH) levels dropped promptly to normal.[19,58,63] These observations appear to identify the drive system dP/dT and the mechanics of valve closure as critical factors responsible for complement activation in long-term Jarvik-7 recipients. Stelzer et al.[58] proposed that exposure of blood to cellular debris, denatured proteins, and activated platelets generated by sheer-induced hemolysis directly activated the alternative complement pathway. The polyurethane/blood contacting surfaces were not considered responsible for direct complement activation. Should this hypothesis be verified, sheer stresses during closure of the mechanical valves may prove to be the source of some of the most important clinical consequences of this device. Reduction of the dP/dT (as in the Utah II driver) may significantly reduce the magnitude of sequelae of TAH implantation such as chronic hemolysis, complement activation, and anaphylatoxin generation and greatly improve the margin of safety in this model of permanent TAH.[58]

LYMPHOCYTES AND T-CELL RESPONSES

Very little is known about the effect of the TAH on the extraerythrocytic elements of circulating blood. DeVries et al. have systematically studied the immunologic function of human recipients. In their four patients with permanent implants, peripheral absolute lymphocyte counts dropped below 200/mm³ without concomitant leukopenia or neutropenia.[58,63] Throughout the implants, absolute lymphocyte counts fluctuated widely, but were below normal in well over half the samples. These fluctuations did not appear to be secondary to transfusions or other phenomenon. The subsets of activated HLA-DR expressing T-cells remained constant, or increased, throughout the implant periods. This may have been, in part, a response to antigen challenge from repeated transfusions.[58]

Although the ratio of helper/inducer to suppressor/cytotoxic cells increased in the first few days following implant, it decreased gradually with time, reaching 1.0 (normal = 2.7) in the chronic phases of implantation.[58] This was associated with a decrease in absolute OKT4 helper/inducer cells, whereas the Leu-2 suppressor/cytotoxic group remained essentially unchanged.[58] It is improbable that such changes could be attributed only to the effects of cardiopulmonary bypass (CPB) during the implant operation. Standard oxygenator bypass does exert a lymphopenic effect, particularly on circulating T-cells and T-helper cells, while the counts of total circulating lymphocytes and B-cell subsets usually remain unchanged.[35] This perioperative effect usually reverses by the seventh day; however, in long-term TAH recipients, marked depression in lymphocytes and T-helper counts remains consistent over a much longer period. In addition, at least two of the patients under study developed significant B-cell lymphopenia as well.[58,63] Serum immunoglobulins were not altered in any of the recipients.

It is still unproved whether these T-cell alterations were in fact the cause, or an end result, of serious infectious complications seen in the permanent Jarvik-7 recipients.[58] It is certainly possible that indirect immunosuppressive side effects of the TAH may contribute significantly to the eventual risk of infectious complications so common in TAH recipients. These immunosuppressive phenomena did not appear to be chronologically (or quantitatively) related to the use of bank blood products.[58] It is still unclear what role is played by the artificial surfaces of the TAH and/or the physical forces induced by blood pumping.

The magnitude of the observed changes in lymphocyte counts is similar to that seen when antilymphocyte globulin is administered to humans.[58] In "bridge" patients, immunosuppressive regimens used for subsequent transplantation may need to be downgraded to accommodate these qualitative effects. TAH recipients have a propensity to develop infections such as mediastinitis,[12,27,43] and this vulnerability may be due in part to the immunosuppressive effects listed above.

Modification of post-bridging transplant protocols, particularly reductions in steroid or antilymphocyte globulin dosage, may be justified to reduce the likelihood of subsequent overwhelming infection.

PLATELETS

Typical platelet counts following any procedure on CPB range from 60,000 to 90,000/mm^3. In addition, the function of circulating platelets are altered by exposure to the cardiopulmonary bypass circuit.[30] These effects are secondary to clumping and sequestration following contact with the artificial surfaces of the oxygenator and pump tubing,[30] and usually resolve 1–2 days following surgery. In Jarvik-7 recipients, more prolonged depression of platelet counts has occasionally been noted. No systematic report has detailed these effects, but a number of anecdotal observations have been made. Recovery of platelet numbers is often delayed several more days beyond the effects of CPB. Current speculation revolves around sequestration and lamination of platelets onto the extensive internal lining of the pump and its conduits.

After platelet counts recover, they often rebound to supranormal levels. This thrombocytosis is probably a nonspecific, physiologic response to stress. Levinson et al. have noted a marked rise in other "acute phase reactants" several days following TAH implantations,[47,48] specifically albumin, factor X, and fibrinogen. These effects occurred synchronously with recovery in circulating platelet numbers. In combination, these changes predispose to hypercoagulability and increased risk for thromboembolic events.[47,48] DeVries has noted curious increases in platelet numbers in chronologic association with neurologic events in long-term Jarvik-7 recipients.[48] Whether this is a nonspecific marker of inflammation, infection, or other thrombotic process is not yet known.

RENAL FAILURE

Marked elevations of BUN and creatinine with oliguria plagued the first few Jarvik-7 patients.[16] Although the etiology still remains unclear, there was initial concern about the potential renal toxicity of the pump and/or its materials. Attempts to reproduce this complication in TAH calves proved unsuccessful despite reductions in cardiac output and other provocative measures.[65] Embolic renal damage has not been confirmed in humans. Patients with devices that fit improperly are prone to low output and subsequent renal failure.[16] The effects of sheer-induced hemolysis and complement activation on renal capillaries have been purported to be nephrotoxic,[16] although these effects have been nearly eliminated since the drive system modification was made in early 1985. DeVries[16] has proposed that sudden restoration of normal cardiac output in patients adapted to a chronic low output state may overperfuse the renal vascular bed with deleterious effects. Joyce et al.[39] reported preimplant renal impairment in over 50% of TAH patients as a consequence of acute cardiac deterioration. The preoperative condition of the patient, particularly prerenal azotemia, hypotension, usage of vasoconstrictor drugs, and prolonged cardiopulmonary bypass all appear to have a cumulative effect on eventual renal function. In 26 TAH patients (all but 8 were Jarvik-7 models), 27% subsequently required temporary dialysis.[39] Of these, four recovered normal renal function while on the TAH device. Dialysis is now infrequently needed in successfully implanted patients, perhaps owing to reductions in the effects of sheer-induced hemolysis and improved patient selection.

In most patients, a salutary effect on renal function is noted shortly after implantation. Creatinine and BUN begin to drop about 1–2 days following restoration of normal blood pressure and cardiac output by the device. Even severe post-implant renal failure has recovered to normal as long as 3 months following the acute onset of anuria.[12,26,40] This implies that direct renal toxicity with this device is not evident. In fact, restoration and maintenance of normal cardiovascular hemodynamics are powerful stimulants to renal tubular regeneration and recovery from anuria.

ATRIAL NATRIURETIC FACTOR

A newly discovered peptide stored and secreted by atrial myocardial cells has been the focus of recent research. Atrial natriuretic factor (ANF) regulates salt and water excretion from the kidney. Distention of the atria during periods of congestive heart failure induces secretion and promotes loss of circulating blood volume through diuresis. Anti-aldosterone activity of this peptide provides "closed-loop" regulation of the salt-retaining properties of the renin-aldosterone axis. The exact control mechanisms for regulation and secretion of ANF have not been clarified.

ANF is stored in secretory granules within atrial myocytes. Normal calves without preexisting heart failure are deficient in ANF response to atrial hypertension following TAH placement.[64] Using transient volume loading along with simulated right heart failure, Jarvik-7 patients demonstrated normal ANF secretion in response to atrial hypertension.[57] However, the renal effects of natiuresis and diuresis were blunted for unclear reasons. Similar data were obtained by Deray et al.,[15] discouraging the ANF hypothesis for renal dysfunction following TAH implantation.

DEVICE REMOVAL AND NON-TRANSPLANTABILITY

Barriers to transplantation often arise during the implant period, which is not unexpected because all BTT candidates are desperately ill. In this respect, use of the TAH or other bridging mechanical devices "preselects" a sick, high-risk subgroup. Patients recently resuscitated from cardiogenic shock with these devices are usually too physiologically impaired to undergo a second major operation for several days. Initial attempts to move immediately with the first available organ donor were disappointing.[11,47,48,61] Death following transplantation in this setting not only spells failure of the bridge attempt, but misappropriation of a valuable donor heart away from another potentially qualified recipient. Most investigators now delay transplantation until the patient can be restored to full transplant candidacy by accepted criteria.[5,12,26,48,51] The absence of persistent infection, renal failure, hepatic insufficiency, respiratory failure, or severe neurologic sequelae is essential before elevating such patients to full transplant status. Absence of infection appears to be the most important determinant of survival following transplantation.[5,26,51]

INDICES OF SURVIVAL

Very few centers have experience with enough cases to analyze survival correlates. Statistically valid information on which subgroups survive TAH implantation and BTT is sparse. Cabrol and associates[5,51] examined their temporary Jarvik-7 recipients for survival parameters. They concluded that younger patients, particularly those with recent onset cardiac dysfunction, are

likely to survive. In their study, 56% of patients < 40 years old survived to leave
the hospital after a Jarvik-7 70cc bridge to transplantation. In contrast, only 18%
of patients > 40 years old survived. The patient sample size was too small to
ascertain whether this difference was due to the greater prevalence of ischemic
cardiac disease in the older group.

It is suspected by these investigators (and others) that younger patients with
idiopathic cardiomyopathy (ICM) provide the best candidates for bridging.
Successful transplantation was possible in 46% of patients with ICM as opposed
to 33% with ischemic heart disease.[5] This may be in part due to their young age,
healthy extracardiac status, and rapid decline prior to TAH implantation.
Statistically, Cabrol et al.[5] were able to demonstrate improved survival in those
with acute cardiac decompensation (44%) when compared to those with chronic
CHF (30%).

Another parameter identified for immediate post-TAH survival was the
duration of mechanical ventilation. Newly implanted TAH patients who remain
on the ventilator more than 2 days appear to be at greater risk, particularly from
infectious complications.[5] The mean duration of intubation in nonsurvivors was
8 days (versus 2 days in survivors). In addition, patients treated with the larger,
100 cc device appear to survive more frequently than those implanted with the
smaller unit (45% vs 27%).[5] This finding remains unexplained, but does not
appear to be directly device-related. Female sex, a known risk factor for coronary
surgery and a correlate with small body size, may play a role in this trend. Other
factors that are reported anecdotally to be associated with a fatal outcome are
summarized in Table 3.

By far, most deaths during implant are secondary to sepsis.[5,16,21,27,28,43]
Mediastinitis and pneumonia appear to dominate in the short term and device
infection and chronic "endocarditis" affect devices in place for long periods.
Infection in the periprosthetic space begins to increase in frequency after the third
week of implant. Although it was initially suspected that such infections were due
to ascending contamination from the percutaneous air drive tubing, it has been
elegantly shown by DeVries and associates[16,21,29,43,62] that primary infection of the
exterior of the device and the surrounding mediastinal spaces can occur in the
absence of ascending tract infection. This finding is probably due to marked
alterations in the host defenses within the mediastinum following removal of the
native heart, creation of complex "dead spaces" filled with prosthetic material

TABLE 3.   Predictors of Poor Outcome Following Interim Jarvik-7 Implantation

Established infection/sepsis
Age > 40
Pre-existing chronic cardiac decompensation (i.e., > 30 days)
Etiologies of cardiac disease
    Coronary artery disease
    Acute viral myocarditis
    Acute rejection
Malfit of TAH
Prolonged CPB (> 5 hours)
Ongoing cardiac arrest/massage
Post-TAH renal failure
Developmental of cytotoxic antibodies

and culture medium (blood), and the numerous potential portals of bacterial entry in debilitated ICU patients connected to so many invasive monitoring lines and ventilator apparati. Interestingly, deep mediastinal infection is less common using paracorporeal VADs as bridging devices,[32] underscoring the role of cardiectomy in altering host defenses against bacterial invasion. Poor penetration of antibiotics into deep mediastinal dead spaces and the extensive surface area of these artificial devices may account for the inability of prophylactic antibiotic coverage to offer protection equivalent to that achieved for coronary and valvular surgery.

Regardless of the mechanisms, the morbidity of post-TAH or post-transplant infection is so apparent that investigators are targeting this complication on multiple fronts. Most will no longer consider bridging in any patient with established infection, especially pneumonias.[5,26,27] Infections established during implantation become contraindications to subsequent transplantation unless they can be eradicated prior to anticipated donor availability.[5,12,51] Despite the temptation to move directly to transplantation, most surgeons now believe that the patient should not be rushed to transplantation while critically ill, especially if infection is present. The common presence of organisms within the mediastinal blood clots and fluid at transplantation, as well as the published incidence of mediastinitis following device removal, has led at least one investigator[13] to propose routine povidone-iodine transmediastinal irrigation for 48 hours following TAH implantation as an attempt to achieve more complete suppression of contaminating bacteria within the mediastinum.

Despite the initial concern that embolic events and strokes would be the leading source of morbidity with this device, debilitating strokes are relatively rare. The current risk of a neurologic event during brief usage of the Jarvik-7 is about 10%, and most patients are left with minimal or no residual deficits. Curiously, the smaller device seems to be associated with a lessened risk of clinical emboli,[46] and fewer thrombi are found in these smaller pumps when inspected following explant.[60] The expanding use of the 70 cc unit may account for some of the recently observed reductions in rates of embolism. Although most explanted devices have thrombi lodged in surface defects and crevices near the connectors or valve mounts of the Jarvik-7,[26,49] the tendency for this material to embolize in particles of sufficient size to cause permanent damage to the brain is far less than originally feared. However, diligent anticoagulation is still required to maintain this relative protection. Current results from the International Artificial Heart Registry are reported in more detail elsewhere in this text.[38]

SUMMARY

One of the remarkable features of the total artificial heart is its ability to instantly resume the entire burden of the circulation. This is surely the reason why clinical recovery and eventual survival have been so remarkable despite the destitute preoperative condition of all these patients. Although the Jarvik-7 and other pneumatic hearts have pioneered mechanical cardiac replacement, the role of air-driven systems will surely diminish in the near future. Permanent, electrically powered systems which do not violate the intact skin will soon be ready for clinical trial. However, major hurdles will still remain, especially the development of portable, high-density power sources that could allow the patient an untethered life for meaningful periods of time. The battles against device infection, thrombogenesis, malfit, and end-organ toxicities must be won before clinical successes with such daring technology are commonplace. Societal and ethical questions, especially the adaptability of human beings to an existence completely dependent upon fabricated equipment, remain to be answered. However, it is now certain that such devices can completely support the circulation and substitute physiologically for the diseased heart. Successful clinical application of this revolutionary concept could open many doors to the future in medicine and patient care.

REFERENCES

1. Akutsu T, Kolff WJ: Permanent substitutes for valves and hearts. Trans Am Soc Artif Intern Organs 4:230, 1958.
2. Artificial Heart and Assist Devices: Directions, Needs, Costs, Societal and Ethical Issues. In: The Working Group on Mechanical Circulatory Support of the National Heart, Lung, and Blood Institute. US Dept of Health and Human Services Publications. Bethesda, MD, Public Health Service, N.I.H. Vol. 85-2723, 1985.
3. Burns GL: The calf as a model for thromboembolic events with the total artificial heart. Trans Am Soc Artif Intern Organs 33:398–403, 1987.
4. Burns GL: Thrombogenesis in and contiguous with pumping chambers. Ann NY Acad Sci 516:662–672, 1987.
5. Cabrol C, Solis E, Muneretto C, et al: Orthotopic transplantation after implantation of a Jarvik 7 total artificial heart. J Thorac Cardiovasc Surg 97:342–350, 1989.
6. Chenoweth DE, Cooper SW, Hugli TE, et al: Complement activation during cardiopulmonary bypass: Evidence for generation of C3a and C5a anaphylatoxins. N Engl J Med 304:497–503, 1981.
7. Chiang BY, Olsen DB, Dries D, et al: An analysis of animals surviving over 100 days on the total artificial heart. In Atsumi K, Naekawa M, Ota K (eds): Progress in Artificial Organs, Vol. 1. Fourth Congress of ISAO, Kyoto, Japan, Nov. 1983, ISAO Press, Cleveland. Vol. 204, 1984, pp 211–216.
8. Cooley DA: Staged cardiac tranplantation: Report of three cases. J Heart Transplant 1:145, 1982.
9. Cooley DA, Akutsu T, Norman JC, et al: Total artificial heart in two-staged cardiac transplantation. 8:305–319, 1981.
10. Cooley DA, Liotta D, Hallman GL, et al: Orthotopic cardiac prosthesis for two-staged cardiac replacement. Am J Cardiol 24:723–730, 1969.
11. Copeland JG, Levinson MM, Smith R, et al: The total artificial heart as a bridge to transplantation: A report of two cases. JAMA 256:2991–2995, 1986.
12. Copeland JG, Smith RG, Icenogle TB, et al: Early experience with the total artificial heart as a bridge to cardiac transplantation. Surg Clin North Am 68:621–634, 1988.
13. Copeland JG, Smith R, Icenogle TB, et al: Orthotopic total artificial heart bridge to transplantation: Preliminary results. Submitted for publication.
14. Demikhov VP: In Haigh B (ed): Experimental Transplantation of Vital Organs. Moscow, Translation-Medquiz, 1969, pp 212–213.
15. Deray G, Maistre G, Cacoub P, et al: Atrial endocrine function in humans with artificial hearts. N Engl J Med 316:1478–1479, 1987.
16. DeVries WC: The permanent artificial heart: Four case reports. JAMA 259:849–859, 1988.
17. DeVries WC: Surgical technique for implantation of the Jarvik-7-100 total artificial heart. JAMA 259:875–880, 1988.
18. DeVries WC, Anderson JL, Joyce LD, et al: Clinical use of the total artificial heart. N Engl J Med 310:273–278, 1984.
19. DeVries WC, Mays BJ, Hastings L, et al: Effect of drive system modification on hematologic profiles of two permanent total artificial heart recipients (abstract). Trans Am Soc Artif Intern Organs 1986.
20. Dew PA, Olsen DB, Kessler TR, et al: Mechanical failures in vivo and in vitro during studies of pneumatic total artificial hearts. Trans Am Soc Artif Intern Organs 30:112, 1984.
21. Dobbins JJ, Johnson S, Kunin CM, DeVries WC: Postmortem microbiological findings of two total artificial heart recipients. JAMA 259:865–869, 1988.
22. Evans RW, Manninen DL, Garrison LP Jr, Maier AM: Donor availability as the primary determinant of the future of heart transplantation. JAMA 255:1892, 1986.
23. Fragomeni LS, Kaye MP: The Registry of the International Society for Heart Transplantation: Fifth Official Report—1988. J Heart Transplant 7:249–253, 1988.

24. Gibbs OS: An artificial heart. J Pharmacol Exp Ther 38:197–215, 1930.
25. Green R, Liska J, Egberg N, et al: Hemostatic disturbances associated with implantation of an artificial heart. Thromb Res 48:349–362, 1987.
26. Griffith BP: Interim use of the Jarvik-7 artificial heart: Lessons learned at Presbyterian-University Hospital of Pittsburgh. Ann Thorac Surg 47:158–166, 1989.
27. Griffith BP, Kormos RL, Hardesty RL, et al: The artificial heart: Infection-related morbidity and its effect on transplantation. Ann Thorac Surg 45:409–414, 1988.
28. Griffith BP, Kormos RL, Wei LM, et al: Use of the total artificial heart as an interim device: Initial experience in Pittsburgh with four patients. J Heart Transplant 5:210–214, 1986.
29. Gristina AG, Dobbins JJ, Giammarra B, et al: Biomaterial-centered sepsis and the total artificial heart: Microbial adhesion vs tissue integration. JAMA 259:870–874, 1988.
30. Harker LA, Malpass TW, Branson HE, et al: Mechanisms of abnormal bleeding in patients undergoing cardiopulmonary bypass: Acquired transient platelet dysfunction associated with selective alpha granule release. Blood 56:824–834, 1980.
31. Henker R, Murdaugh C: Effects of pneumatic artificial heart driver on the rate of isovolumic pressure rise. Artificial Organs 12:513–519, 1988.
32. Hill JD: Bridging to cardiac transplantation. Ann Thorac Surg 47:161–171, 1989.
33. Howard RJ, Crain C, Franzon DA, et al: Effects of cardiopulmonary bypass on pulmonary leukostasis and complement activation. Arch Surg 123:1496–1501, 1988.
34. Hughes SD, Butler MD, Holmberg DL, et al: Comparative hematological data from animals implanted with a total artificial heart containing different valves. Trans Am Soc Artif Intern Organs 31:224–229, 1985.
35. Ide H, Kakiuchi T, Furuta N, et al: The effect of cardiopulmonary bypass on T cells and their subpopulations. Ann Thorac Surg 44:277–282, 1987.
36. Jarvik RK: The total artificial heart. Sci Am 244:74–80, 1981.
37. Jarvik RK, DeVries WC, Semb BKH, et al: Surgical positioning of the Jarvik-7 artificial heart. J Heart Transplant 5:184–195, 1986.
38. Joyce LD, Johnson KE: Total artificial heart as a bridge to transplantation: World results 1989. In Emery RW, et al (eds): Cardiothoracic Transplantation II. Cardiac Surgery: State of the Art Reviews, vol. 3, no. 3. Philadelphia, Hanley & Belfus, Inc., 1989.
39. Joyce LD, Johnson KE, Pierce WS, et al: Summary of the world experience with clinical use of total artificial hearts as heart support devices. J Heart Transplant 5:229–235, 1986.
40. Joyce LD, Pritzker MR, Kiser JC, et al: Use of the mini Jarvik-7 total artificial heart as a bridge to transplantation. J Heart Transplant 5:203–209, 1986.
41. Kolff J, Deeb GM, Cavarocchi NC, et al: The artificial heart in human subjects. J Thorac Cardiovasc Surg 87:825–831, 1984.
42. Kormos RL: Rheologic abnormalities in patients with the Jarvik-7 total artificial heart. Trans Am Soc Artif Intern Organs 33:413–417, 1987.
43. Kunin CM, Dobbins JJ, Melo JC, et al: Infectious complications in four long-term recipients of the Jarvik-7 artificial heart. JAMA 259:860–864, 1988.
44. Levinson MM, Copeland JG: The artificial heart and mechanical assistance prior to heart transplantation. In Cerilli GJ (ed): Organ Transplantation and Replacement. Philadelphia, J.B. Lippincott, 1988.
45. Levinson MM, Copeland JG: Technical aspects of total artificial heart implantation for temporary applications. J Cardiac Surg 2:3–19, 1987.
46. Levinson MM, Copeland JG, Smith RG, et al: Indexes of hemolysis in human recipients of the Jarvik-7 total artificial heart: A cooperative report on fifteen patients. J Heart Transplant 5:236–248, 1986.
47. Levinson MM, Smith R, Cork R, et al: Clinical problems associated with the total artificial heart as a bridge to transplantation. In Andrade J (ed): Artificial Organs: Proceedings of the International Symposium on Artificial Organs, Biomedical Engineering, and Transplantation in Honor of the 75th Birthday of Willem J. Kolff. New York, VCH Publishers, Inc., 1987, pp 169–190.
48. Levinson MM, Smith RG, Cork R, et al: Three recent cases of the total artificial heart before transplantation. J Heart Transplant 5:215–228, 1986.
49. Levinson MM, Smith RG, Cork RC, et al: Thromboembolic complications of the Jarvik-7 total artificial heart: Case report. Artificial Organs 10:236–244, 1986.
50. Magovern JA, Pennock JL, Campbell DB, et al: Bridge to heart transplantation: The Penn State experience. J Heart Transplant 5:196–202, 1986.
51. Muneretto C, Solis E, Pavie A, et al: Total artificial heart: Survival and complications. Ann Thorac Surg 47:151–157, 1989.

52. Olsen DB, Unger F, Oster H, et al: Thrombus generation within the artificial heart. J Thorac Cardiovasc Surg 70:255–278, 1975.
53. Opelz G, Terasaki PI: Improvement of kidney-graft survival with increased numbers of blood transfusions. N Engl J Med 299:799–803, 1978.
54. Pennington DG, Termuhlean DF: Mechanical circulatory support: Device selection. In Emery RW, et al (eds): Cardiothoracic Transplantation II. Cardiac Surgery: State of the Art Reviews, vol. 3, no. 3. Philadelphia, Hanley & Belfus, Inc., 1989.
55. Ring ME, Feinberg WM, Levinson MM, et al: Platelet and fibrin metabolism in recipients of the Jarvik-7 total artificial heart. J Heart Transplant 8:225–232, 1989.
56. Rousou J, Levitsky S, Gonzalez-Lavin L, et al: Randomized clinical trial of fibrin sealant in patients undergoing re-sternotomy or reoperation after cardiac operations: A multicenter study. J Thorac Cardiovasc Surg 97:194–203, 1989.
57. Schwab TR, Edwards BS, DeVries WC, et al: Atrial endocrine function in humans with artificial hearts. N Engl J Med 315:1398–1401, 1986.
58. Stelzer GT, Ward RA, Wellhausen SR, et al: Alterations in select immunologic parameters following total artificial heart implantation. Artificial Organs 11:52–62, 1987.
59. Taenaka T, Olsen DB, Nielsen JD, et al: Mechanical failures of total artificial hearts. Trans Am Soc Artif Intern Organs 31:79–83, 1985.
60. Taylor KD, Gayskowski R, Keate KS, et al: Explant analysis of thirty-three bridge to transplant J7 total artificial heart devices. Trans Am Soc Artif Intern Organs 33:738–743, 1987.
61. Vaughn CC, Copeland JG, Cheng K, et al: Interim heart replacement with a mechanical device: An adjunct to management of allograft rejection. J Heart Transplant 4:502–505, 1985.
62. Ward RA: Thromboembolic and infectious complications of total artificial heart implantation. Ann NY Acad Sci 516:638–650, 1987.
63. Wellhausen SR: Immunologic complications of long term implantation of a total artificial heart. J Clin Immunol 8:307–318, 1988.
64. Westenfelder C, Baranowski RL, Kablitz C, et al: Atrial natiuretic peptide release in calves with artificial hearts. Kidney Int 29:389, 1986.
65. Westenfelder C, England T, Holmberg DL, et al: Renal function in calves with total artificial hearts. Trans Am Soc Artif Intern Organs 31:383–387, 1985.
66. Willshaw P, Nielsen SD, Nanas J, et al: A cardiac output monitor and diagnostic unit for pneumatically driven artificial hearts. Artificial Organs 8:215–219, 1984.

WALTER P. DEMBITSKY, MD[1]
PAT O. DAILY, MD[1]
KENNETH M. MOSER, MD[2]
WILLIAM AUGER, MD[2]

PULMONARY THROMBO-ENDARTERECTOMY AS THE PREFERRED ALTERNATIVE TO HEART-LUNG TRANSPLANTATION FOR CHRONIC PULMONARY EMBOLISM

[1]Sharp Memorial Hospital
San Diego, California

[2]University of California, San
Diego, Medical Center

Reprint requests to:
Walter P. Dembitsky, MD
8010 Frost St. Suite 501
San Diego, CA 92123

Heart-lung transplantation has offered a chance for survival and improved quality of life to the population of patients with chronic pulmonary hypertension. Still, the operative mortality remains high and long-term survival has not yet approached that of heart transplantation alone. Furthermore, the late appearance of bronchiolitis obliterans has continued to erode long-term pulmonary function. Some patients undergoing heart-lung transplantation have had pulmonary hypertension resulting from chronic unresolved pulmonary embolism. In these patients surgical removal of the intra-arterial pulmonary obstruction can result in a significant reduction of pulmonary vascular resistance accompanied by a dramatic recovery of both pulmonary and right ventricular function.[2] Following successful surgery these patients enjoy a marked lasting improvement in functional capacity. The lowered pulmonary artery pressures are expected to improve long-term survival. Failure to relieve obstruction during surgery is associated with a high mortality. Thus, preoperative evaluation and patient selection for this surgery are extremely critical.

CARDIAC SURGERY: State of the Art Reviews—Vol. 3, No. 3, October 1989
Philadelphia, Hanley & Belfus, Inc.

577

Detection of chronic pulmonary emboli is not always simple. Initial screening with careful history and physical examination followed by chest x-ray, lung scan, and pulmonary function tests (if not severely abnormal) select patients who are candidates for pulmonary angiography. Right heart catheterization and detailed pulmonary arteriograms are performed to define more precisely the severity, location, and extent of disease.[4] In the occasional patient with equivocal angiographic findings, intraarterial pulmonary pathology is examined directly using an angioscope.[7]

The apparent evolution of an intrapulmonary arterial embolus involves rapid covering of the embolus by fibrin, which fixes it to the arterial wall, followed by epithelialization on the surface exposed to blood flow. This process is most visible at the attachment of the embolus to the arterial wall. Simultaneously, a thrombus begins to propagate distally to vascular occlusive clots. Smaller emboli often dissolve within 48 hours and, in most cases, the emboli resolve over days to weeks, leaving no residuum. In some patients, especially those with large occlusive emboli, resolution is incomplete, possibly owing to repeated embolization, embolization of organized material, or perhaps, to an associated defect in systemic clot resolution. Cellular in-growth from the arterial wall continues, and the original thrombus may ultimately be reorganized and remain only as a fibroelastic pseudointimal arterial lining.[3] Extensions from the lining usually occupy the lumens of obstructed or stenotic arteries. The surface of the pseudointima has characteristic pits and webs left as evidence of incomplete recanalization. Occasionally, young, often layered, thrombus can be seen adherent to the pseudointima. We speculate that this is due to local stasis thrombosis.

The goal of surgery is to reduce the pulmonary vascular resistance by removing all obstructing intraarterial matter. The most critical aspect of surgery is removal of the pseudointima with its intravascular extensions. This procedure is referred to as "pulmonary thromboendarterectomy" to distinguish it from the less complex "pulmonary embolectomy" performed to remove acute pulmonary emboli.

Pulmonary thromboendarterectomy is performed through a median sternotomy using hypothermic circulatory arrest. Total cardiopulmonary bypass with hemodilution is initiated using ascending aortic and bicaval cannulation. During cooling to 20°C nasopharyngeal temperature, pulmonary artery and left atrial sump catheters are placed to scavenge the copious bronchial circulation often present in these patients. Upon reaching the desired temperature, any remaining central nervous system electroencephalographic activity is quieted using intravenous sodium thiamytal and phenytoin. The aorta is cross-clamped proximal to the innominate artery to facilitate pulmonary artery exposure, reduce the risk of air embolism during subsequent arrests, and eliminate coronary sinus flow, which may obscure the intrapulmonary arterial operative field. Vena caval snares are used to assure profound myocardial hypothermia. Myocardial temperature is monitored and maintained at 5–10° using cardioplegia and a Medtronic-Daily* cooling jacket.

Pulmonary artery dissection is usually begun during the cooling phase. On the right side the vena cava is circumferentially freed from the right pulmonary artery, and the plane between the pulmonary artery and surrounding hilar tissue

* Medtronic Blood Systems, Inc., Subsidiary of Medtronics, Inc., Cardiopulmonary Products Group, 4633 East La Palma Avenue, Anaheim, CA 92807 USA.

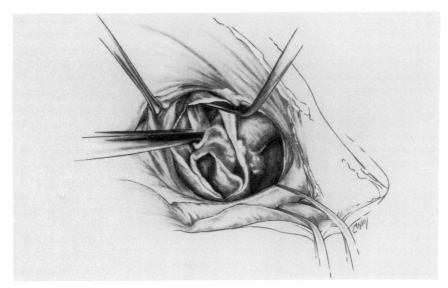

FIGURE 1. The patient's head is to the viewer's right. The superior vena cava is retracted medially and the right superior pulmonary vein is retracted inferiorly. An arteriotomy has been made in the center of the right pulmonary artery at the level of the right upper lobe branch. Dissection is continued distally along the specimen until the first bronchopulmonary segmental artery is encountered. At that point it is essential to dissect around the artery completely circumferentially before proceeding distally. After dissection is extended distally, a vascular forceps is used to grasp the specimen and, by retraction, additional dissection can be carried out distally. Dissection is extended distally into all of the involved subbronchopulmonary segmental arterial branches. Eventually, the specimen will be removed relatively cleanly from each of the bronchopulmonary segmental arteries and divisions.

is entered. The right pulmonary artery is freed anteriorly to identify the origin of the right upper lobe artery superiorly, and distally to identify the origin of the right middle lobe branch. An incision is made in the mid right pulmonary artery at the level of the right upper lobe artery (Fig. 1). If intraluminal thrombus is present, the incision is extended proximally beneath the superior vena cava to clearly visualize the origin of the thrombus. The intraluminal thrombus is removed to facilitate dissection of the underlying pseudointimal membrane that is adherent to the wall of the pulmonary artery. Often, intraluminal thrombus is not present and only the fibrous residuum of the incomplete recanalization process remains. In these cases, the intravascular anatomy may appear normal. Using low magnification, the hallmarks of the remaining pseudointima can be seen, including (1) irregular thickening and ridges in the arterial wall, (2) punctate "dimples" often overlying obstructed arterial orifices and, (3) webs spanning partially obstructed orifices. Atheromatous plaques may be present in hypertensive pulmonary arteries without underlying pseudointima. If present on the pseudointima they serve as a useful guide to identify the proper plane of the intraarterial dissection because they are superficial to it.

In cases where a mature intraarterial thrombus is identified, the proper plane of dissection usually lies in the media of the vessel. It is identified using low magnification, often at the cut arterial edge, using a micro-Penfield elevator.

Once begun, the dissection plane is developed distally using blunt instruments. Circumferential dissection of each distal branch is essential, as is strict maintenance of the proper plane of dissection. If the intra-arterial anatomy is obscured with bronchial blood flow, 20-minute (a time selected empirically) periods of circulatory arrest or reduced systemic flow are used. Flow is resumed between arrests to allow the mixed venous saturation to return to the pre-arrest level which, for 20°C, is 90% or more.

If no thrombus is present and the patient clearly has evidence for peripheral occlusion at the bronchopulmonary segmental level, a more tedious dissection is required. Low ocular magnification and micro-technique are especially helpful in these instances. The same principles of circumferential dissection and maintenance of the proper dissection plane are applied. It is common to remove a 1–2 mm fibrous "plug" from the orifice of a 3–5 mm artery. Following these peripheral dissections, it is often possible to visualize the reticular pattern in lung parenchyma through the remaining transparent arterial wall. Occasionally, separate incisions are made in the right upper lobe to facilitate distal dissection. The arterial incisions are closed with double running 6-0 or 7-0 Prolene sutures.

The left main pulmonary artery dissection is always done through a single, proximal incision near the main pulmonary artery bifurcation that extends distally and inferiorly into the hilum of the lung. The incision is limited distally by the left upper lobe bronchus, which crosses anteriorly and superiorly. The distal incision is directed medial to the left upper lobe branch to enhance visualization and dissection in the left lower lobe (Fig. 2).

After completing the bilateral pulmonary thromboendarterectomy the patient is rewarmed, the aortic clamp is removed, and a search is made for a patent foramen ovale, which has been present in 30% of our patients. A brief period of circulatory arrest can also be used to insert an inferior vena caval filter if one was not previously placed. The patient is weaned from cardiopulmonary bypass. Steroids are given to minimize reperfusion edema and, currently, prostaglandin E_1 is given to facilitate reduction in pulmonary vascular resistance and minimize platelet activation. Careful maintenance of low $PaCO_2$, normal PaO_2 and normal pH is essential to keep the pulmonary vascular resistance as low as possible. Blood transfusions are avoided. A left atrial pressure line and a non-inflated pulmonary artery catheter are left in place to monitor changes in pulmonary vascular resistance. Pulmonary artery pressures may remain somewhat elevated because of the increased pulmonary blood flow following the procedure. All patients are anticoagulated following surgery. Heparin is begun after initial bleeding has ceased, and Coumadin is given long term.

Postoperatively, essentially all patients have some degree of reperfusion pulmonary edema, which varies from minimal radiologic changes to severe, frothy and even hemorrhagic pulmonary edema. This phenomenon is associated with varying degrees of hypoxemia. It is managed by using steroids as well as by changing the patient's position and mode of mechanical ventilation.

Echocardiographic assessment of right ventricular function during the early postoperative period demonstrates favorable changes in right ventricular geometry. All right ventricular biopsies have shown only hypertrophy and no fibrous changes.

We recently have reported an evaluation of risk factors in 127 consecutive patients in whom the methods of myocardial protection and dissection were standardized for pulmonary thromboendarterectomy.[1] The mean age was 50 ±

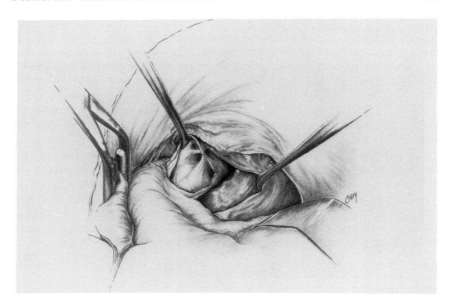

FIGURE 2.   The patient's head is to the viewer's left. As on the right side, the pericardial reflection is divided directly over the left pulmonary artery. A vein retractor is shown retracting the left superior pulmonary vein to the left and inferiorly. The left upper lobe bronchus can be visualized crossing anterior to the left pulmonary artery. The left pulmonary arteriotomy is started within the pericardial reflection and extended approximately 5 cm distally. It is important to extend the incision into the lower lobe branch and to avoid inadvertent extension of the incision into the lower lobe or lingular branches. If necessary, the incision can be extended 1.5–2.0 cm distal to the upper lobe bronchus after the bronchus is dissected free from the pulmonary artery. All bronchopulmonary segmental arteries of the left lung can be endarterectomized through the single incision, as they were in the illustrated case.

16 years and ranged from 20 to 82 years. The majority (62%) were males. Two endpoints were selected for evaluation with respect to potential risk factors. The first factor was respiratory insufficiency as defined by ventilator dependency of five or more days. Of the group, 32% had ventilator dependency. The other endpoint was hospital mortality which, for the entire group, was 13%.

The only preoperative multivariate predictor of ventilator dependency was ascites. Additionally, the percent change in pulmonary vascular resistance, the administration of more than four units of blood, and total cardiopulmonary bypass time were independent predictors of ventilator dependency. There were no preoperative independent predictors of hospital mortality but percent change in pulmonary vascular resistance and total cardiopulmonary bypass time were multivariate predictors. The preoperative group mean pulmonary vascular resistance of 813 ± 365 dyne-sec-cm^{-5} was reduced to 248 ± 233 dyne-sec-cm^{-5} (three operative deaths excluded).

In another reported study from our group, 35 survivors were followed up for an average of 28 months.[5] All but one of these patients were in New York Heart Association functional class I or II, whereas all were in classes III or IV preoperatively. Cardiac catheterization in 17 patients between 4 and 12 months postoperatively revealed a further decline in pulmonary vascular resistance from the postoperative pulmonary vascular resistance recorded during hospitalization for the procedure. Although significant numbers of patients followed up for five years have not been obtained, one can surmise that the level of pulmonary vascular resistance seen postoperatively suggests that these patients may have substantially improved five-year survival as reported by Reidel and others.[6]

When evaluating candidates with pulmonary hypertension for heart-lung transplantation, bilateral lung transplantation, or single lung transplantation, those patients with chronic pulmonary embolism should undergo thromboendarterectomy rather than transplantation. Thromboendarterectomy is currently associated with a lower hospital mortality than heart-lung transplantation. Furthermore, the ravages of immunosuppression are avoided, long-term survival is better, and precious donor organs are spared. Many patients currently undergoing heart-lung transplantation might be well served by single or double lung transplantation alone because the right ventricle is not irreversibly compromised by prolonged exposure to high pulmonary artery pressures.

ACKNOWLEDGMENTS

We extend our appreciation to the Journal of Cardiac Surgery 4:10–24, 1989 for permission to reprint figures and legends 1 and 2 from the manuscript entitled Risk Factors for Pulmonary Thromboendarterectomy.

We would also like to thank Elizabeth Gilpin, M.S., Programmer Analyst at the University of California, San Diego, for her expertise in compiling the statistical analyses described in this manuscript.

FURTHER READING

Daily PO, Dembitsky WP, Peterson KL, Moser KM: Modifications of techniques and early results of pulmonary thromboendarterectomy for chronic pulmonary embolism. J Thoracic Cardiovasc Surg 93:221–233, 1987.

Daily PO, Dembitsky WP, Iverson S: Technique of pulmonary thromboendarterectomy for chronic pulmonary embolism. J Cardiac Surg 4:10–24, 1989.

REFERENCES

1. Daily PO, Dembitsky WP, Iverson S, et al: Risk factors for pulmonary thromboendarterectomy. J Thorac Cardiovasc Surg, in press.
2. Dittrich HC, Nicod PH, Chow LC, et al: Early changes of the right heart geometry after pulmonary thromboendarterectomy. J Am Coll Cardiol 11:937–943, 1988.
3. Dunnill MS: The pathology of pulmonary embolism. Bull Physiopathol Respir 6:7–19, 1970.
4. Nicod PH, Peterson KL, Levine M, et al: Pulmonary angiography in severe chronic pulmonary hypertension. Ann Intern Med 107:565–568, 1987.
5. Moser KM, Daily PO, Peterson K, et al: Thromboendarterectomy for chronic, major-vessel thromboembolic pulmonary hypertension. Ann Intern Med 107:560–565, 1987.
6. Riedel M, Stanek V, Widimsky J, et al: Long-term follow-up of patients with pulmonary thromboembolism: Late prognosis and evolution of hemodynamic and respiratory data. Chest 81:151, 1982.
7. Shure D, Gregoratos G, Moser K: Fiberoptic angioscopy: Role in the diagnosis of chronic pulmonary arterial obstruction. Ann Intern Med 103:844–850, 1985.

FRAZIER EALES, MD

ETHICAL CONSIDERATIONS IN TRANSPLANTATION

Cardiovascular Surgeon
Minneapolis Heart Institute
Chairman, Department of
 Cardiovascular Disease
Abbott Northwestern Hospital
Minneapolis, Minnesota

Reprint requests to:
Frazier Eales, MD
Minneapolis Heart Institute
920 East 28th Street
Minneapolis, MN 55407

The field of cardiac replacement, now a clinical reality for more than 20 years, continues to thrive by virtue of ongoing refinements in this method of treating end-stage cardiac disease.[6] Our successes as well as failures have been and continue to be the focus of an extraordinary level of scrutiny.[7] Indeed, in the history of medical science it is hard to recall any other area that has commanded the attention of public, political, and professional interests in such enduring fashion. Those of us who spend our working lives in this clinical arena are well aware of the vagaries of such attention. We are occasionally pleased, occasionally disgusted, and frequently amused by the repercussions of a relatively high profile. But perhaps most of all, we become numb to much of it. Like an incurable rattle somewhere inside your new car, you either put it out of your mind or fall victim to its perverse tyranny.

A topic such as "Ethical Considerations in Transplantation" has the potential for eliciting a similar reaction of numbness.[5] We are aware of the fact (or at least we should be) that the ethical fundamentals of transplantation are no different from those of any aspect of health care. We try to provide appropriate, safe, and effective treatment to whomever needs it. Issues of fairness in access to medical care or allocation of resources are the same as for any life-threatening illness. Furthermore, perfect solutions to these issues are just as elusive in transplantation as they have proved to be elsewhere, whether it be health care, housing, education, or job opportunity.

CARDIAC SURGERY: State of the Art Reviews—Vol. 3, No. 3, October 1989
Philadelphia, Hanley & Belfus, Inc.

583

What is unique about transplantation is this highly visible crucible in which we work and the high level of accountability to which we are held. We do not have, nor can we be expected to have, perfect solutions to society's larger questions. But we can and must have a firm grasp of what these concerns are. The media have contributed mightily to an enhanced awareness of the field of transplantation. The clinical results, particularly in the last 5 years, have greatly improved the level of acceptance of this form of treatment. But awareness and acceptance do not automatically translate into support, and in order for transplantation to continue to grow, we need large doses of public, professional, political, and financial support. The necessary support is attainable, but only if we systematically address some of society's larger questions. We are in a position to offer valuable guidance and to provide some answers. For the purposes of this discussion, these "larger questions" can be grouped under three headings of progressively narrower focus.

1. Prioritization or allocation of resources
2. Fairness of access and delivery
3. Safety and credentialing issues

SCARCE RESOURCES

In medicine these days, the term "scarce resources" is usually synonymous with scarce money.[4] It is a fact that there is not enough money to go around, particularly when you are talking about meeting everyone's health care needs all of the time. Further, we have all heard that it doesn't make sense to spend $50,000 or $100,000 on one transplant when the same funds would have a greater impact if allocated to disease prevention programs. There may be a good deal of substance to such an argument. Preventive medicine deserves a higher priority than it has traditionally received. But there are two fundamental flaws in such a comparison. The first flaw is the implication that transplantation is somehow different from other "individual-intensive" forms of treatment (e.g., hip replacement, chemotherapy for Stage IV carcinoma, or individual chemical dependency protocols). I would submit that transplantation is fundamentally identical to those types of care (i.e., intensive efforts with one individual directed at appropriate, safe, and effective treatment) and should be considered in the same light. And if, in today's climate, that light is purely one of measuring cost-effectiveness, transplantation would far outstrip the positive economic impact of many other forms of medical intervention.[3]

The second fundamental flaw is the implication that physicians can or should be the ones to prioritize or ration medical care based on the need for financial constraint. We hardly need to be reminded that such a posture, for a clinician, is contrary to our training, contrary to the best interests of our patients, and, in many instances, contrary to the law. In our system of medical care, a physician's first ethical and legal responsibility is the well-being of the patient. First and foremost, we are our patients' advocates. It is tempting to think that such a role is invariably synonymous with the well-being of society at large; unfortunately, it is not. However, if we are to be restrained in our ability to judge who should be cared for, when, and at what cost, such restraint is properly determined by society through its elected representatives. These same officials can then be expected to share in the responsibility for the repercussions of their programs.

While all of us have heard objections to the cost of transplantation, the concerns already voiced would be like a gentle rain compared to the hurricane we would face were it not for another scarce resource in our domain: donor organs. The scarcity of donor organs represents the definitive limit to clinical cardiac transplantation. The increasing numbers of transplants from 1983 to 1987 can largely be attributed to increased donor availability, increased surgical manpower, and better donor organ placement. For the last year or so, increases have come primarily from expanding the donor pool. Over the next few years we can reasonably expect significant, but not dramatic, increases in donor availability. Given the prevalence of cardiovascular disease and the large numbers of people awaiting transplantation, such increases are not likely to alter the fact that 25–35% of patients die while awaiting transplantation. What will change that percentage will be the introduction of a totally implantable, dependable artificial heart. Whether 2 years away or 10, such technology is certainly coming and we had better prepare ourselves for more than just implanting them.

Manpower shortages, a very real issue just 5 years ago, have been largely eliminated as transplant centers have proliferated. From roughly one dozen centers in existence in the United States in 1983, there are today more than 150 institutions that have performed transplants or embarked on formal programs to do so. If HCFA requirements for volume and survival are to be met, probably fewer than one half of these programs will endure. Nevertheless, one serious impediment to the availability of transplantation has been substantially removed.

FAIRNESS

Scarce resources notwithstanding, the wider awareness and acceptance of transplantation have resulted in increased emphasis on the concept of fairness.[1,8] Fairness encompasses issues of patient selection, donor allocation, and access to the health care system in general and donor organs in particular.

The textbook example of a potential cardiac recipient is simple: a young, otherwise healthy individual with end-stage idiopathic cardiomyopathy. It is also an example that is a diminishing fraction of the overall transplant population. Non-ideal modifiers (e.g., advanced age, need for a preoperative ventricular assist device, a history of non-cardiac disease, to name but a few) are present in many candidates who are referred for consideration.[2] Despite these detractors, clinicians are confronted with many patients for whom transplantation represents the best and often the only hope of long-term survival. To be sure, we have expanded the criteria that guide selection for transplantation. The Stanford criteria, which most of us used just 4 years ago, now is a list of primarily historic interest. The extension of transplantation criteria has been gradual and carefully evaluated. Survival and quality of life have not suffered as a result, and continued liberalization and selection parameters can be safely predicted.

Within these changes, there has been a casualty, however, and that is the ease of prioritizing and listing transplant candidates. As the recipient lists have grown and become more heterogeneous, there has been a simultaneous tendency to become more detailed in prioritizing candidates for donors. While this progression may be understandable, it is also confusing and dangerous. It has become confusing to patients because of its complexity, and dangerous to us because of the great potential for confusion and misunderstanding.

The United Network for Organ Sharing (UNOS) spent the greater part of 1988 revamping the old seven-tier system into a cleaner and fairer system.[9] I believe they succeeded. The new system, which was activated in February 1989, features two priority levels for active candidates: Status I (the most critically ill) and Status II, which encompasses all others. The only other pertinent factor is the length of time on the waiting list. While this system is not perfect, it does accomplish three important goals. First, it presents a system that is uniform and simple. It is easy for patients to understand and relatively easy for transplant centers to verify. These are both important contributors to the requirement for fairness. Second, the system is patient-oriented as opposed to center-oriented. In other words, a patient's likelihood of receiving a donor organ is independent of the center providing care. This, too, contributes significantly to fairness. Third, it leaves the selection of transplant candidates entirely in the hands of transplant centers. You can list whomever you deem appropriate, but candidacy, once determined, should be an all-or-none phenomenon. If, for example, my commitment to utilize a donor for a given patient is conditional (e.g., older donor only), I would be well-advised to be very explicit in communicating those conditions to my patient.

The final point to be made with respect to fairness is that of access to the health care system itself. I am not one to suggest that such problems do not exist, nor do I underestimate their importance. I do believe, however, that the transplant centers have gone and continue to go to extraordinary lengths to provide access to everyone in medical need. In some cases this means providing the service at no charge to the patient. In most instances, it means helping patients to martial the financial resources necessary to cover very considerable expenditures of labor and supplies. In point of fact, lack of insurance is less of a problem than inadequate (and in some cases deceptive) insurance. Transplantation may be excluded or inadequately covered by some health care insurers.

SAFETY

Ten years ago when cardiac transplantation was rarely performed and confined to a few centers, safety was not a big issue. The only real comparison made was against the backdrop of 100% mortality for patients who did not receive a transplant. There are now very good reasons to expect that individual risk for those undergoing transplantation should be reasonably low. Similarly, transplant centers can be held to certain standards of performance (i.e., minimum survival percentages and minimum levels of activity). While we might disagree about the specifics of certain standards, there can be no effective argument against the need for quality control. The public demands it, third party payers demand it, and we should be leading the efforts to achieve it.

The most obvious focus for controls is in the certification (and ultimately remuneration) of new centers. Insurers see such controls as a mechanism for assuring quality and controlling costs. The public sees these controls as primarily safety related. Those of us in established centers are in a "catch 22" situation: we obviously have an interest in seeing good results (in most cases we have contributed to them) and yet actions we might take to impose requirements may be interpreted as self-serving and unnecessarily restrictive.

In order to accommodate the somewhat different perspectives involved, the credentialing system needs to incorporate two factors: (1) obstacles to the creation of new centers should be minimized, and (2) requirements for established centers should be tangible. For example, what HCFA has done to date is largely commendable. It has identified and essentially "certified" a core group of cardiac transplantation centers. New centers are subject to a three-year "probationary period" during which time minimum volume and survival statistics must be achieved. As a method of promoting safety, this approach is excellent. Within it, however, lurks the very real danger that the "safety program" can be transformed into a mechanism for rationing. I do not wish to imply that there is anything inherently wrong with rationing. I would simply point out that a rationing program should be identified as such, promoted as such, and its authors should stand accountable.

In the narrower focus of physician certification and training requirements, the same basic principles apply: objectives must be clearly discernible as related to quality control and not to consolidation of "market share."

SUMMARY

Ethical issues have a certain timeless quality. This "timelessness" is at once an asset and a liability. It is an asset in the sense that the underlying principles are largely unchanging. You don't have to learn a new set of ethical principles every year or two. It is a liability in the sense that it masks urgency. It leads us to assume that these issues have been adequately addressed before, which is not necessarily the case. For clinicians involved in cardiac transplantation, I offer these observations:

1. Our first priority is to our individual patients. Our individual and collective professional integrity is solidly centered here.
2. We must do everything we can to cooperate with other transplant centers with whom we compete for both patients and donors.
3. Such a requirement stems from society's legitimate expectations that our services be offered fairly and safely.
4. We must recognize that achieving all three of the above objectives in a given clinical case requires both science and art and, in some cases, a little bit of luck.

REFERENCES

1. Caplan AC: Equity in the selection of recipients for cardiac transplants. Circulation 75:10, 1987.
2. Copeland JC, Emery RW, et al: Selection of patients for cardiac transplantation. Circulation 75:2, 1987.
3. Evans RW: Cost effectiveness analysis of transplantation. Surg Clin North Am 66:603, 1986.
4. Evans RW: The economics of heart transplantation. Circulation 75:63, 1987.
5. Fletcher JC: Cardiac transplants and the artificial heart: Ethical considerations. Circulation 68:1339, 1983.
6. Goodwin JF: Cardiac transplantation. Circulation 74:913, 1986.
7. Qualms About Innovative Surgery (editorial). Lancet 1:149, 1985.
8. Robertson JA: Supply and distribution of hearts for transplantation: Legal, ethical, and policy issues. Circulation 75:77, 1987.
9. UNOS: Heart and Heart/Lung Allocation Policy, February 1989.

THOMAS J. VON RUEDEN, MD, FACS

PRESERVATION OF THE LUNG

Thoracic and Cardiovascular
  Surgeon
Division of Cardiothoracic
  Transplantation
Minneapolis Heart Institute
Minneapolis, Minnesota

Reprint requests to:
Thomas J. Von Rueden, MD
Division of Cardiothoracic
  Transplantation
Minneapolis Heart Institute
920 East 28th Street
Minneapolis, MN 55407

Donor availability remains a major obstacle to pulmonary transplantation. Adding to organ scarcity, approximately only one in ten donor lungs offered for transplant are suitable for implantation.[10] Donor lungs can deteriorate rapidly from neurogenic pulmonary edema and pulmonary sepsis. As with other organs, a local donor pool cannot meet a center's needs and distant procurement becomes a necessity. Protecting the delicate pulmonary structural and functional elements from operative trauma and ischemic damage, facilitating immediate post-transplant function, and allowing distant procurement and maximal utilization of the organ pool are the goals of pulmonary preservation methods.

The development of methods for lung preservation has followed the course of preservation of other organs. Hypothermia and perfusion of the vascular system have received the bulk of attention. However, the lungs have certain unique characteristics, including an airway system, a low-pressure, high-flow network of delicate capillaries, and a bronchial arterial supply, all of which provide other avenues of study.[23] To further complicate matters, the nature of ischemic injury to the lung is not well understood and is often difficult to differentiate from pulmonary allograft rejection.[14,28,48,53]

Numerous animal models have been devised to study pulmonary preservation, including (1) in situ ischemia with or without hypothermia, perfusion, or ventilation, (2) allo- or autotransplantation after various periods of ischemia, and (3) autoperfusion.[1,3–6,8,9,11–14,20,26,29–34,36,37,39–41,44,46,47,50] Many experimental models have used heart-lung transplantation to study preservation of the lung and function thereafter, subjecting the lung to the limiting or damaging side-effects of myocardial preservation. Furthermore, the study of lung preservation has been hampered by the absence of inexpensive methods of screening in small animals, as have been used in heart and kidney preservation research. Implied by the presence of these varied models is the absence of a satisfactory experimental model. Consequently, results have been confusing and contradictory. For a summary of the experimental work in lung preservation, the extensive review by Haverich is recommended.[24]

Notwithstanding methodologic problems, certain principles seem to have emerged. Hypothermic ischemia is better tolerated than normothermic ischemia; thus, topical cooling of the lungs offers limited protection. If cold perfusion of the pulmonary vasculature, either continuous or single flush, is added, the period of protection is extended further. Continuous perfusion methods can be complicated and, as such, add additional problems. Successful preservation perfusates have consisted of intracellular crystalloid, such as Euro-Collins solution, and blood. The addition of certain pharmacologic agents such as prostaglandin or isoproterenol has been beneficial.[21,22,27] However, perfusion of the vasculature and the use of vasodilatory drugs may only serve to facilitate cooling. The use of measures designed to influence the airway system remains controversial. Whether inflation, deflation, or ventilation during flushing and/ or storage enhances preservation remains unanswered.[7,25,35,45,49] Again, airway system pressure may only serve to allow for better cooling by providing more even and thorough distribution of cold perfusates. Currently, combinations of these practices allow satisfactory functional preservation of the lung from 4–6 hours and potentially longer.[6,38,43]

Successful clinical heart-lung and lung transplantation are being carried out at several centers. Distant procurement, which is commonplace, has partially validated experimental findings and provides much of the basis for our present knowledge and methods of pulmonary preservation. The two most common methods of preservation used clinically are single-flush hypothermic perfusion with Euro-Collins solution and continuous hypothermic perfusion with cardiopulmonary bypass prior to organ extraction. Early and late clinical results have been favorable.[2,17–19,51,52] Although autoperfusion systems have been utilized, they are cumbersome because of their complexity and add logistical problems to distant procurement. The single flush with cold Euro-Collins solution is attractive because it is simple and easy to implement. However, cardiopulmonary bypass (CPB) may allow for more uniform cooling, less blood loss, and less time waiting for the preparation of abdominal organs. The organ donor can simply be placed on CPB, cooled systemically, and then the lungs and heart removed, with the pump supporting the rest of the organs during their dissection. Extrathoracic organ procurement teams have historically disapproved of this method, however, for fear of harm to abdominal organs. Nonetheless, given the increase in activity of heart-lung and lung transplantation programs, the use of CPB may prove necessary to protect the lungs from the decline in respiratory mechanics and gas exchange that often occurs during mobilization of the liver, pancreas, and kidneys (lengthy procedures that may require massive transfusion). Whether late function and the development of bronchiolitis obliterans are a result of rejection or preservation techniques is unclear.[42]

Clinical heart-lung and double-lung transplantation provide the ultimate challenge to the technique of lung preservation, as initial survival is dependent on immediate function. We have distilled a method that has provided recipients with excellent immediate and early function of their allografts. The process of donor-lung preservation begins once the organs are offered for donation. This process is diligently overseen by the transplant coordinator and donor surgeon who manage the donor. Communication and coordination with the liver, kidney, and heart teams are required for consistent preservation of all organs.

Direct arterial and central venous pressures must be continuously recorded. Occasionally a Swan-Ganz catheter will be needed. Urine output should be recorded with an indwelling Foley catheter. Central venous pressure should be maintained at 10–12 cm H_2O. Inotropic agents may be judiciously used to keep the systolic blood pressure ≥ 90 torr. Ventilation should be maintained with physiologic volumes and pressures to keep $pO_2 \geq 100$ torr (FiO_2 40%), $pCO_2 \leq 40$ torr, and to sustain normal acid-base equilibrium. Arterial blood gas measurements are obtained every hour once the donor has been accepted. A broad-spectrum antibiotic such as cephalosporin is given prior to operation and methylprednisolone 20 mg/kg is administered.

The chest is opened and the lungs are examined as the abdominal organs are being prepared. The superior (SVC) and inferior vena cava (IVC) are mobilized and looped with tapes. The ascending aorta (AO) is dissected to the innominate artery and secured with a tape. The pulmonary artery (PA) is freed to the bifurcation, and an infusion needle is secured with a pursestring suture in the main PA. The trachea (TR) is mobilized minimally at the level of the innominate artery and circled with a tape. The pericardium (PC) posterior to the SVC and AO is cut with cautery. On the right, the PC is incised to the level of the SVC, and interiorly to the IVC. On the left, the PC is incised to the PA, and inferiorly as lateral as possible without causing hemodynamic instability. The PC is then secured to the chest. Ten minutes prior to AO clamping, the patient is ventilated with 100% oxygen. Two minutes prior to cross-clamp, the patient is heparinized (3 mg/kg) and taken off the ventilator to allow absorption atelectasis to occur. The SVC is stapled and the IVC is transected. After the heart is empty, the AO is clamped and crystalloid cardioplegia (10 ml/kg) at 4°C administered. Simultaneously, Euro-Collins solution (20 ml/kg) at 4°C is delivered by gravity to the PA (Table 1). The left atrial appendage is amputated. The AO and SVC are then transected. At the preference of the surgeon, the heart may be retrieved separately at this point, leaving residual cuffs of PA and left atrium. The inferior pulmonary ligaments and lateral PC pedicles are then divided with cautery. The

TABLE 1. Preservation of the Lung

Euro-Collins Solution	
Travenol electrolyte solution for kidney preservation	930 ml
50% dextrose injection, USP	65 ml
Approximate ionic concentration (mEq/L)	
Potassium	108.0
Magnesium	0.0
Sodium	9.3
Phosphate (HPO_4^{-2})	79.0
Phosphate ($H_2PO_4^{-1}$)	14.0
Sulfate	0.0
Chloride	14.0
Bicarbonate	9.3

TR is stapled and the device left in place. With traction on the stapler, the TR and left mediastinal attachments are sharply divided, followed by the right, until the bloc is out. The organs are then placed in iced saline. The heart may then be separated from the lung bloc if separate heart and lung transplantation are indicated. To facilitate topical cooling on the back table during preliminary trimming, cold laparotomy pads are placed on the lungs to keep them submerged. If, during the operative procedure, the donor becomes unstable from a cardiac or pulmonary aspect, and this cannot be rapidly corrected, the heart-lung block is immediately removed and transported. During implantation, the lungs are covered with cold wet laparotomy pads and iced slush.

This technique has been used by our group for heart-lung (n = 3) and double lung (n = 4) procedures. The ischemic times have ranged from 80–288 minutes (average 205 minutes). Early and late function have been excellent in all cases, as assessed by survival, clinical course, arterial blood gas measurements, roentgen analysis, and time on the respirator.

The success of pulmonary transplantation is primarily dependent on recipient selection and on the condition and preservation of the donor lungs. Cardiopulmonary bypass may have a role in the near future during multiple organ procurement, procedures that tend to traumatize the lungs. However, the logistics of this procedure can be complex. The method we currently utilize is simple, reproducible, and adaptable to distant multiple organ procurements. Just as simplification has greatly advanced conventional cardiopulmonary operations, we anticipate it will improve pulmonary transplantation as well.

REFERENCES

1. Adachi H, Fraser CD, Kontos GJ, et al: Autoperfused working heart-lung preparation versus hypothermic cardiopulmonary preservation for transplantation. J Heart Transplant 6:253–260, 1987.
2. Baldwin JC, Frist WH, Starkey TD, et al: Distant graft procurement for combined heart and lung transplantation using pulmonary artery flush and simple topical hypothermia for graft preservation. Ann Thorac Surg 43:670–673, 1987.
3. Bando K, Teramoto S, Tago M, et al: Core-cooling, heart-perfusion, lung-immersion technique provides successful cardiopulmonary preservation for heart-lung transplantation. Ann Thorac Surg 46:625–630, 1988.
4. Breda MA, Hall TS, Stuart RS, et al: Twenty-four hour lung preservation by hypothermia and leukocyte depletion. Heart Transplant 4:325–329, 1985.
5. Brodman RF, Goldsmith J, Veith FJ, et al: A technique for donor lung procurement and preservation for transplantation after completion of cardiac donation. Surg Gynecol Obstet 166:363–366, 1988.
6. Bruning JH, Bruggeman CA, Van Breda Vriesman PJC: A simple, working heart and lung transplant model for assessing preservation methods in the rabbit. Transplantation 46:624–626, 1988.
7. Burdine J, Heck CF, Shumway SJ, et al: Effects of inflation/deflation of 12 hour preservation of the hypothermic, ischemic, static lung. J Heart Transplant 8:101, 1989.
8. Castagna JT, Shors E, Benfield JR: The role of perfusion in lung preservation. J Thorac Cardiovasc Surg 63:521–526, 1972.
9. Chien S, Todd EP, Diana JN, et al: A simple technique for multiorgan preservation. J Thorac Cardiovasc Surg 95:55–61, 1988.
10. Cooper, JD: The lung donor: Special considerations. Transplant Proc 20:17–18, 1988.
11. Dos SJ, Erdamar I: Orthotopic transplantation of resuscitated canine heart-lung units. Transplant Proc 20:826–831, 1988.
12. Downing TP, Sadeghi AM, Baumgartner WA, et al: Acute physiological changes following heart-lung allotransplantation in dogs. Ann Thorac Surg 37:479–483, 1984.
13. Feeley TW, Mihm FG, Downing TP, et al: The effect of hypothermic preservation of the heart and lungs on cardiorespiratory function following canine heart-lung transplantation. Ann Thorac Surg 39:558–562, 1985.

14. Fraser CD, Tamura F, Adachi H, et al: Donor core-cooling provides improved static preservation for heart-lung transplantation. Ann Thorac Surg 45:253–257, 1988.
15. Goldsmith J, Kamholz SL, Montefusco CM, et al: Clinical and experimental aspects of single-lung transplantation. Heart and Lung 16:231–236, 1987.
16. Griffith BP, Hardesty RL, Trento A, et al: Heart-lung transplantation: Lessons learned and future hopes. Ann Thorac Surg 43:6–16, 1987.
17. Hakim M, Higenbottam T, Bethune D, et al: Selection and procurement of combined heart and lung grafts for transplantation. J Thorac Cardiovasc Surg 95:474–479, 1988.
18. Hakim M, Higenbottam T, English TAH, et al: Distant procurement and preservation of heart-lung homografts. Transplant Proc 19:3535–3536, 1987.
19. Hardesty RL, Griffith BP: Autoperfusion of the heart and lungs for preservation during distant procurement. J Thorac Cardiovasc Surg 93:11–18, 1987.
20. Harjula A, Baldwin JC, Shumway NE: Donor deep hypothermia or donor pretreatment with prostaglandin E-1 and single pulmonary artery flush for heart-lung graft preservation: an experimental primate study. Ann Thorac Surg 46:553–555, 1988.
21. Harjula ALJ, Baldwin JC, Stinson EB, et al: Clinical heart-lung preservation with prostaglandin E-1. Transplant Proc 19:4101–4102, 1987.
22. Harjula ALJ, Starkey TD, Hagberg RC, et al: Intravenous prostaglandin E1, cold crystalloid flush and topical hypothermia for cardiopulmonary graft preservation. Ann Chir Gynaecol 76:56–60, 1987.
23. Haverich A, Aziz S, Scott WC, et al: Improved lung preservation using Euro-Collins solution for flush perfusion. Thorac Cardiovasc Surg 34:369–376, 1986.
24. Haverich A, Scott WC, Jamieson SW: Twenty years of lung preservation—a review. Heart Transplant 4:234–240, 1985.
25. Heimbecker RO, McKenzie N, Stiller C, et al: Guest editorial: Heart and heart-lung transplantation. Heart Lung 13:1–4, 1984.
26. Jones MT, Hsieh C, Yoshikawa K, et al: A new model for assessment of lung preservation. J Thorac Cardiovasc Surg 96:608–614, 1988.
27. Jurmann MJ, Dammenhayn L, Schafers HJ, et al: Prostacyclin as an additive to single crystalloid flush: Improved pulmonary preservation in heart-lung transplantation. Transplant Proc 19:4103–4104, 1987.
28. Kamholz SL: Current perspectives on clinical and experimental single lung transplantation. Chest 94:390–396, 1988.
29. Kontos GJ, Adachi H, Borkon AM, et al: A no-flush core-cooling technique for successful cardiopulmonary preservation in heart-lung transplantation. J Thorac Cardiovasc Surg 94:836–842, 1987.
30. Kontos GJ, Borkon AM, Adachi H, et al: Successful extended cardiopulmonary preservation in the autoperfused working heart-lung preparation. Surgery 102:269–276, 1987.
31. Kontos GJ, Adachi H, Borkon AM, et al: Successful four-hour heart-lung preservation with core-cooling on cardiopulmonary bypass: A simplified model that assesses preservation. J Heart Transplant 6:106–111, 1987.
32. Kontos GJ, Borkon AM, Baumgartner WA, et al: Neurohumoral modulation of the pulmonary vasoconstrictor response in the autoperfused working heart-lung preparation during cardiopulmonary preservation. Transplantation 45:275–279, 1988.
33. Ladowski JS, Kapelanski DP, Teodori MF, et al: Use of autoperfusion for distant procurement of heart-lung allografts. Heart Transplant 4:330–333, 1985.
34. Locke TJ, Hooper TL, Flecknell PA, et al: Comparison of topical cooling and cold crystalloid pulmonary perfusion J Thorac Cardiovasc Surg 96:789–795, 1988.
35. Mancini MC, Griffith BP, Borovetz HS, et al: Static lung preservation. Curr Surg Jan–Feb 1985, pp 23–25.
36. Miyamoto Y, Lajos TZ, Bhayana JN, et al: Physiologic constraints in autoperfused heart-lung preservation. J Heart Transplant 6:261–266, 1987.
37. Morimoto T, Golding LR, Stewart RW, et al: A simple method for extended heart-lung preservation by autoperfusion. Trans Am Soc Artif Intern Organs 30:320–324, 1984.
38. Prieto M, Androne PA, Baron P, et al: Multiple organ retrieval and preservation with normothermic autoperfusion. Transplant Proc 20:827–828, 1988.
39. Prieto M, Baron P, Andreone PA, et al: Multiple ex vivo organ preservation with warm whole blood. J Heart Transplant 7:227–237, 1988.
40. Reichart BA, Novitzky D, Cooper DKC, et al: Successful orthotopic heart-lung transplantation in the baboon after five hours of cold ischemia with cardioplegia and Collins' solution. J Heart Transplant 6:15–22, 1987.

41. Robicsek F, Masters TN, Duncan GD, et al: An autoperfused heart-lung preparation: Metabolism and function. Heart Transplant 4:334–338, 1985.
42. Scott JP, Higenbottam TW, Clelland C, et al: The natural history of obliterative bronchiolitis in heart-lung transplant recipients. J Heart Transplant 8:93, 1989.
43. Semik M, Konertz W, Moller F, et al: Successful 24-hour preservation of the lung—evaluation of viability in a rat model. Transplant Proc 19:4171–4172, 1987.
44. Starkey TD, Sakakibara N, Hagberg RC, et al: Successful six-hour cardiopulmonary preservation with simple hypothermic crystalloid flush. J Heart Transplant 5:291–297, 1986.
45. Stevens GH, Sanchez MM, Chappell GL: Enhancement of lung preservation by prevention of lung collapse. J Surg Res 14:400–405, 1973.
46. Thomas PA, Buchman RJ: Successful 20 hour preservation of ischemic canine lung by hypothermia combined with minimal ventilation. J Thorac Cardiovasc Surg 62:176–182, 1971.
47. Toledo-Pereyra LH, Condie RM: Hypothermic storage for 24 hours in a colloid hyperosmolar solution. J Thorac Cardiovasc Surg 76:846–852, 1978.
48. Veith FJ, Kamholz SL, Mollenkopf FP, et al: Lung Transplantation 1983. Transplantation 35:271–278, 1983.
49. Veith FJ, Sinha SBP, Graves JS, et al: Ischemic tolerance of the lung. J Thorac Cardiovasc Surg 61:804–810, 1971.
50. Wahlers T, Haverich A, Fieguth HG, et al: Flush perfusion using Euro=Collins solution vs. cooling by means of extracorporeal circulation in heart-lung preservation. J Heart Transplant 5:89–98, 1986.
51. Wallwork J, Jones K, Cavarocchi N, et al: Distant procurement of organs for clinical heart-lung transplantation using a single-flush technique. Transplantation 44:654–658, 1987.
52. Wheeldon DR, Biol C, Biol MI, et al: Storage and transport of heart and heart-lung donor organs with inflatable cushions and eutectoid cooling. J Heart Transplant 7:265–268, 1988.
53. Wildevuur CRH, Benfield JR: A review of 23 human lung transplantations by 20 surgeons. Ann Thorac Surg 9:489–515, 1970.

JAMES M. GAYES, MD
LUIS GIRON, MD
MARK D. NISSEN, MD
DAVID A. PLUT, MD

ANESTHESIA AND DOUBLE LUNG TRANSPLANTATION

Department of Anesthesiology
Abbott Northwestern Hospital
Minneapolis Heart Institute
Minneapolis, Minnesota

Reprint requests to:
James M. Gayes, MD
Department of Anesthesia
Abbott Northwestern Hospital
800 E. 28th Street
  at Chicago Avenue
Minneapolis, MN 55407

Nearly a quarter century has passed since Barnard performed the first human heart transplantation. At that time, few would have foreseen the success that cardiac transplantation has grown to enjoy throughout the world. During the 22 years since Barnard's historic operation, numerous clinical studies and advances in basic science research have allowed significant breakthroughs in cardiothoracic organ transplantation. As experience with heart transplantation grew, surgical options for patients with high pulmonary vascular resistance and right ventricular failure were being investigated. In 1981, the Stanford group successfully performed the first combined heart and lung transplantation.[42]

The patient with endstage pulmonary disease and normal cardiac function presented thoracic surgeons with a different set of challenges. The first human lung transplant was performed by Hardy in 1963.[22] During the following 20 years, approximately 50 lung transplant operations were performed, with the longest patient survival being 8 months.[54] Because of this poor long-term survival rate, lung transplantation was performed only rarely until the mid 1980s. With the advent of new immunosuppressive agents, omental tracheal wrapping, and the delaying of the onset of steroid therapy, the survival rates have subsequently improved.[10] In 1988, the Toronto Lung Transplant Group published a technique that allowed double-lung transplantation without the heart.[38] Between 1979 and 1986, the total age standardized mortality rate in the United States declined by 8%. The largest decreases were for stroke followed by coronary artery disease. In contrast, the portion of obstructive lung disease likely related to smoking increased by 33%.[33] In 1985, chronic obstructive lung disease was the fifth leading cause of death in the U.S., claiming the lives of nearly 75,000 Americans.[36,50] Double lung transplantation has provided treatment for endstage obstructive pulmonary disease for selected patients in which medical therapy has been unable to maintain adequate pulmonary function.[9]

In the United States during 1988, 17 double lung transplantations were performed at nine medical centers.[8] The overall national survival rate has been 57%, with the longest survivor living 2½ years to date.[8] Severe chronic obstructive lung disease has accounted for about 90% of recipient lung pathology.[10] Restrictive lung disease has played a minor role as a preoperative recipient diagnosis. This chapter reviews the limited literature on double lung transplantation and the pathophysiology of the denervated lung, and concentrates on anesthetic considerations for the recipient operative procedure. A discussion of criteria for donor utilization and recipient selection has been presented elsewhere.[15,21]

PATHOPHYSIOLOGY OF THE DENERVATED LUNG

Anesthetic concerns relating to the physiology of the transplanted lung center around three areas: vagal denervation, absence of lymphatics, and risk of oxygen toxicity. There has been little written regarding the changes in pulmonary physiology of patients undergoing double lung transplantation. However, much can be learned from experimental animal studies and human heart-lung transplant patients.

Phillipson et al.[39] showed that the effect of vagal blockade on the regulation of breathing in awake dogs results in no change in resting carbon dioxide (CO_2) tension. There is, however, a reduction in the ventilatory response to hypercapnia. Hence, the rise in $PaCO_2$ secondary to narcotic depression might not be met with an increase in respiratory rate in patients following double lung transplantation. This is especially important in patients given high-dose narcotic anesthesia.

Cutting the vagal nerve pathways leads to bronchodilation.[35] This might lead one to conclude that bronchoconstriction in double lung transplant recipients is unlikely. However, there have been at least two reports of severe bronchoconstriction in patients who have undergone heart-lung transplantation.[4,5] The etiology of the bronchoconstriction remains unclear, but early rejection was postulated in one patient.

Theodore et al.[52] compared pulmonary function tests in nine patients before and after heart-lung transplant surgery and found significant increases in PaO_2 over pre-transplant levels and progressive improvement in pulmonary function after surgery. Gas exchange was maintained at near normal levels. Dawkins et al.[12] studied a long-term follow-up of 22 patients who had undergone heart-lung transplantation and found that their values for arterial blood gases were within normal range 1 year after the transplantation procedure.

Denervation of the lungs not only affects bronchomotor tone but also pulmonary clearance mechanisms and cough reflexes. Pulmonary denervation causes a loss of the cough reflex. Patients can consciously cough, but secretions or foreign bodies that may accumulate in the trachea and bronchi produce no cough reflex. Damage to the recurrent laryngeal nerve may occur during surgery.[17] Loss of laryngeal innervation and the cough reflex places the double lung transplant recipient at great risk for aspiration. Extubation should be performed only when the patient is fully awake, in order to assure the ability to cough and to clear secretions on command.

Reinnervation of the lungs after transplantation is known to occur only in animals.[13,41] Reinnervation does not occur in human lung transplant recipients possibly because immunosuppressants are thought to inhibit regrowth of preganglionic nerve fibers.[58]

Pulmonary lymphatics are disrupted during the procurement of the donor lungs. This lack of lymphatic drainage allows for large amounts of fluid volume, required immediately after bypass, to accumulate, resulting in interstitial pulmonary edema. Lymphatics also provide an important filtering process. The blood and blood products given during the post-bypass period are inadequately filtered by the lung, promoting pulmonary congestion and hypoxemia. The right atrial pressure (CVP) must thus be maintained at the lowest level to provide adequate renal perfusion and hemodynamic stability. Two-stage 40-micron filters should be used for all homologous blood products. Although some lymphatic channels may reform months after lung transplantation, their extent and significance are currently unclear.[25]

Donor lungs suffer from manipulation trauma and ischemia during the period between procurement and transplantation. Superoxide radicals are thought to play a major role in the oxygen toxicity seen in ischemic tissues.[20,30] It has been suggested that in order to avoid the development of alveolar capillary leak seen in hyperoxia, the lowest oxygen concentration compatible with maintaining a PaO_2 of 70–80 mm Hg be routinely used after the implantation of donor lungs.[16,25] We prefer to keep the PaO_2 between 100 and 120 mm Hg. Acute changes in cardiac output and/or the formation of interstitial pulmonary edema may cause sudden and significant decreases in PaO_2. Increases in pulmonary vascular resistance leading to right ventricular dysfunction may further add to hypoxemia.

PREOPERATIVE PREPARATION

A very strict technique of protective isolation should be followed by all personnel involved in the care of the lung transplant recipient. Clean scrub suits, shoe covers, hood and mask, along with clean or sterile gloves, should be worn prior to patient contact. Sterile technique should be used prior to starting all intravenous and intra-arterial lines. Betadine preparations to cleanse the injection sites of intravenous tubing should be used before each intravenous injection.

Anesthesia equipment consists of basic anesthesia supplies for cardiac surgery and a special cart containing the sterile equipment for the heart-lung transplant patient (gas-sterilized intubation kit: laryngoscope handle, blades, airways, stylet, Magill forceps and PEEP valves). The batteries for the laryngoscope are not sterilized. A selection of oral and nasal endotracheal tubes, esophageal stethoscope, temperature probes, and suction catheters are available in clean packages.

Anesthesia machines must be equipped with ventilators capable of delivering different levels of PEEP. Gas-sterilized hoses and appropriate connections should be available.

Routine drugs prepared for each case include: lidocaine 2% solution for intravenous use, 100 mg vial; sodium bicarbonate, 50-mEq vials; Neo-synephrine,

1 mg/ml dilution and 0.1 mg/ml dilution; calcium chloride, 1-mg vials; heparin, protamine sulfate, furosemide, bumetanide, potassium chloride, desmopressin, 0.3 μg/kg, diluted to 50 ml in normal saline solution. Methylprednisolone, 500 mg for intravenous use.

Intravenous inotropic/vasoactive solutions for drip infusion include: dopamine, 400 mg/250 ml D5W; dobutamine, 250 mg/250 ml D5W; epinephrine, 1 mg/250 ml D5W; sodium nitroprusside, 50 mg/250 ml D5W; nitroglycerine, 50 mg/250 ml D5W.

The following anesthetic drugs should be readily available: diazepam, midazolam, sodium pentothal, ketamine, ethomidate, fentanyl, sufentanil, isoflurane, pancuronium, vecuronium, and succinylcholine. Antibiotics most commonly used are a cephalosporin, vancomycin, and imipenem.

PREOPERATIVE EVALUATION

Optimally, the patient undergoing double lung transplantation should be interviewed during one of the early evaluation visits. This initial meeting establishes good patient rapport, allows time for discussion between the anesthesiologist and surgeon about any specific potential concerns, and also allows time for ordering additional preoperative laboratory tests. The preoperative visit should instill the patient with confidence and encourage cooperation.[14] A careful and calm description of the preoperative sequence of events, including monitoring lines, possible intraoperative awareness,[43] and postoperative respiratory care, usually allays patient anxiety.

A review of the patient's chart should reveal information regarding previous anesthetic experiences, operations, response to sedative medications, recent cardiovascular and respiratory evaluation, present medication, drug sensitivities, laboratory data, psychological status, and information on remaining major organ function. Right ventricular function can be evaluated noninvasively with echocardiography and nuclear angiography.[1] Near normal cardiac function should be present before patients are considered candidates for double lung transplantation.

A careful psychological evaluation is also important in that preexisting psychological problems may be exacerbated postoperatively. A supportive family environment is needed to help the patient maintain the strict long-term postoperative medical regimen necessary.[16]

The anesthesiologist should pay special attention to the examination of the airway. Immunosuppressant drugs (cyclosporine and azathioprine) are started prior to patient arrival to the operating room, necessitating emphasis on careful management of the patient's full stomach. We recommend that cyclosporine be given with a small amount of water or antacids (sodium citrate). Antibiotics are given intravenously during the immediate preoperative period.

The timing of donor organ procurement is such that most lung transplantations occur in the middle of the night and on short notice. Consequently, the multiple medications patients are receiving allow for very little manipulation. Importantly, because of the adverse effects of steroids on tracheal anastomotic healing,[1,11] all recipients are weaned from corticosteroid therapy prior to transplantation.

INTRAVASCULAR ACCESS
AND HEMODYNAMIC MONITORING

Intravascular access is usually not a problem because lung transplant recipients are frequently emaciated secondary to pulmonary cachexia. Faced with the realization of a long-awaited transplant, patients may present with acute anxiety causing vasoconstriction and hyperventilation. Judicious use of benzodiazepines and/or narcotics may be helpful, but only with the simultaneous use of pulse oximetry monitoring. Critically ill lung transplant recipients are frequently receiving oxygen therapy, and this should be continued throughout the period of intravascular line access and transfer to the operating room.

Difficult vascular anastomosis and pleural adhesions as well as surgical dissection make blood loss a significant problem before, during, and after the procedure. Therefore, at least two large-bore peripheral intravenous catheters are mandatory initial preparation. These should be connected to blood administration sets and equipment to warm intravenous fluids and blood products.

After a Betadine preparation, radial artery catheterization is performed under local anesthesia for purposes of blood sampling and blood pressure monitoring. An arterial catheter kit (Arrow Product #NS04100) has been used because the 5-inch, 20-gauge catheter provides better stability in the operating room and intensive care unit. The left radial artery is used in the unlikely event that the surgeon would find it necessary to clamp the right subclavian artery. Routine femoral artery catheterization has not been done at our institution.

The debate continues about the use of central venous versus pulmonary artery flow directed catheters in cardiac surgical patients.[2,53,57] The multiple issues in this very timely controversy are beyond the scope of this review. In an account of a single lung transplantation by Conacher et al.,[7] a pulmonary artery catheter was employed. Sale et al. described the anesthetic management of 20 heart and lung transplant recipients managed with only central venous catheters.[46] In their original six double lung transplantations, Patterson et al.[37] used pulmonary artery catheters for patient management.[37] Hemodynamic values were not presented in this article and the authors did not comment on the utility of the data.

Cardiac output measurements derived from transthoracic electrical bioimpedance have close correlation with that obtained by Fick's method and thermodilution.[18,24,31,44,49,51] Spivale[51] has suggested that, because of its noninvasive nature and absence of potential infection, bioimpedance might be used to obtain postoperative hemodynamic information in cardiothoracic transplant recipients. Impedance cardiography has also been found to be a sensitive indicator of changes in the volume of fluid within the thoracic cavity.[3,40,47] The postoperative accumulation of interstitial pulmonary fluid seen in lung transplant recipients could be followed by impedance cardiography. Such monitoring may be useful in the future.

In our experience with double lung transplantation, multi-lumen central venous catheters have been employed for pressure monitoring and delivery of anesthetics and vasoactive drugs. We arrived at this decision for several reasons. First, all of our patients had preserved cardiac function. Measurement of left-sided filling pressures and cardiac output during anesthetic induction and prior to cardiopulmonary bypass has not been considered necessary. Increased pulmonary artery pressures are assumed to be present in all cases. All empirical efforts to avoid increases in pulmonary vascular resistance are employed. It is not clear that measurement of these elevated values would be of any significant benefit to the patient. In addition, the pulmonary artery catheter would need to be withdrawn almost entirely in order to perform the vascular anastomosis. Significant manipulation of the lungs and heart after cardiopulmonary bypass and the new vascular anastomosis would create additional risks of infection and perforation during re-advancement of the catheter to the pulmonary artery position. Unlike heart and lung transplant patients, myocardial biopsies are not needed in double lung transplant recipients. Therefore, the right internal jugular vein can be used for central venous access. As in any transplant candidate about to receive immunosuppressive drugs, strict sterile technique must be used in all vascular access procedures.

INTRAOPERATIVE ANESTHETIC MANAGEMENT

The induction of anesthesia in the double lung transplant recipient may be the most critical period of the perioperative course. The patient may enter the operating room in the sitting position, unable to tolerate the usual supine position for anesthetic induction. In this case, the patient is pre-oxygenated in the upright position. When medication is given to begin induction of anesthesia, crichoid pressure is applied along with cervical and occiput support during placement of the patient in the supine position.

The intubation of the patient is usually performed using a modified rapid-sequence induction technique with succinylcholine, vecuronium, or pancuronium. Lidocaine (1 mg/kg) is given intravenously prior to intubation in an attempt to blunt the potential of pulmonary hypertension during airway manipulation. A sterile, large spiral (wire-wound) endotracheal tube is placed under direct vision with the cuff just below the vocal cords. The cuff should be inflated only to prevent an air leak. The cuff is checked frequently during surgery to make sure tracheal ischemia is avoided. It is important to maintain sterile technique during intubation. An assistant with sterile gloves may facilitate handling sterile airway equipment. Care must be made not to hyperinflate the lungs during the induction of anesthesia. The potential for bleb rupture to lead to tension pneumothorax and cardiovascular collapse is always present. Immediate availability of the thoracic surgeon is imperative, because emergency sternotomy may become necessary.

A nasogastric tube is inserted after successful intubation of the trachea. The nasogastric tube is not connected to suction because cyclosporine may be removed with the stomach contents. Anesthesia is maintained during the pre-bypass period with additional narcotics, benzodiazepines, or a low-dose inhalational agent.

Anesthetic induction and maintenance has been undertaken using any of the following medications: fentanyl, sufentanil, diazepam, midazolam, pentobarbital, ketamine (in drip form), pancuronium, vecuronium and succinylcholine. Narcotics or muscle relaxants that may have the potential of causing broncho-constriction through histamine release are avoided.[17] Nitrous oxide is omitted in order to avoid possible air embolism or an increase in bleb size. Nitrous oxide may also exacerbate hypoxemia or increase pulmonary vascular resistance in recipients with preexisting pulmonary hypertension.[27,48] A high resting sympathetic tone may account for the majority of the recipient's tachycardia and high systemic vascular resistance. Too rapid administration of sedatives and/or narcotics may lead to vasomotor collapse when sympathetic tone is ablated.

Inotropic and/or vasoactive drugs may be needed to maintain perfusion during the periods of minimal patient stimulation. Hypertension occurring after the onset of surgical stimulation is treated by increasing anesthetic depth and/ or using vasodilators. The venodilation and subsequent decreased venous return caused by nitroglycerine may be useful if right ventricular dysfunction occurs intraoperatively. Prior to bypass, arterial blood gases, potassium, and baseline

ACT are determined. Heparin (300 U/kg) is administered via a central venous line. Adequate anticoagulation is checked before cardiopulmonary bypass is initiated. A loop diuretic and mannitol is given to encourage diuresis on bypass.

During cardiopulmonary bypass, the anesthetic requirements are usually decreased as a result of the effects of hypothermia. Either inhalational or intravenous agents have been used with good results. Bypass flows are kept higher than 2.5 L/min/m² to maintain mean arterial pressure greater than 75 mm Hg, and thus provide adequate perfusion to the heart during the pulmonary dissection as well as adequate tracheal blood supply, avoiding the possibility of airway necrosis.

A Betadine solution (15–20 cc) is placed into the endotracheal tube after bilateral pneumonectomy but prior to transection of the trachea. The solution is removed by gentle suction before the tracheal anastomosis is sutured. After the donor lungs are implanted, ventilation is initiated with small tidal volumes and a low rate. Subsequently, the tidal volumes and rate are gradually increased until the desired values are achieved. The FiO_2 and PEEP are kept at the lowest values that maintain a PaO_2 in the range of 100–120 mm Hg in order to decrease the possibility of hyperoxic pulmonary injury in the transplanted lungs[16] and to maintain pulmonary vasodilation. The heart begins to beat spontaneously during the warming period but may need the chronotropic support of an isoproterenol infusion. Other inotropic agents (calcium chloride, dopamine, epinephrine, dobutamine) and/or vasodilator agents (nitroprusside, nitroglycerine) may be needed to terminate cardiopulmonary bypass to keep cardiac filling pressures as low as possible, yet maintain systemic perfusion.

Prior to separation from cardiopulmonary bypass, every attempt is made to maintain the serum potassium at or near 5.0 mEq/L. In contrast to that of others,[48] it is our clinical experience that maintaining serum potassium at these levels on bypass appears to minimize the incidence of ventricular ectopy and other cardiac arrhythmias during the early post-bypass period.

Thorough re-warming is important, because hypothermia can cause pulmonary vasoconstriction, peripheral vasoconstriction, and metabolic acidosis.[56] We place an additional oximeter probe in a central location (ear or nose) in the event that the digital pulse oximeter probe is unable to detect a peripheral pulse. A poor peripheral pulse detected by oximetry after bypass may be due to peripheral vasoconstriction from residual hypothermia or vasoconstrictor/inotropic drugs.

When extracorporeal support is terminated and the hemodynamic conditions are stable, a diluted solution of protamine sulfate is administered via a peripheral intravenous line over 15–20 minutes.[23] Relatively long bypass periods and hemodilution most often result in a bleeding diathesis after the heparin has been reversed. The necessity for large amounts of blood, fresh frozen plasma, cryoprecipitate and platelets is commonplace. During these instances, we have seen significant increases in right atrial and peak airway pressure (Fig. 1). This right ventricular dysfunction and pulmonary edema result from surgical manipulation of the ischemic lung, increased volume load from blood and blood products, and loss of lymphatic drainage in the transplanted lung.[17] Right ventricular failure and pulmonary edema are treated with vasopressors/vasodilators, diuretics, and PEEP. After bypass methylprednisolone (500 mg), desmopressin (0.3 μg/kg),[28,45] and possibly a diuretic and potassium are given intravenously. Vasoactive drugs (i.e., dopamine and epinephrine) are used to maintain peripheral perfusion at the lowest level of central venous pressure possible.

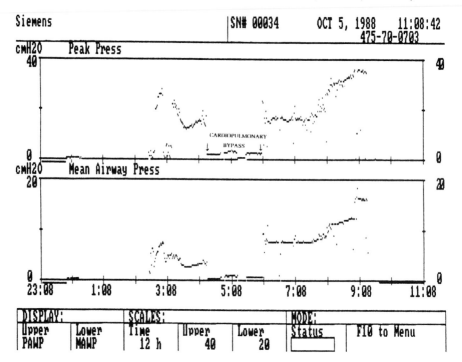

FIGURE 1. Computer-aided ventilation printout records of mean and peak airway pressures. Information obtained with a 900 SERVO Anesthesia System, 940 Lung Mechanics Calculator, and SERVO Computer Module 990. Note rise in both peak and mean airway pressures toward the end of the transplant procedure.

POSTOPERATIVE MANAGEMENT

Patients are transported to the cardiothoracic intensive care unit, anesthetized, paralyzed, intubated, and ventilated. Transport using complete anesthesia machine circuits was initially employed. Currently, a portable oxygen source and manual breathing circuit capable of delivering positive end expiratory pressure are used. Monitoring of intraarterial and right atrial pressures along with EKG and pulse oximetry is used during transfer to the intensive care unit.

Significant amounts of fluid and blood components continue to be administered during the immediate postoperative period. Much attention is given to the preservation of coagulation. Inotropic and vasoactive drugs are administered as indicated; however, only low doses of dopamine to assist in the maintenance of splanchnic blood flow and encouragement of diuresis is considered routine.

Postoperative ventilatory management of these patients is reminiscent of cardiac surgical patients. Matthay and Wiener-Kronish recently discussed the effects of anesthesia, thoracic surgical procedures, and cardiopulmonary bypass on postoperative pulmonary function.[29] Decreases in functional residual capacity and atelectasis are common problems after general anesthesia and thoracic surgery. Interstitial pulmonary edema can be seen in patients after cardiopulmonary bypass. The mechanisms for all of these effects are not completely understood. Additional insults to the lungs have occurred during the variable period of pre-implantation ischemia and profound manipulation during the surgical procedure.

We have consistently seen rises in peak and mean airway pressures in the hours following cardiopulmonary bypass (see Fig. 1). Presumably, multiple mechanisms are responsible for this consistent observation. Viitanen et al. point out that significant increases in pulmonary vascular resistance are caused by hypercarbia in patients after cardiopulmonary bypass.[55] Whether this finding can be extrapolated to lung transplant recipients is not known, but hypercarbia would be an undesirable occurrence in these patients; therefore, ventilation to low normal levels of $PaCO_2$ is necessary.

Bear MA-2 ventilators have been employed in the assist control or SIMV modes. Tidal volumes have ranged from 10 to 14 ml/kg with 5 to 10 cm H_2O of PEEP. FiO_2 levels are kept as low as possible to provide adequate PaO_2, which frequently requires high levels of FiO_2 immediately postoperatively. Respiratory rates of approximately 8–18 breaths/min are adjusted to keep the $PaCO_2$ in the low 30 mm Hg range.

Compounding the complex issue of postoperative ventilation is the presence of a fresh tracheal anastomosis. The integrity of this critical ring of suture material may depend upon low airway pressures and minimal airway manipulation and trauma. The desire for adequate ventilation and ideal blood gases must be weighed against the requisite need for extubation as early as is safely possible. We have been able to successfully wean and extubate our patients 12–36 hours postoperatively. Weaning from mechanical ventilatory support proceeds in the usual manner. The patient must be alert and cooperative, and ventilatory parameters must be achievable by spontaneous breathing. The vital capacity and peak negative inspiratory force must be adequate, and the patient should be able to maintain a satisfactory level of $PaCO_2$ This final point must take into account the preoperative status of the patient, because CO_2 retention preoperatively may necessitate tolerating a significant level of hypercarbia in the early postoperative period.

Because patients with transplanted lungs lack a cough reflex, and blood and fluid accumulation is a constant problem, airway management postoperatively frequently requires diagnostic and therapeutic bronchoscopy. Initial selection of large (Nos. 8.5–9.0) endotracheal tubes facilitates bronchoscopy both in the operating room and in the intensive care unit. Spiral wound tubes have provided some degree of increased ease in passing a bronchoscope; however, the "memory" of these tubes once kinked mandates the use of an oral airway whenever the patient is capable of biting the tube. Changing and manipulating endotracheal tubes and reintubating patients under these circumstances should be approached with extreme care and under sterile precautions. Chronic elevations of pulmonary artery pressure may impinge upon the left recurrent laryngeal nerve which, coupled with surgical trauma, may lead to vocal cord paralysis and an increased risk of aspiration in the postoperative period. Sterile reintubation trays are kept at the patient's bedside.

Although not needed in our experience, facilities for providing extracorporeal membrane oxygenation, jet ventilation, and advanced levels of circulatory support may be required. Any center capable of undertaking a transplant program should be able to provide these support services.

ANESTHETIC DRUG INTERACTIONS AND PRECAUTIONS

The immunosuppressive drugs prednisone, cyclosporine, and azathioprine as well as OKT3 and gamma globulin are used in these patients. Cyclosporine is given orally immediately prior to the induction of anesthesia, and provides a "full stomach" situation in virtually every instance. However, cyclosporine may cause renal dysfunction and alterations in drug clearance, which must be kept in mind when choosing renally cleared drugs. Cyclosporine has been reported to enhance the neuromuscular blockade of atracurium and vecuronium,[19] although the mechanism of this enhancement is presently unknown. Analgesia potentiation of fentanyl by cyclosporine has also been reported in animal studies.[6] An extensive review of drug interactions with cyclosporine may be found elsewhere.[26]

Long-term survival rates for double-lung transplantation is beginning to approach that of cardiac transplantation. Additional surgical experience and advances in immunosuppressive therapy will continue to narrow this gap. Lung transplantation has offered end-stage pulmonary patients a surgical option when medical therapy has been unable to maintain adequate pulmonary function. Transplantation of the lungs without the heart has aided in thoracic organ conservation during this current time of limited donor availability. The medical and surgical indications for lung transplantation appear to be nearly fully defined. The economic impact on our society, however, will continue to be a matter of ongoing debate.[32]

REFERENCES

1. Barash PG: Non-invasive intraoperative monitoring. Thirty-fourth Annual Refresher Course Lectures, American Society of Anesthesiologists, 1983.
2. Bashein G, Ivey TD: Con: A pulmonary artery catheter is not indicated for all coronary artery surgery. J Cardiothorac Anesth 1:362–365, 1987.
3. Berman IR, Scheetz WI, Jenkins EB, et al: Trans-thoracic electrical impedance as a guide to intravascular overload. Acct Surg 102:61–64, 1971.
4. Burke CM, Morris A, Hawkins CGA, et al: Late airflow obstruction in heart-lung transplant recipients. Heart Transplant 4:437, 1985.
5. Casella ES, Humphrey LS: Bronchospasm after cardiopulmonary bypass in a heart-lung transplant recipient. Anesthesiology 69:135–137, 1988.
6. Cirella VN, Pantuck CB, Lee YJ, et al: Effects of cyclosporine on anesthetic action. Anesth Analg 66:703, 1987.
7. Conacher ID, McNally B, Choudhry AK, et al: Anesthesia for isolated lung transplantation. Br J Anaesthesiol 60:588–591, 1988.
8. Cooper JD: Personal communication.
9. Cooper JD, Patterson GA, Grossman Ronald, Maurer J, Toronto Lung Transplant Group: Double-lung transplant for advanced chronic obstructive lung disease. Am Rev Respir Dis 139:303–307, 1989.
10. Cooper JD, Pearson FG, Patterson GA, et al: Technique of successful lung transplantation in humans. J Thorac Cardiovasc Surg 93:173–181, 1987.
11. Dark J, Cooper JD: Transplantation of the lungs. Br J Hos Med May 1987, pp 443–445.
12. Dawkins KD, Jamieson SW, Hunt SA, et al: Long term results, hemodynamics and complications after combined heart and lung transplantation. Circulation 71:919–926, 1985.
13. Edmunds LH, Graf PD, Nadel JA: Reinnervation of the reimplanted canine lung. J Appl Physiol 31:722–727, 1971.
14. Egbert LD, Battit GE, Turndorf H, et al: The value of the preoperative visit by an anesthesiologist. JAMA 185:553–555, 1963.
15. Emery RW, Eales F, VonRueden TJ, Joyce LD: The cardiothoracic donor. In Emery RW, Pritzker MR (eds): Cardiothoracic Transplantation. Cardiac Surgery: State of the Art Reviews, vol. 2, no. 4. Philadelphia, Hanley & Belfus, Inc., 1988, pp 547–554.
16. Finch EL, Jamieson SW: Anesthesia for combined heart and lung transplantation. In Brown BR (ed): Anesthesia an Transplant Surgery. Philadelphia, F.A. Davis Co., 1987, pp 109–131.
17. Gallo JA: Anesthesia for thoracic transplantation in cardiac surgery. In Emery RW, Pritzker MR (eds): Cardiothoracic Transplantation. Cardiac Surgery: State of the Art Reviews, vol. 2, no. 4. Philadelphia, Hanley & Belfus, Inc., 1988, pp 555–564.

18. Gotshall RW, Miles DS: Non-invasive measurement of cardiac output by impedance cardiography in the newborn canine. Crit Care Med 17:63–65, 1989.
19. Gramstad L, Gjerlow JA, Hysing, et al: Interaction of cyclosporine and its solvent, cremphor, with atracurium and vecuronium. Br J Anaesthesiol 58:1149, 1986.
20. Granger ND, Gianfranco R, McCord JM: Superoxide radicals in feline intestinal ischemia. Gastroenterology 81:22–29, 1981.
21. Hale K, Pritzker MR: The single and double lung recipient: Patient selection. In Emery RW, Pritzker MR (eds): Cardiothoracic Transplantation. Cardiac Surgery: State of the Art Reviews, vol. 2, no. 4. Philadelphia, Hanley & Belfus, Inc., 1988, pp 571–574.
22. Hardy JD, Webb WR, Dalton ML, et al: Lung homo-transplantation in man. JAMA 186:1065–1074, 1963.
23. Horrow JC: Protamine allergy. J Cardiothorac Anesth 2:225–242, 1988.
24. Intiona RP, Pruett JK, Crumrine RC, et al: Use of transthoracic bioimpedance to determine cardiac output in pediatric patients. Crit Care Med 16:1101–1105, 1988.
25. Jamieson SW: Recent developments in heart and heart-lung transplantation. Transplant Proc 17:199, 1985.
26. Lake KD: Cyclosporine drug interactions: A review. In Emery RW, Pritzker MR (eds): Cardiothoracic Transplantation. Cardiac Surgery: State of the Art Reviews, vol. 2, no. 4. Philadelphia, Hanley & Belfus, Inc., 1988, pp 617–630.
27. Lappas DA, Buckley MJ, Laver MB, et al: Left ventricular performance and pulmonary circulation following addition of nitrous oxide to morphine during coronary-artery surgery. Anesthesiology 43:61–69, 1975.
28. Mannucci PM: Desmopressin: A non-transfusional form of treatment for congenital and acquired bleeding disorders. Blood 72:1449–1455, 1988.
29. Matthay MA, Wiener-Kronish JP: Respiratory management after cardiac surgery. Chest 95:424–434, 1989.
30. McCord JM: Oxygen radicals and lung injury. Chest 83:355–375, 1983.
31. Miles DS, Gotshall RW, Golden JC, et al: Accuracy of electrical impedance cardiography for measuring cardiac output in children with congenital heart defects. Am J Cardiol 61:612–616, 1988.
32. Moore FD: The desperate case: CARE (Costs, Applicability, Research, Ethics). JAMA 10:1483–1485, 1989.
33. Mortality Trends—U.S., 1979–1986. Morbidity and Mortality Weekly Report 38(12):189–191, 1989.
34. Moyers JR, Tinker JH: Emergence from cardiopulmonary bypass. Controversies about physiology and pharmacology in cardiopulmonary bypass. In Tinker JH (ed): Current Concepts and Controversies. Society of Cardiovascular Anesthesiologists Monograph. Philadelphia, W.B. Saunders Co., 1989, pp 109–113.
35. Nadel JA: Adoration of the vagi. N Engl J Med 311:463–464, 1984.
36. National Data Book and Guide to Sources, Statistical Abstract of the United States, 108th ed. U.S. Department of Commerce, Bureau of Census, 1988, pp 77–78.
37. Patterson GA, Cooper JD, Goldman B, et al: Technique of successful clinical double-lung transplantation. Ann Thorac Surg 45:626–633, 1988.
38. Patterson GA, Cooper JD, Park JH, Jones MT: The Toronto Lung Transplant Group: Experimental and clinical double-lung transplantation. J Thorac Cardiovasc Surg 95:70–74, 1988.
39. Phillipson E, Hickey RF, Bainton CR, et al: Effect of vagal blockade on regulation of breathing in conscious dogs. J Appl Physiol 29:475–479, 1970.
40. Pomerantz MR, Baumgartner J: Transthoracic electrical impedance for early detection of pulmonary edema. Surgery 66:260–268, 1970.
41. Popovich B, Mikm FG, Hilberman M, et al: Reinnervation of the lungs after transplantation. Anesthesiology 57:A491, 1982.
42. Reitz BA, Hunt SA, Gaudiani V, et al: Clinical heart lung transplantation. Transplant Proc 15:1256, 1983.
43. Robinson RJS, Boright WA, Ligier B, et al: The incidence of awareness and amnesia for perioperative events after cardiac surgery with lorazepam and fentanyl anesthesia. J Cardiothorac Anesth 1:524–530, 1987.
44. Salandin V, Zussa C, Risica G, et al: Comparison of cardiac output estimation by thoracic electrical bioimpedance, thermodilution and fick methods. Crit Care Med 16:1157–1158, 1988.
45. Salcman EW, Weinstein MJ, Weintraub RM, et al: Treatment with desmopressin acetate to reduce blood loss after cardiac surgery. N Engl J Med 314:1402–1406, 1986.

46. Sale JP, Patel D, Duncan B, et al: Anesthesia for combined heart and lung transplantation. Anesthesia 42:249–258, 1987.
47. Saunders CE, The use of transthoracic electrical bioimpedance in assessing thoracic fluid status in emergency department patients. Am J Emerg Med 6:337–340, 1988.
48. Schulte-Sasse U, Hess W, Tarnow J: Pulmonary vascular responses to nitrous oxide in patients with normal and high pulmonary vascular resistance. Anesthesiology 57:9–13, 1982.
49. Shoemaker W, Appel P, Kram HB, et al: Multicomponent non-invasive physiologic monitoring of circulatory function.
50. Silberberg E, Lubera JA (eds): Statistics: 1989 Estimates of cancer incidence by site and sex. CA: A Cancer Journal for Clinicians 39:1–15, 1989.
51. Spivale FG, Reenes H, Crawford FA: Comparison of bioimpedance and thermodilution methods for determining cardiac output: Experimental and clinical studies. Ann Thorac Surg 45:421–425, 1988.
52. Theodore J, Jamieson SW, Burke CM, et al: Physiologic aspects of human heart-lung transplantation. Chest 86:349–357, 1984.
53. Tuman KJ, McCarthy RJ, Spiess BD, et al: Effect of pulmonary artery catheterization on outcome in patients undergoing coronary artery surgery. Anesthesiology 70:199–206, 1989.
54. Vieth FJ, Kamhotz SL, Mullenkopf FL, et al: Lung transplantation 1983. Transplantation 35:271–278, 1983.
55. Viitanen A, Salmenpera M, Heinonen J, et al: Pulmonary vascular resistance before and after cardiopulmonary bypass: The effect of $PaCO_2$. Chest 95:773–778, 1989.
56. Vitez TS, Soper LE, Wong KC, et al: Chronic hypokalemia and intraoperative dysrhythmias. Anesthesiology 63:130–133, 1985.
57. Weintraub AC, Barash PG: Pro: A pulmonary artery catheter is indicated in all patients for coronary artery surgery. J Cardiothorac Anesth 1:358–361, 1987.
58. Wyner J, Finch EL: Heart and heart-lung transplantation. In Gelman S (ed): Anesthesia and Organ Transplantation. Philadelphia, W.B. Saunders Co., 1987, pp 111–137.

JOHN B. O'CONNELL, MD
DALE G. RENLUND, MD

IMMUNE MECHANISMS OF ACUTE CARDIAC ALLOGRAFT REJECTION AND MODIFICATION BY IMMUNOSUPPRESSION

From the UTAH Cardiac
  Transplant Program
Salt Lake City, Utah

Reprint requests to:
John B. O'Connell, MD
Medical Director
UTAH Cardiac Transplant
  Program
Division of Cardiology
University of Utah Medical Center
50 North Medical Drive
Salt Lake City, UT 84132

The operative technique of orthotopic cardiac transplantation developed by Lower and Shumway achieved resounding success from initiation of clinical application.[10] However, the major limitation to long-term survival was the lack of successful control of immunologic responses which, if left unmodified, result in the destruction of the allograft. Nonspecific immunosuppressive therapy, corticosteroids, antimetabolites, and crude cytolytic agents predispose the recipient to infection when used in doses that control rejection. Even though selectivity in immunosuppression has improved survival, rejection and infection remain the major causes of death.[5] A more definitive understanding of the immune mechanisms responsible for rejection may lead to development of effective new agents with allospecificity.

CLASSIFICATION OF REJECTION

The clinical classification of rejection that was established for renal transplantation has been applied to cardiac transplantation.[8] "Hyperacute" rejection is manifested by the rapid development of allograft dysfunction resulting from the presence of preformed antibodies to donor alloantigens in the recipient's serum. Antibodies to human histocompatibility antigens may result from exposure to fetal (paternal) antigens during pregnancy or from previous blood transfusions. Once established, hyperacute rejection is usually irreversible. Because careful screening with a random panel of donor lymphocytes identifies the requirement for a donor-specific crossmatch in sensitized recipients, this type of rejection can generally be avoided. "Acute" cardiac allograft rejection is common, occurring with increasing frequency beginning 1 week following cardiac transplantation. Unlike hyperacute rejection, acute rejection is diagnosed by endomyocardial biopsy and, in most cases, responds to intensification of immunosuppression. "Chronic" cardiac allograft rejection is slowly progressive and results in vascular endothelial damage, culminating in the development of allograft coronary artery disease. The true incidence of allograft coronary artery disease is unknown because coronary angiography, the only accurate technique for making the diagnosis, has limited sensitivity because the lesions develop initially in the microvasculature. Whether hyperacute, acute, or chronic, the principal steps in the rejection cascade are antigen presentation, cell activation, allograft destruction, and the induction of allograft tolerance. Each step is discussed below.

ANTIGEN PRESENTATION

The proteins eliciting the immune response following cardiac transplantation are the major histocompatibility (MHC) Class I and Class II antigens (Table 1).[13] The MHC antigens are coded on the sixth chromosome in man and serve to regulate immune responses. The MHC Class I antigens (HLA-A, B, and C) are the major targets of CD8+ (cytotoxic) lymphocytes. The MHC Class II antigens (HLA-DP, DQ, and DR) are the major targets of CD4+ (helper) lymphocytes. The mesenchymal cells of solid organs, including cardiac myocytes, express Class I antigens. The major stimuli for induction of Class I antigen expression are the interferons. Alpha and beta interferon are cytokines released by activated macrophages and fibroblasts, whereas gamma interferon is released by T-helper cells (CD4+) following MHC Class II alloantigen activation or virus infection.

Class II antigens are more restricted in their distribution and are generally not expressed by cardiac myocytes. Helper T-cells (CD4+) respond selectively to Class II antigens, which are expressed on B-lymphocytes, activated T-lymphocytes, dendritic cells, monocytes, macrophages, and endothelial cells. Post-transcription regulation of Class II expression is induced by gamma interferon, which is released by activated CD4+ cells, but not by alpha or beta interferon. The expression of MHC antigens is the rate-limiting step in the initiation of cardiac allograft rejection. The inhibition of antigen expression will, therefore, attenuate allograft rejection.

TABLE 1. Characteristics of the Human Major Histocompatibility Antigens (MHC)

	Class I	Class II
HLA Loci	A.B,C	DP,DQ,DR
Lymphocyte response specificity	CD8+ (suppressor/cytotoxic)	CD4+ (helper/inducer)
Cellular expression	Most cells in allograft (including cardiac myocytes)	B-cells, activated T-cells, monocytes, macrophages dendritic cells, endothelial cells
Mode of expression	Alpha, beta, gamma, interferon	Mostly gamma interferon

The alloantigen binds to a specific receptor (T-cell receptor, TCR) that is complexed with the pan T-cell, CD3 membrane proteins.[12] Stimulation of the TCR-CD3 complex by alloantigen results in the induction of interleukin-2 synthesis by helper T-lymphocytes and the transmission of the activating signal to the cytotoxic T-cell. Monoclonal antibodies with specificity for the CD3 proteins (OKT3) modulate lymphocytes, so the TCR-CD3 complex is not expressed.[2] The net result is the prevention of allospecific activation of CD4+ and CD8+ cells.

CELL KINETICS

Following alloantigen binding to the TCR-CD3 complex on CD4+ cells, the T-helper cell is activated. The major allogeneic cells responsible for this activation are endothelial cells of capillary origin, dendritic cells, and passenger leukocytes that densely express Class II antigens.[6] Activation of the T-helper cell requires both alloantigen and interleukin-1 from activated macrophages. The CD4+ cell synthesizes and releases interleukin-2, which initiates a receptor-mediated positive feedback loop, leading to release of lymphokines, which in turn activate macrophages (further increasing interleukin-1), cytotoxic T-lymphocytes, and B-lymphocytes. Interferons produced by activated cells further augment expression of MHC Class I and Class II antigens. CD4+ cells exert their modulatory effect principally by release of these mediators.

The effector mechanisms responsible for graft destruction are cytotoxic T-lymphocyte activation and alloantibody-mediated vascular injury.[3] The diagnosis of rejection and determination of its mechanism depend upon the characteristics of the infiltrating cells in the allograft. Although the cellular infiltrate consists predominantly of T-lymphocytes, the percentage of CD4+ and CD8+ varies.[13] When cardiac allograft dysfunction occurs in the absence of classic light microscopic evidence of rejection, alloantibody formation may be the primary mechanism of rejection (Table 2).[7] Immunofluorescence microscopic examination is required to identify immunoglobulin and complement deposition and the vascular endothelial injury to implicate these humoral mechanisms. Therefore, vascular (humoral) rejection, which fortunately is unusual, may go undetected by conventional light microscopic techniques.

IMMUNOLOGIC TOLERANCE

The frequency of acute cardiac allograft rejection drops precipitously after approximately 6 months following transplantation. The reasons for this apparent tolerance remain obscure. In the rat, transplanted kidneys survive indefinitely when retransplanted from a primary to a secondary recipient of the same genotype and do not induce T-lymphocyte immune responses.[1] The immunogenicity of

TABLE 2.   Characteristics of Acute Rejection Based on Mechanism

	Cellular	Vascular (Humoral)
Frequency	Common	Rare
Diagnosis	Light microscopy	Immunofluorescence
Primary target	Cardiac myocyte	Endothelial cells
Treatment	Corticosteroids, cytolytic agents	B-cell specificity
Therapeutic result	Easily reversed	May be irreversible

these allografts can be restored by the injection of afferent lymph cells from genotypically identical donors, suggesting that dendritic (interstitial support matrix) cells and passenger leukocytes may serve as the major source of alloantigen presentation.[9] Clearance of these cells over time may explain long-term tolerance. Dendritic cells and passenger leukocytes express MHC Class II antigens in high density and form aggregates with CD4+ cells.[4] Early intense immunosuppression, which blocks antigen recognition until these highly antigenic cells are cleared, may greatly enhance the development of tolerance.

The development of tolerance may also be due to recipient factors.[6] Specific unresponsiveness may be induced by active enhancement with the administration of low-dose alloantigen prior to transplant, which induces anti-idiotypic antibodies or a clone of alloantigen-specific suppressor T-lymphocytes. This is the rationale for donor-specific blood transfusions prior to renal transplantation.

Another mechanism that may induce tolerance is reendothelialization of allografts with recipient endothelial cells.[14] In a report wherein biopsies from transplanted blood group compatible donor kidneys were studied to determine the ABO characteristics of the endothelial cells, 23% of the allografts expressed the ABO characteristics of the recipient rather than the donor, suggesting that reendothelialization with recipient endothelial cells occurred. The authors concluded that reendothelialization reflected injury to the allograft. It is attractive to postulate that following dendritic cell elimination, recipient reendothelialization promotes tolerance by eliminating the major source of MHC Class II antigens.

EFFECT OF IMMUNOSUPPRESSION

The ideal immunosuppressive agent should induce specific unresponsiveness without requiring nonspecific immunosuppression. Current immunosuppressive regimens utilize agents that affect immunoactivation distal to antigen expression and presentation. As a result, multiple agents in combination are required. If agents that selectively block induction of MHC alloantigens could be developed, tolerance would result, eliminating the necessity for chronic immunosuppression.

Current immunosuppressive regimens incorporate combinations of corticosteroids, azathioprine, cyclosporine, and cytolytic agents.[11] Corticosteroids inhibit interleukin-1 release by preventing transcription of messenger RNA, preventing interleukin-2 production and T-helper cell activation. Azathioprine, converted in the liver to 6-mercaptopurine, inhibits DNA and RNA synthesis in actively dividing cells. Therefore, T and B lymphocyte proliferation is attenuated. Cyclosporine blocks transcription of the interleukin-2 gene, thereby inhibiting release of gamma interferon and B and cytotoxic T-cell stimulating factors. Because these agents inhibit antigen-driven T-cell activation at distinct points in the immunologic cascade, this combination appears rational. The polyclonal cytolytic agents (antithymocyte and antilymphoblast globulins) nonspecifically opsonize T-lymphocytes, inducing clearance by the reticuloendothelial system. Murine monoclonal anti-CD3 antibody (OKT3), however, not only opsonizes T-cells bearing the CD3 proteins but also modulates the cells so that the TCR-CD3 complex is no longer expressed on the membrane surface, rendering the T-cell incapable of recognizing antigen. Although OKT3 is very effective in the treatment of allograft rejection, it may also be of value as a prophylactic agent, blocking antigen recognition during the critical time when MHC Class II antigen density is expressed to its greatest extent on dendritic cells and passenger leukocytes.

CONCLUSION

The primary steps in the development of acute cardiac allograft rejection consist of antigen presentation, activation of T-helper cells, release of lymphokines by T-helper cells that augment immune response and further induce antigen expression, and graft destruction by cytotoxic T-cells and occasionally alloantibodies. Although the commonly prescribed immunosuppressive regimens are rational, these combinations will not specifically inhibit antigen presentation without affecting mechanisms responsible for clearance of infective agents or cancer cells. Future research should, therefore, be directed at promoting the induction of tolerance via allospecific mechanisms.

REFERENCES

1. Batchelor JR, Welsh KI, Maynard A, Burgos H: Failure of long surviving passively enhanced allografts to provoke T-cell immunity. I. Retransplantation of (AS × AUG) F$_1$, kidneys into secondary AS recipients. J Exp Med 150:455–464, 1979.
2. Bristow MR, Gilbert EM, Renlund DG, et al: Use of OKT3 monoclonal antibody in heart transplantation: Review of the initial experience. J Heart Transplant 7:1–11, 1988.
3. Cramer DV: Cardiac transplantation: Immune mechanisms and alloantigens involved in graft rejection. CRC Crit Rev Immunol 7:1–30, 1987.
4. Forbes RDC, Parfrey NA, Gomersall M, et al: Dendritic cell-lymphoid cell aggregation and major histocompatibility antigen expression during rat cardiac allograft rejection. J Exp Med 164:1239–1258, 1986.
5. Fragomeni LS, Kaye MP: The Registry of the International Society for Heart Transplantation: Fifth Official Report—1988. J Heart Transplant 7:249–253, 1988.
6. Hall BM: Mechanisms of specific unresponsiveness to allografts. Transplant Proc 16:938–943, 1984.
7. Hammond EH, Yowell RL, Nunoda S, et al: Vascular (humoral) rejection in cardiac transplantation: Pathologic observations and clinical implications. J Heart Transplant (in press).
8. Kirkpatrick CH: Transplantation immunology. JAMA 258:2993–3000, 1987.
9. Lechler RI, Batchelor JR: Restoration of immunogenicity to passenger cell-depleted kidney allografts by the addition of donor strain dendritic cells. J Exp Med 155:31–41, 1982.
10. Lower RR, Shumway NE: Studies on orthotopic homotransplantation of the canine heart. Surg Forum 11:18–19, 1960.
11. O'Connell JB, Renlund DG, Lee HR, et al: New techniques of immunosuppression in cardiac transplantation. Cardiac Surgery: State of the Art Reviews 2:607–615, 1988.
12. Oettgen HC, Terhorst C: The T-cell receptor-T3 complex and T-lymphocyte activation. Human Immunol 18:187–204, 1987.
13. Rose ML, Yacoub MH: The immunology of cardiac rejection in man. In Spry CJF (ed): Immunology and Molecular Biology of Cardiovascular Diseases. Boston, MTP Press Ltd., 1987, pp 177–197.
14. Sedmak DD, Sharma HM, Czajka CM, Ferguson RM: Recipient endothelialization of renal allografts: An immunohistochemical study utilizing blood group antigens. Transplantation 46:907–909, 1988.

KATHLEEN D. LAKE, PharmD

CYCLOSPORINE: MECHANISM OF ACTION

Program Director
Division of Cardiothoracic
  Transplant Surgery and
  Research
Minneapolis Heart Institute
Abbott Northwestern Hospital
Minneapolis, Minnesota

and

Clinical Assistant Professor
College of Pharmacy
University of Minnesota
Minneapolis, Minnesota

Reprint requests to:
Kathleen D. Lake, Pharm D
Division of Cardiothoracic
  Transplant Surgery and
  Research
Abbott Northwestern Hospital
800 E. 28th St.
Minneapolis, MN 55407

In 1970, two strains of fungi imperfecti, Cylindrocarpum lucidum Booth and Tolypocladium inflatum Gams, both of which synthesized cyclosporine (CsA), were isolated. Because the latter grows in submerged culture, it was selected to be used for large-scale production of CsA by fermentation.

Initial studies on a crude extract of this fungus by Borel[7] and coworkers[8] described a potent immunosuppressive activity and an apparent selective action on T-lymphocytes. Based on these reports and on the results in animal models, the first clinical trials were conducted in 1978.[13,80] In 1983 CsA was approved for use in the United States.

Since its introduction, CsA has revolutionized clinical transplantation and contributed as an investigational tool in the understanding of cellular immunology. Impressive success rates have been reported for heart, heart and lung, kidney, liver, and bone marrow transplantation.[11,12,14,16,20,29,63,73,84,91,98] Clinical trials are under way to evaluate the efficacy of CsA in preventing graft-vs-host disease in mismatched bone marrow transplants[99] and in treating various autoimmune disorders.[3,4,43,102]

The precise mechanism of CsA action at the cellular and molecular level remains controversial. This knowledge is critical for optimal use of CsA in combination with other immunosuppressive drugs. Further studies identifying the mechanism of action may also elucidate the potential role of CsA in tolerance induction to organ allografts in man.

THE IMMUNE RESPONSE

The immune response involved in organ rejection is discussed in more detail in an earlier chapter of this volume but a brief review is warranted.[75] Rejection of the transplanted organ is thought to begin with recognition of foreign human leukocyte antigens (HLA) (Fig. 1), glycoproteins present on many cell surfaces. Class I HLA antigens (e.g., HLA-A, B, and C) are recognized by receptors on the surface of the suppressor/cytotoxic T-cell precursor.[71] The receptors are also antigenic, and include the T3 and T8 proteins. Class II HLA antigens (e.g., HLA-DR) are recognized by receptors on the surface of the helper T-cell precursor and include the T3 and T4 proteins.

While macrophage processing of antigenic material appears to be necessary for lymphocyte response to an infectious agent, lymphocytes respond directly to incompatible HLA antigens without macrophage intervention. Macrophages still play a role in the rejection process, because helper T-cells activated by class II HLA antigens prompt the release of an intercellular mediator, a lymphokine, by

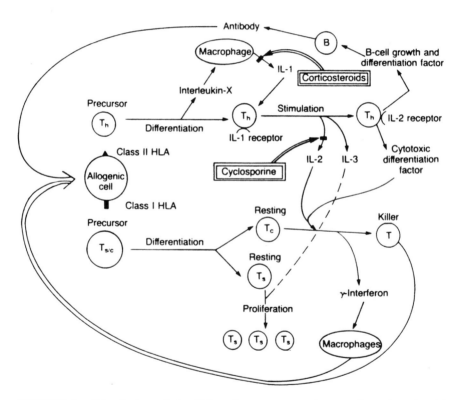

FIGURE 1. Stimulation of the T-lymphocyte system by an allogenic cell with subsequent attack on the cell by the immune system. Points of blockade of the system by corticosteroids and by cyclosporine are included. HLA, human leukocyte antigens; T, T-lymphocyte; T_h, helper T-lymphocyte; $T_{s/c}$, suppressor/cytotoxic T-cell; T_c, cytotoxic T-cell; T_s, suppressor T-cell; IL, interleukin; B, B-lymphocyte. (From Ptachcinski RJ, Venkataraman R, Burckart GJ: Drug therapy in transplantation. In DiPiro JT, et al (eds): Pharmacotherapy: A Physiologic Approach. New York, Elsevier, 1987, p 76, with permission.)

the lymphocyte. This lymphokine is a macrophage stimulant called interleukin-X, which causes the stimulated macrophage to release another mediator, interleukin-1 (IL-1).[72] The secreted IL-1 stimulates (1) the release of interleukin-2 (IL-2) by stimulated helper T-cells, (2) the formation of IL-1 receptors on helper T-cells, and (3) the formation of IL-2 receptors on helper T-cells and stimulated suppressor/cytotoxic T-cells. Under the influence of IL-1, the helper T-cell, which was previously stimulated by the class II HLA antigen, secretes IL-2 in addition to a variety of other lymphokines, including cytotoxic differentiation factor, IL-3 (suppressor cell differentiation/amplification factor), and IL-4 (B-cell growth factor).[95]

The secretion of IL-2 is a key step in the process of continuing the immune response and subsequent rejection of the transplanted organ. The precursor suppressor/cytotoxic T-lymphocytes are uncommitted and, given the appropriate stimulus, can differentiate into clones of either suppressor cells, which suppress the immune system, or cytotoxic cells, which evolve to killer cells that attack and destroy the antigenic material. The form of cell that predominates, either suppressor or cytotoxic T-cell, dictates the overall immune response. In conjunction with both the promotion of IL-2 receptors by IL-1 and the elaboration of cytotoxic differentiation factor by stimulated helper T-cells, IL-2 promotes clonal proliferation and differentiation, resulting in a population of mature and committed cytotoxic T-cells of defined specificity. To balance this effect of IL-2, activated helper T-cells elaborate IL-3, which promotes maturation and clonal expansion of suppressor T-cells, ultimately leading to feedback suppression of the immune response. Damage to the transplanted organ is produced not only by the direct action of cytotoxic T-lymphocytes, which attach to the class I HLA antigens on the cell surface, but also by macrophages, which have been stimulated by gamma-interferon produced by the cytotoxic T-cells.[30]

The Role of Cyclosporine in the Immune Response

CsA is a cyclic endecapeptide ($C_{62}H_{111}N_{11}O_{12}$, MW 1202.64) with several N-methylated amino acids and a characteristic unsaturated C-9 amino acid that is unique to this substance (Fig. 2). It exhibits potent immunosuppressive, antiparasitic, fungicidal, and chronic anti-inflammatory properties. The structural requirements for immunosuppressive activity have been reviewed elsewhere.[105] CsA is neutral and insoluble in water but highly soluble in many organic solvents and lipids.

CsA represents a new class of clinically important immunosuppressive agents. It is not an alkylating, antimitotic, or lymphocytotoxic agent. Its action at the molecular level appears to be highly specific for lymphoid cells. It is not cytotoxic and does not produce significant inhibition of either erythroid or myeloid colony formation and consequently lacks bone marrow toxicity.[8,100]

By selectively inhibiting lymphocyte function, CsA limits clonal expansion of specific T-cell subsets and the subsequent immunologic response (see Fig. 1), predominantly affecting the distinct T-lymphocyte subsets responsible for graft rejection and autoimmunity. In general, CsA inhibits helper and cytotoxic T-lymphocyte function while sparing suppressor T-cell subpopulations.

The inhibition of IL-2 elaboration by stimulated helper T-cell appears to be a major mechanism of action of CsA.[45] Recent studies have demonstrated that the metabolites of CsA (M17, M1, and M21) are also active immunosuppressive substances, as determined in mitogen-induced lymphocyte responses, mixed

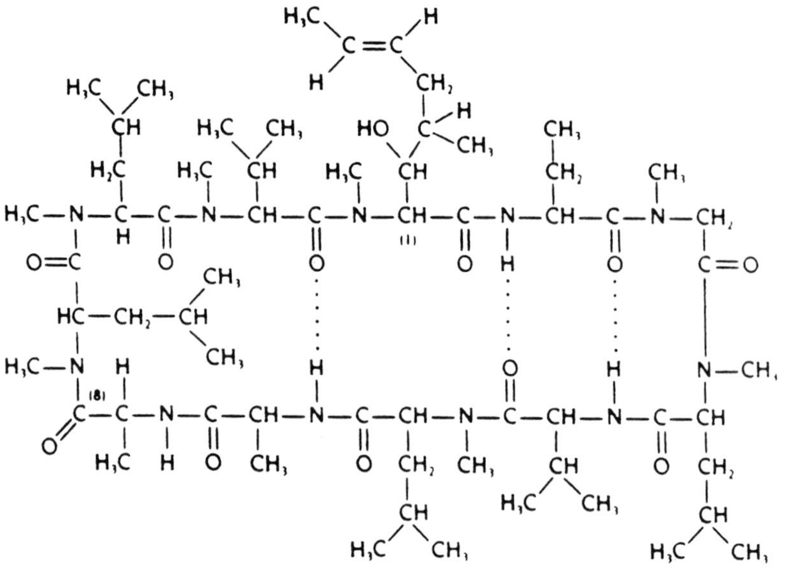

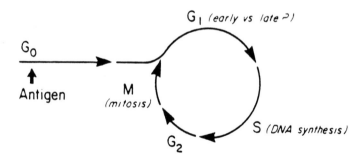

FIGURE 2. The molecular structure of CsA.

lymphocyte reaction cultures, and the IL-2 release assays.[32,107] CsA and its primary metabolite, M17, may inhibit IL-2 release in a synergistic manner.[107] In the absence of IL-2, blastogenesis may occur, but cells are unable to enter the S-phase of their growth cycle (Fig. 3).[68]

FIGURE 3. The phases of the cell cycle. Following stimulation by an antigen, or other type of mitogen, small lymphocytes are activated. They are converted from the resting G_0 phase to the active G_1 phase. The G_1 phase lasts 10 hours (h) or longer before DNA synthesis (S phase) begins. The S phase lasts about 10 h and is followed by a short (2 to 4 h) G_2 phase before mitosis (M phase). M phase is relatively brief, usually less than 2 to 3 h, after which the cells are returned to the G_1 phase. The susceptibility of the cell to the immunosuppressive agents used in transplantation varies with the phase of the cycle. Periods of most intense nucleic acid synthesis, particularly S phase, are most vulnerable to the antimetabolites. The resting G_0 lymphoctye is also susceptible to several of the clinically used immunosuppressive agents. (From Ascher N, Simmons RL, Najarian JS: Principles of immunosuppression. In Sabiston DC Jr (ed): Textbook of Surgery. Philadelphia, W.B. Saunders, 1986, p 440, with permission.)

CsA inhibits the clonal differentiation of precursor suppressor/cytotoxic T-cells into cytotoxic T-cells through its blockade of IL-2. IL-3 is not inhibited by cyclosporine, thereby allowing the expansion of the suppressor T-cell population and increasing the ratio of host suppressor to cytotoxic cells. The persistence of suppressor cells in vivo suggests that these cells are critical to the induction and maintenance of allograft specific tolerance.[60] CsA has been reported to induce tolerance to organ allografts in certain nonhuman species;[21,44,45,93,101] however, this finding has not been observed in humans. There appears to be wide tissue and species variability observed with this phenomenon.[39] In a recent study of renal transplant patients a low incidence of rejection correlated with the presence of donor-specific suppressor T-cells.[56]

Unlike the cytotoxic drugs and corticosteroids, cyclosporine exerts its effect without killing or lysing effector cells and is therefore ineffective once antigenic stimulation has occurred. CsA must be present during the early phase of mitogen or alloantigen stimulation to prevent sensitization of precursor cytotoxic lymphocytes. Maximal benefit is generally seen with initiation of therapy at the time of primary antigen exposure.[84] This is because CsA does not inhibit the proliferation of cells that have developed the ability to respond to lymphokines.[18] Thus, mature cytotoxic cells are refractory to CsA even at high concentrations,[55] just as CsA is ineffective against primed helper T-cells.[7,104] Similarly, pretreatment of T-lymphocytes, followed by removal of the drug before antigen exposure, has no effect on subsequent responsiveness.[47] Because CsA is not lymphocytotoxic, its discontinuation is followed by a prompt reversal of its immunosuppressive effect.

Studies examining the cell cycle events of T-lymphocytes following mitogen stimulation demonstrated that CsA prevented cells from proceeding from the G_0/G_1 phase to the S phase in the cell cycle. (see Fig. 3).[58] Based on these observations, it appears that CsA may interfere with the events of T-cell activation prior to DNA synthesis and cell division. The mechanism of T-helper cell activation to produce a lymphokine, such as IL-2, is a multistep process: (1) dual binding of IL-1 and of antigen to a clonotypic T-cell receptor; (2) membrane translation of the activation message; (3) cytoplasmic signaling to the nucleus via a derepressor; (4) uncovering of the IL-2 DNA; (5) transcription of IL-2 mRNA; (6) translation of the message on ribosomes; and (7) secretion of the IL-2 peptide product (Fig. 4).[52]

The overall effect of CsA therapy is to suppress the immune response to the allograft without debilitating the antibacterial defenses of the recipient (i.e., it leaves preformed immunity and the humoral immune system intact),[51] whereas cytotoxic drugs and steroids suppress all immunocompetent cells, thus altering the ability of the organism to fight bacterial infection.

Effect of Cyclosporine on T-Lymphocytes

Activation of T-lymphocytes triggers a complex cascade of ionic and enzymatic events. The process culminates in DNA synthesis/replication and cell division and maturation with acquisition of special effector function. The precise sequence of events from membrane to nucleus has not been clearly defined; however, a generalized schema has been proposed for the events in T-cell activation (Fig. 5).[46]

Recent work suggests that a two-step activation sequence for T-lymphocytes is involved. The first step involves the binding of mitogen or alloantigen to the T-cell receptor in association with macrophage class II antigen (HLA-DR) and a subsequent rise in intracellular calcium.[66] The secondary rise in intracellular

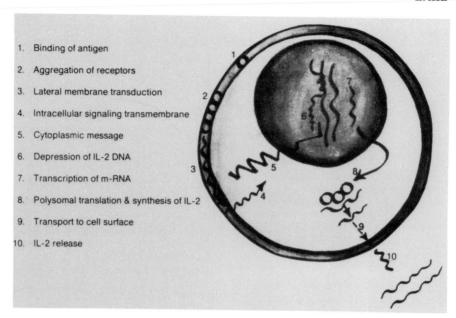

1. Binding of antigen
2. Aggregation of receptors
3. Lateral membrane transduction
4. Intracellular signaling transmembrane
5. Cytoplasmic message
6. Depression of IL-2 DNA
7. Transcription of m-RNA
8. Polysomal translation & synthesis of IL-2
9. Transport to cell surface
10. IL-2 release

FIGURE 4. Steps in the generation of IL-2 upon antigen-stimulated activation of a helper T-cell. (From Kahan BD: Cyclosporine: The agent and its actions. Transplant Proc 17(4 Suppl 1):1985. In Kahan BD (ed): Cyclosporine: Diagnosis and Management of Associated Renal Injury. Orlando, Grune & Stratton, 1985, p 7, with permission.)

calcium facilitates the activities of a number of cell proteins or enzymes (e.g., calmodulin, phospholipase A_2, phospholipase C), each of which has been reported to play a key role in cell activation and in the regulation of many cellular activities through various second messenger systems.[17,74]

The second important step involves the activation of protein kinase C, by diacylglycerol, phospholipids, and calcium.[49] IL-1 and IL-2 may provide the necessary second signal for full T-cell activation through activation of protein kinase C.[22] Protein kinase C phosphorylates a number of enzymes, which results in the activation and/or enhancement of their enzymatic activity.

A variety of studies suggest that the primary effect of CsA is on the calcium-dependent pathway.[53,54,58] Further evidence suggests that CsA may act along this calcium-dependent pathway: (1) T-lymphocyte proliferation (CsA sensitive) requires a rise in intracellular calcium, whereas some B-lymphocyte proliferative responses (CsA resistant) may progress in a calcium independent fashion.[5] (2) Lymphokine production by the T-helper cells is calcium dependent, whereas expression of IL-2 receptors is much less calcium dependent.[34] (3) The inhibitory effect of CsA on T-lymphocyte proliferation appears to be potentiated by calcium channel blockers.[77] The evidence is consistent with the hypothesis that CsA primarily affects the calcium-dependent activation pathway of both T- and B-lymphocytes subsequent to the rise in intracellular calcium.

Several specific early events do not appear to be blocked by CsA. CsA does not compete for binding of mitogens to T-cells,[88] does not block the increase in intracellular Ca^{++}[106] or phospholipid breakdown,[92] and does not affect protein kinase C activity.[70]

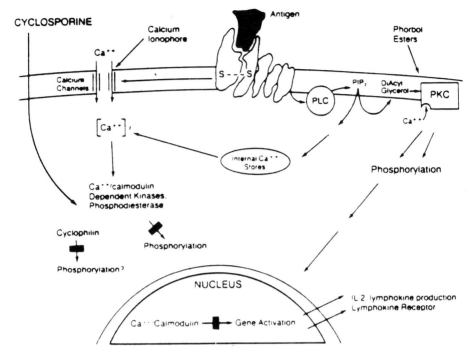

FIGURE 5. Schema of T-cell activation and the effect of CsA. Schematic representation of T-lymphocyte activation. PLC, phospholipase C; PKC, protein kinase C; PIP$_2$, phosphatidylinositol diphosphate, CsA blockade. Calcium ionophores mimic signal 1, while phorbol esters mimic signal 2. (From Hess AD, Esa AH, Colombani PM: Mechanism of action of cyclosporine: Effect on cells of the immune system and on subcellular events in T-cell activation. Transplant Proc 20(2 Suppl 2):29, 1988. In Kahan BD (ed): Cyclosporine: Nature of the Agent and Its Immunologic Actions. Philadelphia, Grune & Stratton, 1988, p 34, with permission.)

Following the cytoplasmic activation of the proteins and enzymes, the T-lymphocyte activation sequence progresses to nuclear induction of ornithine decarboxylase (ODC) and polyamine synthesis, necessary for gene activation and expression, mRNA and DNA synthesis, and cell cycle progression to cell division. CsA has been shown to inhibit the induction of ODC, inhibit the synthesis of mRNA and new proteins, and prevent cells from proceeding to the S phase of the cell cycle.[58] CsA may inhibit an early intracellular enzymatic event in the polyamine cascade involved in ODC induction.[31] Several investigators have proposed that CsA selectively acts at the level of lymphokine mRNA[25,35,36] and does not affect mRNA involved in total protein synthesis. These results have been supported by data suggesting that CsA acts after antigen binding and before transcription of lymphokine-encoding mRNA.[50,59,76] This action results in reduced expression of several lymphokines, including IL-2,[25,35,59,106] interferon-gamma,[35,106] and IL-4.[38]

Membrane-related Hypothesis

It has been suggested that immunosuppression is achieved by partitioning of the hydrophobic portion of the CsA molecule into the cell membrane lipid bilayer of the target cell, thereby disturbing homeostatic control of membrane function.[64] The effect of CsA on the membrane can affect fluidity and various protein-lipid interactions.[85] These interactions may influence membrane-related immunologic processes such as recognition, activation, and release of lymphokines.[9]

Inhibition of IL-2 Receptor Expression Hypothesis

It has been proposed that CsA inhibits the expression of IL-2 receptors; however, other authors have found conflicting results.[6,62,67,77] This controversy may actually be due to variable affinity exhibited by the IL-2 receptors, whereby CsA selectively inhibits the expression of low affinity IL-2 binding sites on activated lymphocytes.[89]

Receptor Binding Hypotheses

Investigations continue in an attempt to locate a specific receptor for CsA binding to explain its mechanism of action. The failure to observe drug sequestration in a nondisplaceable location on either resting or alloantigen-stimulated lymphocytes suggests a surface site;[64] however, no specific surface receptor has been found.

It is highly likely that the action of CsA is multifactorial. Citterio and Kahan recently reported that CsA exerts both cytoplasmic and nuclear effects on cellular activation.[15] CsA may diffuse passively through the cell membrane into the cytoplasm where it could interact with one or more cytosolic receptor proteins.

Surface Receptor. The initial hypothesis that CsA inhibits HLA-DR antigen binding to its clonotypic T-cell receptor was not confirmed.[78] The proposed mechanism suggested a binding site identical to, or in close proximity to, the surface receptor responsible for cell activation.[77] The hypothesis that T-helper cells display specific CsA receptors has also been refuted. CsA binds reversibly to all peripheral human lymphocytes and no CsA-specific surface receptors have been identified.[90]

Prolactin Receptor. Several investigators have reported that CsA competes with prolactin for the same cell surface receptor on human lymphocytes,[48,61,86] suggesting that part, if not all, of the inhibitory action of CsA is exerted by displacement of prolactin, thus rendering the lymphocyte unresponsive to antigenic stimulation. Recent experience indicates that prolactin binding exerts an amplifying effect on lymphocyte activation and may play a fundamental role in the development of the immune response.[87] Carrier et al.[14a] have correlated serum prolactin levels with the development of rejection in heart transplant patients. Several studies have indicated that CsA may enter the cell by binding to the prolactin receptor, thereby leading to inhibition of the polyamine bio-synthetic pathway. One of the major enzymes in this pathway is ornithine decarboxylase (ODC), and activation of the enzyme leads to DNA synthesis. CsA has been shown to inhibit the induction of ODC.[31,58]

Cyclophilin and Calmodulin Receptors. The finding that the effect of CsA appears to be distal to the initial influx of calcium suggests that CsA primarily affects an intracellular protein.[46] CsA is localized within the cytosol and binds reversibly to two proteins, cyclophilin and calmodulin. These observations give rise to the idea that CsA mediates its action within the cell rather than at the cell membrane level.

Calmodulin, a ubiquitous constituent of all eukaryotic cells, mediates the activation of calcium in intracellular metabolism and therefore is essential to normal cell function.[19,24] The activation of calmodulin secondary to the rise in intracellular calcium results in the increase of enzymatic activities within the cytoplasm of the cell. CsA has been reported to interfere with the binding of Ca^{++} by calmodulin and prevent the activation of the second messengers that are necessary to initiate the synthesis of proteins, mRNA, DNA, and prostaglandins.[19]

Whether inhibition of calmodulin-dependent processes is sufficient to explain the immunosuppressive properties of CsA remains controversial.[65] Non-immunosuppressive derivatives of CsA also bind to calmodulin, so it is unlikely that CsA interacting with calmodulin is the primary mechanism of action. Other authors have been unable to demonstrate that CsA is a calmodulin inhibitor.[41,53] A further conclusion that CsA inhibits the active gene transcription process dependent on calmodulin binding to the nuclear matrix cannot explain the CsA selectivity for lymphokine genes.

The specific function of the cytoplasmic binding protein cyclophilin is unknown.[42] Cyclophilin is possibly responsible for the uptake and concentration of CsA by lymphoid cells.[42] Cyclophilin has a higher binding affinity for CsA than does calmodulin. Cyclophilin binding has been found to parallel immuno-suppressive activity in vitro.[24] It has been proposed that CsA resistance or sensitivity may be determined by the relative concentration of cyclophilin vs. calmodulin.[44] High concentrations of cyclophilin prevent CsA from interacting with calmodulin, whereas low levels allow CsA to bind to calmodulin and inhibit the enzymatic processes necessary for protein synthesis; however, this theory has been disputed based on analytical differences.[24]

Cyclophilin may bind to the CsA active site in a stereospecific manner, which could lead to the CsA-cyclophilin complex being recognized by other receptor molecules specific for T-cells or selectively involved in T-cell activation.[82] Interaction with this receptor would presumably prevent generation of the lymphokine depressor necessary to trigger transcription (see Fig. 4). However, it is clear that CsA does not affect the events distal to gene transcription, i.e., mRNA translation and synthesis and release of interleukins.

Effects on Accessory Cells or Antigen Presenting Cells

Immunoregulation may begin at the level of antigen presentation.[27,28,37,40] Cells responsible for antigen presentation include peripheral blood monocytes, tissue macrophages, and dendritic, Langerhan's, and endothelial cells. These cells synthesize and elaborate a variety of immunomodulators necessary for the induction and maintenance of immune responsiveness. In vitro studies suggest that CsA inhibits antigen presentation;[26,79,97] however, the mechanism is not known.

Esa et al.[27] demonstrated the existence of two functionally distinct human peripheral blood monocyte populations. Functionally, large monocytes present antigens poorly but are more effective in the activation of suppressor cells, whereas small monocytes present antigen efficiently. The larger monocyte subset appears to be more resistant than the small monocyte subset to the effects of CsA. When exposed to CsA, the smaller monocytes release significantly more arachidonate metabolites, prostaglandin E_2 (PGE_2) and thromboxane (TXB_2), than large monocytes. PGE_2 is a powerful mediator that affects many of the suppressive pathways known to be affected by CsA. PGE_2 inhibits IL-2 production, diminishes the expression of class II HLA antigens, and facilitates the activation of T suppressor cells.[69,83,96] PGE_2 causes an elevation of cAMP and inhibits ODC, a potentially important enzyme that has also been reported to be inhibited by CsA.[31]

Conflicting reports exist for the effect of CsA on IL-1. Early studies suggested that CsA inhibited the release of IL-1 from macrophages and also rendered T-cells refractory to exogenous IL-1.[1,10,78] In contrast, Wagner[103] reported that IL-1 produced by macrophages was unaffected by CsA.

Effect on B-Lymphocyte Responses

Initial studies of CsA suggested that B-lymphocytes were relatively resistant to its effects. Recent studies have demonstrated that there are two distinct subsets of B-lymphocytes based on sensitivity or resistance to CsA. Distinct activation pathways may exist for CsA-resistant and CsA-sensitive responses.[23] The major mechanism by which CsA inhibits B-cells appears to be interference with a calcium-dependent step.[57] The CsA-resistant responses appear to be activated by an alternative, calcium-independent pathway. The effect of CsA on B cells may be concentration dependent. Results to date suggest that low concentrations inhibit B-cell IgG production, whereas higher concentrations are needed to suppress B cell proliferation and IgM production.[33]

SUMMARY

CsA has contributed dramatically to the field of clinical transplantation and has proved to be a useful investigational tool in the study of cellular immunology. The main advantages of CsA include its lack of bone marrow toxicity, its specificity relative to other immunosuppressive agents, and its reversibility. The inhibition of IL-2 elaboration by stimulated helper T-cells appears to be the major mechanism of action of CsA. The exact mechanism by which CsA blocks transmission of the antigen signal before lymphokine messenger mRNA transcription remains to be determined. The primary theory is that CsA interferes with the calcium-dependent second messenger pathway, which results in the inhibition of protein synthesis and cell division. The overall effect is that CsA blocks the release of lymphokines and prevents the activation of cytotoxic T-lymphocytes.

Identifying the mechanism of action of CsA and the contribution of its active metabolites at the molecular level will provide useful insight into its role in combined immunosuppressive regimens and its potential for inducing allograft tolerance in man, as well as provide information for the design of future generations of selective immunosuppressive agents.

REFERENCES

1. Andrus L, Lafferty KJ: Inhibition of T cell activity by CsA. Scand J Immunol 14:499, 1982.
2. Ascher N, Simmons RL, Najarian JS: Principles of immunosuppression. In Sabiston DC (ed): Textbook of Surgery: The Biological Basis of Modern Surgical Practice, 13th ed. Philadelphia, W.B. Saunders, 1986, p 440.
3. Bach JF: Cyclosporine in autoimmunity. Transplant Proc 20(Suppl 4):379, 1988.
4. Belendiuk G, Solch S: Cyclosporine in neurological autoimmune disease. Clin Neuropharmacol 11:291, 1988.
5. Bijsterbosch MK, Klaus GG: Cyclosporine does not inhibit mitogen-induced inositol phospholipid degradation in mouse lymphocytes. Immunology 56:435, 1985.
6. Bloemena E, van Oers MH, Weinreich S, et al: Cyclosporine A does not prevent expression of biologically active IL-2 receptors in vitro. Transplant Proc 20(Suppl 2):131, 1988.
7. Borel JF: Comparative study of in vitro and in vivo drug effects on cell-mediated cytotoxicity. Immunology 31:631, 1976.

8. Borel JF, Feurer C, Gubler HU, Stahelin H: Biological effects of cyclosporine A: A new antilymphocytic agent. Agents Actions 6:468, 1976.
9. Britton S, Palacios R: Cyclosporin A—usefulness, risks and mechanism of action. Immunol Rev 65:5, 1982.
10. Bunjes D, Hardt C, Rollinghoff M, Wagner H: CsA mediates immunosuppression of primary cytotoxic T cell responses by impairing the release of IL-1 and IL-2. Eur J Immunol 11:657, 1981.
11. Calne RY: Immunosuppression for organ grafting—observations on cyclosporin A. Immunol Rev 46:113, 1979.
12. Calne RY: Pancreas transplantation. Prog Allergy 38:395, 1986.
13. Calne RY, White DJG, Evans DB, et al: Cyclosporin A in patients receiving renal allografts from cadaver donors. Lancet 2:1323, 1978.
14. Canadian Multicentre Transplant Study Group: A randomized clinical trial of cyclosporine in cadaveric renal transplantation. N Engl J Med 309:809, 1988.
14a. Carrier M, Russell DH, Wild JC, et al: Prolactin as a marker of rejection in human heart transplantation. J Heart Transplant 6:290, 1987.
15. Citterio F, Kahan BD: Effects of cyclosporine on nuclear function. Transplant Proc 20(Suppl 2):75, 1988.
16. Cohen DJ, Loertscher R, Rubin MF, et al: Cyclosporine: A new immunosuppressive agent for organ transplantation. Ann Intern Med 101:667, 1984.
17. Coffey RG, Hadden EM, Hadden JW: Evidence for cyclic GMP and calcium mediation of lymphocyte activation by mitogens. J Immunol 119:1387, 1977.
18. Colombani PM, Donnenberg AD, Robb A, Hess AD: Use of T lymphocyte clones to analyze cyclosporine binding. Transplant Proc 17:1413, 1985.
19. Colombani PM, Robb A, Hess AD: CsA binding to calmodulin: A possible site of action on T lymphocytes. Science 228:337, 1985.
20. Deeg HJ, Storb R, Thomas ED, et al: Cyclosporine prophylaxis for graft-versus-host disease: A randomized study in patients undergoing marrow transplantation for acute non-lymphoblastic leukemia. Blood 65:1325, 1985.
21. Deeg HJ, Storb R, Appelbaum FR, et al: Combined immunosuppression with cyclosporine and methotrexate in dogs given bone marrow grafts from HLA-haploidentical littermates. Transplantation 37:62, 1984.
22. Depper JM, Leonard WJ, Kronke M, et al: Regulation of interleukin 2 receptor expression: effects of phorbol diester, phospholipase C, and re-exposure to lectin or antigen. J Immunol 133:3054, 1984.
23. Dongworth AW, Klaus GG: Effects of cyclosporin on the immune system of the mouse. I. Evidence for a direct selective effect of cyclosporin A on B cells responding to anti-immunoglobulin antibodies. Eur J Immunol 12:1018, 1982.
24. Durette PL, Boger J, Dumont F, et al: A study of the correlation between cyclophilin binding and in vitro immunosuppressive activity of cyclosporine A and analogues. Transplant Proc 20(Suppl 2):51, 1988.
25. Elliot JF, Lin Y, Mizel SB, et al: Induction of IL-2 mRNA inhibited by CsA. Science 226:1439, 1984.
26. Esa AH, Converse PJ, Hess AD: Cyclosporine inhibits soluble antigen and alloantigen presentation by human monocytes in vitro. Int J Immunopharmacol 9:893, 1987.
27. Esa AH, Noga SJ, Donnenberg AD, Hess AD: Immunological heterogeneity of human monocyte subsets prepared by counterflow centrifugation elutriation. Immunology 59:95, 1986.
28. Esa AH, Paxman DG, Noga SJ, Hess AD: Sensitivity of monocyte subpopulations to cyclosporine arachidonate metabolism and in vitro antigen presentation. Transplant Proc 30(Suppl 2):80, 1988.
29. European Multicentre Trial Group: Cyclosporine in cadaveric renal transplantation: One-year follow-up of a multicentre trial. Lancet 2:986, 1983.
30. Farrar WL, Johnson HM, Farrar JJ: Regulation of the production of immune interferon and cytotoxic T lymphocytes by interleukin 2. J Immunol 126:1120, 1981.
31. Fidelus RK, Laughter AH, Twomey JJ, et al: The effect of cyclosporine on ornithine decarboxylase induction with mitogens, antigens and lymphokines. Transplantation 37:383, 1984.
32. Freed BM, Rosano TG, Lempert N: In vitro immunosuppressive properties of cyclosporin metabolites. Transplantation 43:123, 1988.
33. Freed BM, Stevens C, Zhang G, et al: A comparison of the effects of cyclosporine and steroids on human T lymphocyte responses. Transplant Proc 20(Suppl 2):233, 1988.

624   LAKE

34. Gelfand EW, Cheung RK, Grinstein S, Mills GB: Characterization of the role for calcium influx in mitogen-induced triggering of human T cells: Identification of calcium-dependent and calcium-independent signals. Eur J Immunol 16:907, 1986.
35. Granelli-Piperno A, Andrus L, Steinman RM: Lymphokine and non-lymphokine mRNA levels in stimulated human T cells. Kinetics, mitogen requirements, and effects of cyclosporin A. J Exp Med 163:922, 1986.
36. Granelli-Piperno A, Inaba K, Steinman R: Stimulation of lymphokine release from T lymphoblasts—requirement for mRNA synthesis and inhibition by CsA. J Exp Med 160:1782, 1984.
37. Granelli-Piperno A, Keane M: Effects of cyclosporine A on T lymphocytes and accessory cells from human blood. Transplant Proc 20(Suppl 2): 136, 1988.
38. Granelli-Piperno A, Keane M, Steinman R: Evidence that cyclosporine inhibits cell-mediated immunity primarily at the level of the T lymphocyte rather than the accessory cell. Transplantation 46(Suppl):53S, 1988.
39. Green GJ: Experimental transplantation and cyclosporine. Transplantation 46(Suppl):3S, 1988.
40. Gullberg M, Smith KA: Regulation of T cell autocrine growth. T4+ cells become refractory to interleukin 2. J Exp Med 163:270, 1986.
41. Hait WN, Harding MW, Handschumacher RE: Calmodulin, cyclophilin and CsA. Science 233:987, 1986.
42. Handschumacher RE, Harding MW, Rice J, et al: Cyclophilin: A specific cytosolic binding protein for CsA. Science 226:544, 1984.
43. Harrison WB, von Graffenried B: Ciclosporin in rheumatoid arthritis: A review. Agents Actions 24(Suppl):236, 1988.
44. Hess AD, Colombani PM, Esa AH: Cyclosporine and the immune response: Basic aspects. CRC Crit Rev Immunol 6:123, 1986.
45. Hess AD, Esa AH, Colombani PM: Mechanism of action: In vitro studies. Prog Allergy 38:198, 1986.
46. Hess AD, Esa AH, Colombani PM: Mechanisms of action of cyclosporine: Effect on cells of the immune system and on subcellular events in T cell activation. Transplant Proc 20(Suppl 2):29, 1988. In Kahan BD (ed): Cyclosporine: Nature of the Agent and Its Immunologic Actions. Philadelphia, Grune & Stratton, 1988.
47. Hess AD, Tutschka PJ: Effect of cyclosporin A on human lymphocyte responses in vitro. I. CsA allows for the expression of alloantigen-activated suppressor cells while preferentially inhibiting the induction of cytolytic effector lymphocytes in MLR. J Immunol 123:2601, 1980.
48. Hiestand PC, Mekler P: Mechanisms of action: Ciclosporin- and prolactin-mediated control of immunity. Prog Allergy 38:239, 1986.
49. Hirano T, Fujimoto K, Teranishi T, et al: Phorbol ester increases the level of interleukin 2 mRNA in mitogen-stimulated human lymphocytes. J Immunol 132:2165, 1984.
50. Hodgkin PD, Hapel AJ, Johnson RM, et al: Blocking of delivery of the antigen-mediated signal to the nucleus of T cells by cyclosporine. Transplantation 43:685, 1987.
51. Janco RL, English D: Cyclosporine and human neutrophil function. Transplantation 35:501, 1983.
52. Kahan BD: Cyclosporine: The agent and its actions. Transplant Proc 17(Suppl 1), 1985. In Kahan BD (ed): Cyclosporine: Diagnosis and Management of Associated Renal Injury. Orlando, Grune & Stratton, 1985.
53. Kay JE: The cyclosporin-sensitive event in lymphocyte activation. Ann Inst Pasteur Immunol 138:622, 1987.
54. Kay JE, Benzie CR, Borghetti AF: Effect of CsA on lymphocyte activation by the calcium ionophore A32187. Immunology 50:441, 1983.
55. Keown PA, Stiller CR, Carruthers G, et al: Cyclosporine: Mechanism of action, measurement and clinical use. Br J Clin Pract 40:149, 1986.
56. Kerman RH, Fleckner SM, Van Buren CT, et al: Immunoregulatory mechanisms in cyclosporine-treated renal allograft recipients. Transplantation 43:205, 1987.
57. Klaus GG: Cyclosporine-sensitive and cyclosporine-insensitive modes of B cell stimulation. Transplantation 46(Suppl):11S, 1988.
58. Koponen M, Grieder A, Loor F: The effects of cyclosporine on the cell cycle of T lymphoid cell lines. Exp Cell Res 140:237, 1982.
59. Kronke M, Leonard WJ, Depper JM, et al: Cyclosporin A inhibits T cell growth factor gene expression at the level of the mRNA transcription. Proc Natl Acad Sci USA 81:5214, 1984.
60. Kupiec-Weglinski JW, Filho MA, Strom TB, Tilney NL: Sparing of suppressor cells: A critical

action of cyclosporine. Transplantation 38:97, 1984.

61. Larson DF: Cyclosporine. Mechanisms of action: Antagonism of the prolactin receptor. Prog Allergy 38:222, 1986.

62. Larsson EL: CsA and dexamethasone suppresses T cell responses by selectively acting at distinct sites of the triggering process. J Immunol 128:2828, 1980.

63. Laupacis A, Keown PA Ulan RA, et al: Cyclosporin A: A powerful immunosuppressant. Can Med Assoc J 126:1041, 1982.

64. LeGrue SJ, Friedman AW, Kahan BD: Binding cyclosporin by human lymphocytes and phospholipid vesicles. Immunology 131:712, 1983.

65. LeGrue SJ, Turner R, Weisbrodt N, Dedman JR: Does the binding of cyclosporin to calmodulin result in immunosuppression? Science 234:68, 1986.

66. Lichtman AH, Segal GB, Lictman MA: The role of calcium in lymphocyte proliferation (an interpretative review). Blood 61:413, 1983.

67. Lillehoj HS, Malek TR, Shevach EM: Differential effect of CsA on the expression of T and B lymphocyte activation antigens. J Immunol 133:244, 1984.

68. Maizel AL, Mehta SR, Hauft S, et al: Human T lymphocyte/monocyte interaction in response to lectin: Kinetics of entry into the S-phase. J Immunol 127:1058, 1981.

69. Makoul GT, Robinson DR, Bhalla AK, Glimcher LH: Prostaglandin E2 inhibits the activation of cloned T cell hybridomas. J Immunol 134:2645, 1985.

70. Manger B, Hardy KJ, Weiss A, Storbo JD: Differential effect of cyclosporin A on activation signaling in human T cell lines. J Clin Invest 77:1501, 1986.

71. Meuer SC, Schlossman SF, Reinherz EL: Clonal analysis of human cytotoxic T lymphocytes: T4+ and T8+ effector T cells recognize products of different major histocompatibility complex regions. Proc Nat Acad Sci USA 79:4395, 1982.

72. Moore RN, Oppenheim JJ, Farrar JJ, et al: Production of lymphocyte-activating factor (interleukin 1) by macrophages activated with colony-stimulating factors. J Immunol 125:1302, 1980.

73. Morris RJ: Cyclosporin A. Transplantation 32:349, 1981.

74. Nishizuka Y: The role of protein kinase C in cell surface signal transduction and tumour promotion. Nature 308:693, 1984.

75. O'Connell JB, Renlund DG: Immune mechanisms of acute cardiac allograft rejection and modification by immunosuppression. In Emery RW, et al (eds): Cardiothoracic Transplantation. Cardiac Surgery: State of the Art Reviews, Vol. 3, no. 3. Philadelphia, Hanley & Belfus, Inc. 1989.

76. Palacios R: Cyclosporin A inhibits antigen- and lectin-induced but not constitutive production of interleukin 3. Eur J Immunol 15:204, 1985.

77. Palacios R: Mechanisms of T cell activation: Role and functional relationship of HLA-DR antigens and interleukins. Immunol Rev 63:73, 1982.

78. Palacios R, Moller G: Cyclosporin A blocks receptors for HLA-DR antigens on T cells. Nature 290:792, 1981.

79. Paley DA, Cluff CW, Wentworth PA, Ziegler HK: CsA inhibits macrophage-mediated antigen presentation. J Immunol 136:4348, 1986.

80. Powles R, Barrett AJ, Clink H, et al: Cyclosporine A for the treatment of graft-versus-host disease in man. Lancet 2:1327, 1978.

81. Ptachcinski RJ, Venkataramanan R, Burckart GJ: Drug therapy in transplantation. In DiPiro JT (ed): Pharmacotherapy: A Pathophysiologic Approach. Elsevier, New York, 1989, p 76.

82. Quesniaux VF, Schreier MH, Wenger RM, et al: Cyclosporine-cyclophilin interaction. Transplant Proc 20(Suppl 2):58, 1988.

83. Rappaport RS, Dodge GR: Prostaglandin E inhibits the production of human interleukin 2. J Exp Med 155:943, 1982.

84. Rietz BA, Bieber CP, Raney AA, et al: Orthotopic heart and combined heart and lung transplantation with cyclosporin A immune suppression. Transplant Proc 13:393, 1981.

85. Rossaro L, Dowd SR, Ho C, Van Thiel DH: ^{19}F Nuclear magnetic resonance studies of cyclosporine and model unilamellar vesicles: Where does the drug sit within the membrane? Transplant Proc 20(Suppl 2):41, 1988.

86. Russell DH, Kibler DH, Matrison L, et al: Prolactin receptors on human T and B lymphocytes: Antagonism of prolactin binding of cyclosporin. J Immunol 134:3027, 1985.

87. Russell DH, Larson DF: Prolactin-induced polyamine biosynthesis in spleen and thymus: Specific inhibition by cyclosporine. Immunopharmacology 9:165, 1985.

88. Ryffel B, Gotz U, Heuberger AD: Cyclosporin receptors on human lymphocytes. J Immunol 129:1978, 1982.

89. Ryffel B, Muller S, Foxwell B: CsA allows the expression of high affinity IL-2 binding sites on anti-T cell antibody activated human T lymphocytes. Transplant Proc 19:1199, 1987.
90. Ryffel B, Willard-Gallo KE, Tammi K, Loken MR: Quantitative fluorescence analysis of cyclosporine binding to human leukocytes. Transplantation 37:276, 1984.
91. Santos GW, Brookmeyer R, Saral R, Tutschka PJ: Cyclosporine (CsA) versus cyclophosphamide (CY)—prevention of graft-versus-host disease (GVHD). Exp Hematol 13:45, 1985.
92. Schleuning M, Reem G: The Second International Congress on Cyclosporine. Washington, DC, Nov 4–7, 1987 (abstract).
93. Shevach EM: The effects of CsA on the immune system. Ann Rev Immunol 3:397, 1985.
94. Simons JW, Noga SJ, Colombani PM, et al: CsA, an in vitro calmodulin antagonist induces nuclear lobulations in human T lymphocytes and monocytes. J Cell Biol 102:145, 1986.
95. Smith KA, Lachman LB, Oppenheim JJ, Favata MF: The functional relationship of the interleukins. J Exp Med 151:1551, 1980.
96. Snyder DS, Beller DI, Unanue ER: Prostaglandins modulate macrophage Ia expression. Nature 299:163, 1982.
97. Snyder DS, Wright CL, Ting C: Inhibition of human monocyte antigen presentation, but not HLA-DR expression, by cyclosporine. Transplantation 44:407, 1987.
98. Starzl TE, Hakala TR, Iwatsuki S, et al: Cyclosporin A and steroid treatment in 104 cadaveric renal transplantations. In White DJG (ed): Cyclosporin A. Amsterdam, Elsevier, 1982, p 365.
99. Tollemar J, Ringden O, Heimdahl A, et al: Decreased incidence and severity of graft-versus-host disease in HLA matched and mismatched marrow recipients of cyclosporine and methotrexate. Transplant Proc 20(Suppl 3):470, 1988.
100. Tutschka PJ: Cyclosporin A: A new outlook for immunosuppression in clinical transplantation. Blut 39:81, 1979.
101. Tutschka PJ, Beschorner WE, Allison AC, et al: Use of cyclosporin A in allogeneic bone marrow transplantation in the rat. Nature 280:148, 1979.
102. von Graffenried B: Sandimmun (ciclosporin) in autoimmune diseases. Overview on early clinical experience (status September 1987). Am J Nephrol (Suppl 1):51, 1989.
103. Wagner H: CsA: Mechanism of action. Transplant Proc 15:523, 1983.
104. Wang BS, Heacock EH, Collins KH, et al: Suppressive effects of cyclosporin A on the induction of alloreactivity in vitro and in vivo. J Immunol 127:89, 1981.
105. Wenger RM: Cyclosporin and analogues: Structural requirements for immunosuppressive activity. Transplant Proc 18:213, 1986.
106. Wiskocil R, Weiss A, Imboden J, et al: Activation of a human T cell line: A two-stimulus requirement in the pretranslational events involved in the coordinate expression of interleukin 2 and gamma-interferon genes. J Immunol 134:1599, 1985.
107. Zeevi A, Eiras G, Burckart G, et al: Immunosuppressive effect of cyclosporine metabolites from human bile on alloreactive T cells. Transplant Proc 20(Suppl 2):115, 1988.

ROBERT W. EMERY, MD
DAN R. HOLDER, PharmD
KATHLEEN D. LAKE, PharmD

MODIFIED IMMUNOSUPPRESSION IN PATIENTS BRIDGED TO TRANSPLANTATION

Robert W. Emery, MD
Director, Cardiothoracic
    Transplantation
Cardiovascular and Thoracic
    Surgeon
Minneapolis Heart Institute
Minneapolis, Minnesota

Dan R. Holder, PharmD
Research Associate
Cardiothoracic Transplantation
Minneapolis Heart Institute
Minneapolis, Minnesota

Kathleen D. Lake, PharmD
Program Director
Division of Cardiothoracic
    Transplantation and Research
Minneapolis Heart Institute
Minneapolis, Minnesota
        and
Clinical Assistant Professor
University of Minnesota College
    of Pharmacy
Minneapolis, Minnesota

Reprint requests to:
Robert W. Emery, MD
920 E. 28th Street
Suite 420
Minneapolis, MN 55407

Since the first mechanical bridge with a ventricular support device in 1984[11] and subsequent success with a total artificial heart in 1985,[4] an array of mechanical devices have been utilized as interim means to support patients in whom ventricular function would not allow a wait for an organ to become available for transplantation.[17] In this population, an increased incidence of secondary organ system dysfunction occurs because of the critical pre-bridge condition of patients in circulatory collapse and in part because of the bridge devices as well.[9,12] Mediastinal, wound, and systemic infections occur commonly following the bridge.[9] Nutrition is often poor before and during mechanical support, and wound healing is delayed after transplantation. In addition to these problems multiple surgical procedures are required in the difficult course from serious end-stage cardiac disease to mechanical bridging to successful transplantation. The use of mechanical support, especially the Jarvik-7 device, results in leukopenia and lymphopenia akin to what occurs with the administration of antilymphocyte globulin.[23] Because the toxic side effects of the numerous immunosuppressive agents necessary to prevent organ rejection compound these problems, a modified approach to antirejection therapy in these patients is warranted.

OKT3, a murine monoclonal antibody directed at the CD-3 molecule of immunocompetent T-lymphocytes, causes cell lysis and

CARDIAC SURGERY: State of the Art Reviews—Vol. 3, No. 3, October 1989
Philadelphia, Hanley & Belfus, Inc.

627

TABLE 1.   Toxic Effects of Commonly Used Immunosuppressive Agents

Steroids	Azathioprine	Cyclosporine
Cushingoid appearance	Bone marrow suppression	Renal dysfunction
Impeded wound healing	Hepatotoxicity	Hepatotoxicity
Osteoporosis	Pancreatitis	Hypertension
Sodium retention		Hirsutism
Weight gain		Tremor
Diabetes mellitus		
Serum lipid increase		
Inhibition of inflammation		

opsonization.[7] This antibody is therefore more specific than antilymphocyte globulin or antithymocyte globulin, which are pan-cellular depleting. The antibacterial action of B-cells and leukocytes may thus be spared. Earlier studies indicated the effectiveness of OKT3 in preventing or reversing rejection prospectively.[2,6,14,19,25]

In order to minimize toxic effects of commonly used antirejection agents (Table 1), we have devised a protocol for multidrug immune suppression in patients who have been mechanically supported prior to human heart transplant. The basis of this support, the use of the murine monoclonal antibody OKT3, allows other drugs to be administered initially at lower doses to minimize toxic side effects yet enhance immunosuppression.

METHODS

A regimen consisting of the three standard drugs—cyclosporine, azathioprine, and prednisone—tailored to use with OKT3 in the early post-transplant period is shown in Table 2. Note that OKT3 is begun on the second postoperative day, after diuresis has reduced the patient's weight to <10% over ideal and central venous pressure is ≤15 torr. Low-dose steroids (0.15 mg/kg/day) to prevent the development of anti-murine antibodies, is administered simultaneously with OKT3 on post-transplant days 2–14. One day prior to the last dose of OKT3, bolus methylprednisolone is administered and, on the 14th day of OKT3, a steroid taper is started (1.5 mg/kg/day). The patient is fully weaned from steroids

TABLE 2.   Modified Immunosuppression in "Bridge" Patients

Drug	Dose
OKT3	5 mg IV PTD 2–16
Azathioprine	4 mg/kg po preoperatively
	1.5–3 mg/kg/day WBC 3–5000
Cyclosporine	3 mg/kg/dose (b.i.d.), increasing slowly
	(Trough 200 ± 25 ng/ml 12 hr)
Methylprednisolone	500 mg IV after CPB
Methylprednisolone	125 mg IV q12h × 3 doses
Prednisone	0.15 mg/kg q.d. PTD 2–14
Methylprednisolone	250 mg IV PTD 15
Prednisone	1.5 mg/kg/day in divided doses
	decrease by 5 mg/dose to 0.5 mg/kg/day
	then decrease by 2.5 mg/week until off
Dopamine	1 mg/kg/min for 7 days

CPB = cardiopulmonary bypass, PTD = post-transplant day.

by 12 weeks after transplantation. Cyclosporine is administered in a low preoperative dose and continued in the immediate post-transplant period via nasogastric tube if necessary. The dose is slowly titrated to therapeutic levels over 14 days, depending on urine output, renal function tests, and whole blood high-power liquid chromatography (HPLC) trough concentration to 200 ± 25 ng/ml. Azathioprine 1.5–3 mg/kg/day is administered to maintain WBC at 3–5,000/mm³. Dopamine, an inhibiter of prolactin release (1 mg/kg/min intravenous), is administered peripherally for 1 week after transplantation.[3]

RESULTS

From October 1985 through January 1989 11 patients have undergone bridge to transplant at the Minneapolis Heart Institute Cardiothoracic Transplant Program. Eight of 11 patients have been managed with a modified immunosuppressive regimen. All devices used are listed in Table 3. These patients are discussed in detail elsewhere.[12] There have been two deaths: one due to multisystem organ failure 9 months post transplantation in the first Jarvik-7 bridge patient not receiving OKT3, and the second due to acute rejection in a patient who was bridged with a biventricular assist device followed by a Jarvik-7 total artificial heart. This patient received OKT3 therapy early in our experience. She was never started on steroids and on postmortem examination was found to have severe rejection emanating from the epicardium toward the endocardium at her death 29 days after transplantation. Multiple premortem endomyocardial biopsies had been considered negative.

Of the patients treated with OTK3, one suffered a major systemic complication before transplantation. This 15-year-old patient was placed on cardiopulmonary bypass (CPB) emergently following cardiac arrest. The ventricles were found to be filled with clot at the time of excision and there was free clot trapped in the aortic clamp. He awoke on the Jarvik-7 with a dense left hemiparesis. Four

TABLE 3.   Results in 11 Patients Undergoing Bridge to Transplantation at the Minneapolis Heart Institute

Patient	Age	Sex	Etiology	Device	Modified Regimen	Survival
PH	24	M	Marfan's	LVAD	(–)	Yes
ML	40	F	ICM	J-7-70	(–)	9 mo
NC	28	F	ICM	J-7-70	(–)	Yes
CL	15	M	ICM	J-7-70	(+)	Yes
PT	50	M	CAD	J-7-70	(+)	Yes
LF	44	M	CAD	BIVAD	(+)	Yes
SG	45	F	RHD	BIVAD J-7-70	(+)	29 days
DM	19	M	DHF	BIVAD J-7-70	(+)	Yes
TI	40	M	CAD	BIVAD	(+)	Yes
BV	16	M	ICM	J-7-70	(+)	Yes
BK	19	M	ICM	J-7-70	(+)	Yes

ICM = idiopathic cardiomyopathy, CAD = coronary artery disease, RHD = rheumatic heart disease, DHF = donor heart failure, LVAD = left ventricular assist, RVAD = right ventricular assist, and BIVAD = biventricular assist.

patients had mediastinal contamination at the time of transplantation, yet no frank mediastinal infection occurred in the post-transplantation period. Four patients had renal dysfunction in the pre-transplantation period; because management consisted of lower dose cyclosporine during the early post-transplantation period, renal failure was not encountered and moderate renal dysfunction of the preoperative period resolved rapidly with implantation of the donor heart. No patient receiving OKT3 required dialysis. Three patients had transient hepatic dysfunction and three had pancreatitis.

The incidence of rejection has been 0.25 episodes/patient, the two episodes occurring at 29 days and 368 days. One patient died and the late asymptomatic episode resolved with a steroid taper. The incidence of infection has been 0.6 episodes/patient, consisting of no bacterial and four viral infections. Three patients had cytomegalovirus and one had mumps. All were treated successfully with appropriate antiviral medication.

Six patients treated with this modified regimen are not taking steroids. The one patient remaining on steroids is managed by another program because of insurance coverage. Serum cholesterol in those patients not taking oral steroids at 6 (n = 6) and 12 (n = 5) months post transplant was 151 ± 11 (± SEM) and 171 ± 23 mg/dl, respectively. This differed from the serum cholesterol of 35 other patients having heart transplantation during the same time frame but managed on a standard triple-drug regimen of 249 ± 10 (8 < .001) and 238 ± 30 mg/dl (p ≤ .001), respectively. The serum triglyceride levels at similar intervals in the patients off steroids of 153 ± 30 and 183 ± 83 mg/dl did not differ from patients on the triple-drug regimen. In a follow-up period of 6–27 months, seven patients are functional Class 1; one is functional Class 2 with a residual pre-bridge neurologic deficit, although he attends school.

COMMENTS

With the increased incidence of postoperative complications and prolonged recovery following bridge situations,[1,5,9,15,16,21] reduction of the additional toxic side effect of immunosuppressive agents is desirable to allow organ system recovery and systemic antibacterial activity (see Table 1). Although OKT3 has undesirable side effects, including "flu-like" syndrome, nausea, vomiting, diarrhea, hypotension, and rarely non-cardiogenic pulmonary edema, these problems are associated with the first and second doses and decrease dramatically with subsequent doses.[22] The acute side effects can be minimized by holding the first administration until the patient is within 10% of dry weight and pre-treating the patient with a modified prophylactic regimen described in Table 4 (J.B. O'Connell, personal communication). Late effects such as antibody development can be minimized by administering a small dose of steroid (prednisone, 0.1 mg/kg/dose) over the duration of OKT3 therapy. The monitoring of T-cell subsets is used to determine OKT3 effectiveness, with an early fall in T_3 cells to <0.1% of total lymphocytes and a late rebound in T-11 cells.[7] The presence of a positive cytotoxic screen after the first several doses may also be a useful indicator of excess murine antibody and OKT3 effect (C. DeWitt, personal communication).

As OKT3 specifically affects lymphocytes, granulocytic and B-cell function remains intact and early bacterial contamination may be combatted in conjunction with the appropriate or prophylactic antibiotic therapy. It is of interest that four patients had mediastinal contamination based on positive intraoperative cultures, one of these with preoperative gram-negative rods growing from chest

TABLE 4. Prophylactic Regimen for Administration of OKT3

Pre-medication regimen prior to FIRST dose of OKT3:
_____ A. Benadryl (diphenhydramaine) 50 mg IV × 1 (within 15 minutes of dose)
_____ B. Ranitidine 100 mg IVBP × 1 (within 30 minutes of dose)
_____ C. Tylenol (acetaminophen) 650 mg po/(R) × 1 (30–60 minutes prior to first dose)
_____ D. Methylprednisolone 1.0 mg/kg IV (within 15 minutes prior to first dose)
_____ E. Hydrocortisone 100 mg IV × 1 (30 minutes after first dose)

Medication regimen up to time of FOURTH dose:
_____ A. Ranitidine 50 mg IVPB q8h
_____ B. Benadryl (diphenhydramine) 25 mg IV q6h p.r.n.
_____ C. Tylenol (acetaminophen) 650 mg po/(R) q6h p.r.n.
_____ D. Hydrocortisone 100 mg IV × 1 prior to second dose

tube drainage, yet none of the patients developed mediastinal infection. Although others have noticed a trend toward increased infections in patients receiving OKT3, this was not the case in our series.[20]

In spite of low postoperative doses of traditional immunosuppressive medications, there has been no incidence of acute cardiac rejection during OKT3 therapy. The one death resulting from rejection on post-transplant day 29 occurred early in our experience, and the patient had not been started on steroids because of concern for mediastinal contamination with gram-negative rods. While endocardial biopsies were negative, at postmortem examination an intensive T-cell infiltrate was found to emanate from the epicardium inward, sparing the subendocardial layers. Myocardial necrosis was present in the mid-myocardium. Retrospectively, this event was the rebound response occasionally seen after OKT3 administration and caused our conversion to the present regimen of steroid bolus on the next to last day of OKT3 and prednisone taper beginning the last day of OKT3.

The incidence of viral infection, particularly CMV, has been high (43%) and of concern.[8] The incidence of rejection has not increased following CMV infection nor has the incidence of graft atherosclerosis. These data may differ from those reported by Grattam et al. because of our short-term of follow-up and possibly because of the early and aggressive use of DHPG to combat viral infections not addressed in that publication.[8] The one-year survival rate of 88% compares favorably with our non-bridge patients (90%).

Secondary organ system problems have been minimal following transplant, and the prolonged recovery process associated with the OKT3 regimen has primarily been due to the need for intensive physical rehabilitation. Outpatient administration of OKT3 has been prescribed, and hospital stay has not been increased because of the use of this drug.[10] The steroid taper has been accomplished completely on an outpatient basis.

On long-term follow-up, steroid-related complications in bridge patients are absent. Serum cholesterol levels are within the normal range and, as previously reported, are lower than the levels of patients taking steroids as part of the immunosuppressive regimen.[18,24] The management of cholesterol and weight in these patients is eased.[13]

Because of the success encountered with this modified regimen, we have expanded the use to include: patients with preoperative organ system dysfunction, diabetics, pediatric patients, females, and post-transplant patients who have required mechanical assist devices. The advantages of early low-dose immunosuppressive therapy and the success achieved in weaning patients from prednisone,

sparing them the long-term complications of steroids and associated hypercholesterolemia, have persuaded us to continue using the regimen of post-transplant
immunosuppression in selected patients.

REFERENCES

1. Bolman RM, Cox JL, Marshall W, et al: Circulatory support with a centrifugal pump as a bridge to cardiac transplantation. Ann Thorac Surg 47:108–112, 1989.
2. Bristow MR, Gilbert EM, Renlund DG, et al: Use of OKT3 monoclonal antibody in heart transplantation: Review of the initial experience. J Heart Transplant 7:1–11, 1988.
3. Carrier M, Emery RW, Mobley-Wild J, et al: Prolactin as a marker of rejection in human heart transplantation. Transplant Proc 19:3442–3443, 1987.
4. Copeland JG, Levinson MM, Smith R, et al: The total artificial heart as a bridge to transplantation: A report of two cases. JAMA 256:2991–2995, 1986.
5. Copeland JG, Smith R, Icenogle TB, et al: Orthotopic total artificial heart bridge to transplantation: Preliminary results. J Heart Transplant 8:124–137, 1989.
6. Gay WA, O'Connell JG, Nelson BA, et al: OKT3 monoclonal antibody in cardiac transplantation. Ann Surg 208:287–290, 1988.
7. Gilbert EM, DeWitt C, Eiswirth CC, et al: Treatment of refractory cardiac allograft rejection with OKT3 monoclonal antibody. Am J Med 82:202–206, 1987.
8. Grattan MT, Moreno-Cabral CE, Starnes VA: Cytomegalovirus infection is associated with cardiac allograft rejection and atherosclerosis. JAMA 261:3561–3566, 1989.
9. Griffith BP: Interim use of the Jarvik-7 artificial heart: Lessons learned at Presbyterian University Hospital of Pittsburgh. Ann Thorac Surg 47:158–166, 1989.
10. Herrick CM, Mealey PC, Hagan ME, et al: Rejection prophylaxis with murine monoclonal CD-3 antibody (OKT3): Considerations for early discharge. J Heart Transplant 8:67–70, 1989.
11. Hill JD, Farrar DJ, Hershon JJ, et al: Use of a prosthetic ventricle as a bridge to cardiac transplantation for post-infarction cardiogenic shock. N Engl J Med 314:626–628, 1986.
12. Joyce LD, Emery RW, Eales F, et al: Mechanical circulatory support as a bridge to transplantation. Submitted for publication.
13. Keogh A, Simons L, Spratt P: Hyperlipidemia of the heart transplant. J Heart Transplant 7:171–175, 1988.
14. Konertz W, Wegand M, Friedl A: Prophylactic use of OKT3 in cardiac transplantation. Transplant Proc 21:2494–2496, 1989.
15. Levinson MM: The spectrum of pathophysiology and complications in human Jarvik-7 artificial heart recipients. In Emery RW, et al (eds): Cardiothoracic Transplantation II. Cardiac Surgery: State of the Art Reviews, vol. 3, no. 3. Philadelphia, Hanley & Belfus, Inc., 1989.
16. Oaks TR, Wismann CB, Pae WE, et al: Results of mechanical circulatory assistance before heart transplant. J Heart Transplant 8:113–115, 1989.
17. Pennington DG, Termuhlen DF: Mechanical circulatory support: Device selection. In Emery RW, et al (eds): Cardiothoracic Transplantation II. Cardiac Surgery: State of the Art Reviews, vol. 3, no. 3. Philadelphia, Hanley & Belfus, Inc., 1989.
18. Renlund DG, Bristow MR, Crandall BG, et al: Hypercholesterolemia after cardiac transplantation: Amelioration by corticosteroid-free maintenance immunosuppression. J Heart Transplant 7:70, 1988.
19. Renlund DG, O'Connell JB, Gilbert EM, et al: A prospective comparison of murine monoclonal CD-3 (OKT3) antibody-based and equine antithymocyte globular based rejection prophylaxis in cardiac transplantation. Transplantation 47:599–605, 1989.
20. Sinnott JT, Cullison JP, Sweeney MS, Weinstein SS: Infections in patients receiving OKT3 monoclonal antibody for cardiac rejection. Texas Heart Inst J 15:102–106, 1988.
21. Starings VA, Oyer PA, Portner F, et al: Isolated left ventricular assist as a bridge to cardiac transplantation. J Thorac Cardiovasc Surg 96:62–71, 1988.
22. Stein KL, Ladowski J, Kormos R, Armitage J: The cardiopulmonary response to OKT3 in orthotopic cardiac transplant recipients. Chest 95:817–821, 1989.
23. Stelzer GT, Wand RA, Wellhausen SR, et al: Alterations in select immunologic parameters following total artificial heart implantation. Artificial Organs 11:52–62, 1987.
24. Taylor DO, Thompson JA, Hastillo A, et al: Hyperlipidemia after clinical heart transplantation. J Heart Transplant 8:209–213, 1989.
25. Weiman W, Essed CE, Balk Ahum et al: OKT3 delays rejection crisis after heart transplantation. Transplant Proc 21:2497–2498, 1989.

JEANNE D. OLSON, RDMS
IRVIN F. GOLDENBERG, MD
MARC R. PRITZKER, MD
ROBERT W. EMERY, MD

DOPPLER ECHOCARDIOGRAPHIC INDICES AS MARKERS OF ACUTE CARDIAC REJECTION

Minneapolis Heart Institute
Abbott Northwestern Hospital
Minneapolis, Minnesota

Reprint requests to:
Irvin F. Goldenberg, MD
Director of Research
Minneapolis Heart Institute
920 East 28th Street, Suite 160
Minneapolis, MN 55407

Rejection following cardiac transplantation may lead to changes in cardiac systolic and diastolic function. Previous investigators have suggested that Doppler echocardiographic indices of diastolic function such as pressure half-time and isovolumic relaxation time may show a significant decrease during acute myocardial rejection.[2,9] It has also been reported that following treatment for cardiac rejection that these indices return toward baseline.[2] The purpose of this study is to confirm prior reports that Doppler echocardiographic indices of cardiac function are useful as a noninvasive method of evaluating patients for myocardial rejection.

METHODS

Patient Population

Forty-six patients who underwent orthotopic cardiac transplantation had serial surveillance studies for rejection consisting of endomyocardial biopsy and Doppler echocardiographic examinations. Doppler echocardiographic examinations were performed within 24 hours of endomyocardial biopsy. An average of 6.8 examinations per patient were performed within 22 months after transplantation. There were 39 men and 7 women, whose average age was 49 years (range 18 to 61 years). Patients underwent transplantations between 1 week and 22 months prior to entry into the study.

CARDIAC SURGERY: State of the Art Reviews—Vol. 3, No. 3, October 1989
Philadelphia, Hanley & Belfus, Inc.

633

Twelve patients who had a baseline normal biopsy developed an episode of moderate rejection. In these 12 patients an endomyocardial biopsy and Doppler echocardiographic examination were obtained prior to rejection, during rejection, and following treatment for rejection.

Doppler echocardiographic examinations were obtained with an Irex Meridian. A 3 MHz transducer was used to perform the M-mode and two-dimensional recordings. A 3.5 MHz dual frequency transducer was used to obtain the pulsed Doppler recordings. All paper recordings were taken at a speed of 100 mm/s.

MEASUREMENTS

M-mode images of the left ventricle were taken from the long axis view at the level of the papillary muscles.[7] The left ventricular end-diastolic and end-systolic dimensions were obtained for calculation of fractional shortening (FS).[5] Pulsed Doppler recordings of the mitral inflow were taken from the apical four-chamber view, with the sample volume located at the tips of the leaflets for measurement of the peak early mitral flow velocity (M1), mitral valve pressure half-time (PHT), and mitral valve modified deceleration time (DT).[5] The modified deceleration time was measured from the peak early mitral flow velocity (M1) to the arm of the mitral closure. Pulsed Doppler interrogations were obtained by placing the sample volume midway between the left ventricular outflow tract and the anterior mitral valve leaflet, enabling visualization of a crisp closure of the aortic valve in conjunction with the opening click of the mitral valve for measurement of the isovolumic relaxation time (IVRT).[4]

Measurements were taken by three blinded observers on 7 consecutive beats. We did not exclude mitral beats with recipient atrial contractions during diastole, as other authors have.[10]

ENDOMYOCARDIAL BIOPSIES

Myocardial biopsies were graded as no rejection (NR); mild rejection (mild R): rejection with mild cellular infiltrate only; and moderate rejection (mod R): rejection with more extensive cellular infiltrate with or without necrosis. The biopsy results were compared to the Doppler echocardiographic findings. Therapy for rejection was undertaken for biopsy findings of moderate rejection with necrosis.

Statistical Analysis

Data was analyzed using an unpaired t-test when comparing echocardiographic indices against graded endomyocardial biopsy (Table 1). When patients served as their own control, comparing echocardiographic indices in biopsy-proven rejection and the treatment thereof, a Student's paired t-test was conducted.

Results

Table 1 shows indices by biopsy results. There is a significant decrease in isovolumic relaxation time, mitral valve pressure half-time as well as modified mitral valve deceleration time during both mild and moderate rejection, as compared to patients with no rejection, indicating that significant changes in Doppler echocardiographic indices accompany rejection. We also found a significant decrease in left ventricular fractional shortening (LVFS) associated

TABLE 1.   Doppler Indices Correlated with Endomyocardial Biopsy

	NR	Mild R	Moderate R
IVRT (msec)	102±2	89±2*	80±3*
DT (msec)	112±2	88±1*	75±2*
M1 (msec)	1.2±0.02	0.8±0.02	0.8±0.03
PHT (msec)	50±1	44±1*	37±1*
LVFS (%)	37±1	34±1**	30±2**

* P = < .001 – mild or moderate R vs NR.
** PNR = < 0.05 – mild or moderate R vs NR.
DT = modified deceleration time, IVRT = isovolumic relaxation time, LVFS = left ventricular fractional shortening, M1 = early peak mitral flow velocity, Mild R = mild rejection, Moderate R = moderate rejection, NR = no rejection, and PHT = pressure half time.

with mild or moderate rejection. However, the LVFS values were within accepted normal limits, indicating the importance of following trends for each individual patient.

Table 2 shows Doppler echocardiographic indices in 12 patients with moderate rejection by endomyocardial biopsy and Doppler echocardiographic examination. During rejection there is a decrease in the pressure half-time, fractional shortening, modified deceleration time, and isovolumic relaxation time. Following treatment these indices return toward normal.

DISCUSSION

These data confirm prior reports that Doppler echocardiographic indices of diastolic function are useful for detecting cardiac rejection.[2,9] As suggested previously, substantial shortening of the isovolumic relaxation time is helpful in predicting cardiac rejection,[2,9] is quite easily and rapidly reproduced on serial examinations, and is easily measured even with an increased heart rate. In the present study, the IVRT times were longer than those previously reported,[9] most likely due to the longer follow-up in our patient group (up to 22 months) than in the other studies.[9] St. Goar et al. noted a gradual lengthening of the IVRT with increasing length of follow-up time after transplant, possibly because of changes in left ventricular diastolic function in the early postoperative period.[8]

TABLE 2.   Doppler Echocardiographic Indices in Patients Treated for Cardiac Rejection

	Baseline	Mod R	After T
IVRT (msec)	113	75**	111*
DT (msec)	105	78**	105*
PHT (msec)	46	40†	48*
LVFS (%)	42	34‡	36*

* P = NS—After T vs baseline.
** P = 0.0001—Mod R vs baseline.
† P = 0.08—Mod R vs baseline.
‡ P = 0.05—Mod R vs baseline.
After T = after treatment, Baseline = baseline normal, DT = modified declaration time, IVRT = isovolumic relaxation time, LVFS = left ventricular fractional shortening, Mod R = moderate rejection, and PHT = pressure half time.

The mitral inflow diastolic indices appear to be somewhat more problematic. Even though pressure half-time showed a decrease during rejection, we found that these indices often varied between consecutive beats possibly owing to the recipient atrial contraction during diastole.[10]

In order to circumvent this problem, we attempted to measure a modified deceleration time, a measurement easy to make and quite reproducible. The modified deceleration time, like mitral valve pressure half-time, showed significant shortening during organ rejection.

Left ventricular fractional shortening also decreased with mild to moderate rejection. This differs from previous studies, which have shown systolic function may remain unchanged during rejection.[3]

The peak early mitral flow velocity was not increased during rejection, complementing the findings of Desruennes et al.,[2] who also found no change in peak early mitral flow velocity, but differing from the data of Valantine et al.,[9] who found the early mitral peak flow velocity increased with cardiac rejection. Desruennes et al. indicated that their results may have differed from those of Valentine et al. because of the use of pulsed-wave Doppler as opposed to continuous-wave Doppler in the latter.

The current study also is consistent with other reports that Doppler echocardiographic indices of diastolic function shorten during moderate rejection and return toward baseline following treatment.[2] For effective use of this diagnostic test, however, patients must be used as their own control.

The determination and treatment of cardiac rejection remain a primary clinical and financial obstacle in the care of transplant patients. Although endomyocardial biopsy is the gold standard, it suffers from well-defined technical, financial, and sampling problems.[1] Thus techniques that would allow a decrease in the frequency of endomyocardial biopsy without sacrificing sensitivity would aid in patient management. Nuclear magnetic resonance imaging and monoclonal antibody basal imaging are newer techniques that may be of help but their lack of availability and high cost will continue to be drawbacks in the foreseeable future. Echocardiography is widely available and generally reasonably priced when compared with other available modalities for the detection of acute cardiac rejection. Serial Doppler measurements of diastolic and systolic function utilizing each patient as his or her own control provides a high index of suspicion for rejection episodes that may subsequently be confirmed by endomyocardial biopsy. Unfortunately, changes in Doppler echocardiographic indices of diastolic and systolic function are not specific to rejection and may be altered by such factors as loading conditions, time from surgery, etc. In addition, not all patients with biopsy proven rejection had significant changes in Doppler echocardiographic indices. Thus a negative echocardiographic examination does not exclude rejection, and these indices must be viewed in context with other associated signs and symptoms of rejection.

ACKNOWLEDGMENTS

We wish to acknowledge the assistance of Karen Calvin and Donna Hunn, RN in the preparation of the manuscript.

REFERENCES

1. Billingham ME: Endomyocardial biopsy interpretation in cyclosporine-treated cardiac recipients. In Emery RW, Pritzker MR (eds): Cardiothoracic Transplantation. Cardiac Surgery: State of the Art Reviews, vol. 2, no. 4. Philadelphia, Hanley & Belfus, Inc., 1988.
2. Desruennes M, Corcos T, Cabrol A, et al: Doppler echocardiography for the diagnosis of acute cardiac allograft rejection. J Am Coll Cardiol 12:63–70, 1988.
3. Greenberg ML, Uretsky BF, Reddy S, et al: Long-term hemodynamic follow-up of cardiac transplant patients treated with cyclosporine and prednisone. Circulation 71:487–494, 1985.
4. Hatle L, Angelsen B, Tromsdal A: Noninvasive assessment of atrioventricular pressure half-time by Doppler ultrasound. Circulation 60:1096–1104, 1979.
5. Kronik G, Slany J, Mosslacher H: Comparative value of eight M-mode echocardiographic formulas for determining LV stroke volume. Circulation 60:308, 1979.
6. Kurland RJ, West J, Kelley S, et al: Magnetic resonance imaging to detect heart transplant rejection: Sensitivity and selectivity. Transplant Proc 21:2537–2544, 1989.
7. Sahn DJ, DeMaria A, Kisslo J, Weyman A: The Committee on M-mode Standardization of the American Society of Echocardiography. Recommendations regarding quantization of M-mode echocardiography: Results of a survey of echocardiographic measurements. Circulation 58:1072–1083, 1978.
8. St. Goar FG, Gibbons R, Schnittger I, et al: Left ventricular diastolic function—Doppler changes in early post cardiac transplant recipients (abstract). J Am Coll Cardiol 13 (Suppl A).
9. Valantine HA, Appleton CP, Hatle LK, et al: A hemodynamic and Doppler echocardiographic study of ventricular function in long-term cardiac allograft recipients. Circulation 79:66–75, 1989.
10. Valantine HA, Appleton CP, Hatle LK, et al: Influence of recipient atrial contraction on left ventricular filling dynamics of the transplanted heart assessed by Doppler echocardiography. Am J Cardiol 59:1159–1163, 1987.

KATHRYN R. LOVE, MD

DONOR-TRANSMITTED INFECTIONS

Clinical Assistant Professor
  of Medicine
University of Minnesota Medical
  School

Infectious Diseases Consultant
  and Hospital Epidemiologist
Abbott Northwestern Hospital
Minneapolis, Minnesota

Reprint requests to:
Kathryn R. Love, MD
2545 Chicago Avenue South
Suite 211
Minneapolis, MN 55404

The phenomenon of microbial latency allows the transmission of infected donor "passenger" cells along with a transplanted organ. Subsequent anti-rejection therapy tips the balance in favor of the microbe, and donor organisms reactivate in the allograft causing primary infection in the recipient. The seronegative recipient (SNR) of an organ from a seropositive donor (SPD) will become infected 80–100% of the time, and disease (infection with clinical manifestations) results in 60–80% of these primary infections. A donor strain of organism introduced into a seropositive recipient (SPR) can also cause a primary infection which tends to cause fewer symptoms, presumably because of preexisting immunity to the similar recipient strain. This chapter highlights organisms documented to be transmitted by transplantation of heart and/or lungs (listed below) and focuses on primary infection and disease.

 *Cytomegalovirus (CMV)
 *Epstein-Barr virus (EBV)
  Hepatitis B virus (HBV)
  Delta virus (DV)
  Non-A, non-B hepatitis virus (NANB)
 *Human immune deficiency virus (HIV-1)
 *Toxoplasma gondii (TG)

 * = documented transmission in thoracic
     transplantation

CYTOMEGALOVIRUS

Viral Pathogenesis
Cytomegalovirus (CMV), a DNA virus that is classified as human herpesvirus 5, replicates best in fibroblasts and less well in epithelial and

other cells. It is generally accepted that white blood cells are the carriers of latent virus. Replication of CMV is a relatively slow process and it can take 4 days for release of progeny virus, which may contribute to the long incubation period between infection and disease.[1]

Immunosuppressive regimens interfere with the cell-mediated mechanisms that check the activation and expression of virus-infected cells. The frequency of CMV infections, however, has decreased in the cyclosporine era, particularly with low-dose triple regimens,[2] and there is no good evidence that prophylactic OKT3 (Orthoclone, Ortho Pharmaceuticals, Raritan, NJ) results in a higher incidence of CMV disease.

Clinical Syndromes

In primary infection the incubation period is 2–8 weeks with a mean of 6.5 weeks. Ninety percent of symptomatic infection occurs within 4 months.[3] Reactivation of latent recipient infection takes longer, owing to the time it takes to induce cell-mediated immune deficiency with anti-rejection therapy, added to the usual incubation period.

Primary infections occur in 80–100% of SNR receiving organs from SPD, and are more likely to be symptomatic (CMV disease as opposed to infection) than reactivation infections, except in heart lung/lung transplant recipients (HL/LTR), in whom all CMV infection tends to symptomatic and severe. This may be due to the large inoculum size transferred with transplantation of lungs and the more intense immunosuppression required by these patients.

Dummer et al.[4] have defined a classification of CMV disease that provides a standardized approach:

1. CMV Syndrome
   Fever of 38°C for at least 1 week without any other source
   Laboratory evidence of CMV infection (see Diagnosis)
   One or more of the following:
   • white blood count $\leq$ 4000/mm³
   • platelets $\leq$ 100,000/mm³
   • atypical lymphocytes $\geq$ 3%
   Myalgias, arthralgias, and headache are nonspecific but often present, as is anemia.
2. Localized CMV disease
   Tissue invasion of a single organ, proven histologically; and/or positive tissue culture
3. Disseminated CMV disease
   Tissue involvement of two or more non-contiguous sites

Common CMV infections in transplantation are enteritis, pneumonitis, and hepatitis. Rare CMV infections in transplantation include retinitis, myocarditis, and encephalitis with or without meningitis.

Enteritis. Cytomegalovirus can cause mucosal disease anywhere along the gastrointestinal (GI) tract, including the oral cavity. Upper GI presentation consists of epigastric pain often exacerbated by movement, nausea, vomiting, and anorexia. Esophageal involvement may cause odynophagia. Colonic infection presents with diarrhea and lower abdominal pain. In both instances, occult or overt bleeding may occur. CSA levels tend to decrease, reflecting absorption abnormalities.

Pneumonitis. Patients with pneumonitis present with constitutional illness, dyspnea, tachypnea, dry cough, and a bilateral interstitial infiltrate on chest roentgenogram.

Diagnosis

A CMV workup should include blood, urine, and throat cultures for CMV, and IgG and IgM serology. Endoscopy for CMV enteritis will reveal nonspecific findings of inflammation, erosions, and aphthous ulcerations; the presence of large antral folds seems to be more specific for CMV disease.[5] Histopathology shows inflammation and characteristic perinuclear inclusion bodies of CMV. Cultures are usually positive.

The diagnosis of CMV pneumonia is made by bronchoscopy with bronchoalveolar lavage (BAL) and brushings. Although biopsied tissue showing compatible pathology and growing CMV would add to the sensitivity of diagnosis, it is no longer necessary as a requirement for obtaining the experimental drug ganciclovir (Syntex Laboratories, Mountainview, CA), and the added risk is therefore prohibitive. One report stated that the isolation of CMV from BAL fluid is insufficient evidence of CMV pneumonitis and described a technique for establishing specifically the infection of alveolar macrophages which seems more accurately to indicate invasive CMV infection.[24]

Isolation Technique. Rapid diagnostic techniques have contributed to improvement in the results of treatment of CMV disease. Monoclonal antibody specific for the immediate-early and early antigens that are produced within hours of CMV infection can be applied directly to clinical material[6-8] or indirectly to tissue culture at 24–48 hours to provide prompt diagnosis. The direct technique can give an answer within a few hours but is not yet in widespread use. Some centers perform an immunoperoxidase stain on BAL material.

New techniques being evaluated include *in situ* hybridization with DNA probes,[9] which detects specific viral genomes, and the polymerase chain reaction method, whereby viral genomes are amplified to increase the sensitivity of detection.[10,11] Neither technique has demonstrated increased diagnostic sensitivity over rapid fluorescent monoclonal antibody methods for non-latent infection (C. Jordan, personal communication).

The ultimate diagnostic tool is still a positive culture, which takes 1–4 weeks and is characterized by a typical cytopathic effect (CPE) on human foreskin or embryonic fibroblast culture.

Serology. Seroconversion (negative to positive) or a four-fold rise of CMV IgG antibody titer is supportive evidence of CMV infection. Although neutralizing antibody (NA) is produced early and the NA test is exquisitely sensitive, levels are low. The test is technically difficult and takes 2 weeks to perform. The complement fixation test for IgG is therefore the most widely used serologic test for CMV. It is specific but less sensitive, although it is comparable to other tests if the glycine-extracted antigen is used.[12] The detection of specific IgM is indicative of recent infection, as IgM antibodies rise early and subside quickly in contrast to long-standing, if not life-long, IgG titers. However, IgM antibody can be nonspecific in terms of correlating with clinical disease, or may not be generated at all in immunosuppressed patients.

Treatment

The advent of ganciclovir has had a great impact on the previously poor outcome of CMV disease in transplant recipients. Cumulative data indicate almost universal resolution of CMV enteritis and a 50–60% cure rate for CMV pneumonia.[25-29]

Decreasing immunosuppression, particularly azathiaoprine, is also advisable, but careful reinstitution of higher doses must be undertaken when the infection and its immunosuppressive effects are resolving, as rejection can occur. CMV hyperimmunoglobulin (CMVIG) alone has not proved beneficial in treating serious CMV disease.[30] Ganciclovir given with CMVIG[31] or high-dose commercially available intravenous immune globulin (IVIG)[32] resulted in a significantly higher response rate in bone marrow transplant recipients with CMV pneumonia.

Jordan et al. recently reported three patients in whom ganciclovir-resistant CMV was isolated; in one, resistance emerged on therapy. Ganciclovir was ineffective in eradicating virus from the blood and all three patients (2 with AIDS, 1 with chronic lymphocytic leukemia) died with active CMV disease. Trisodium phosphonoformate (Foscarnet, Astra), a virostatic agent, has been used with some success in the treatment of CMV disease in immunocompromised hosts, including a heart transplant recipient.[33] This drug could serve as an alternative in the patient with ganciclovir-resistant CMV.

Prevention

Although matching donor and recipient by CMV serostatus reduces the incidence of CMV disease in renal transplant recipients,[14] this approach is not an option in thoracic transplantation. Seronegative recipients should receive seronegative blood, however.[15]

Passive Immunization. There is evidence in bone marrow transplant recipients and in renal transplant recipients that intramuscular (IM) and intravenous (IV) CMVIG, IV CMV hyperimmune plasma, and unselected IVIG may prevent CMV disease or at least attenuate it.[15-20] Doses of IVIG have ranged from 20 ml/kg given once every two weeks[18] to 500 mg/kg every week.[21]

More recently, attention has focused on neutralizing antibodies (NA). All hyperimmunoglobulin preparations have been produced from high anti-CMV antibody titer plasma selected by enzyme-linked immunosorbent assay (ELISA), complement fixation (CF), or indirect hemagglutination (IHA) techniques. ELISA titers do not, however, correlate well with neutralization activity.[22] Emanuel et al. showed that commercially available IVIGs were as effective as "hyperimmune" globulins in neutralizing CMV.[23] In France, Gibert et al. have demonstrated that IMIG of placental origin offers similar ELISA antibody titers and neutralizing activity equal to or greater than that of plasma-derived "hyperimmune" CMVIG.[22] At several centers prophylactic and therapeutic trials of newly developed human monoclonal CMV antibodies with high levels of neutralizing activity will be undertaken.[23,24] A readily available highly active product that is not prohibitively expensive is needed. An IM preparation would be particularly useful. At present, CMVIG or IVIG prophylaxis of thoracic transplant recipients should be reserved for the highest risk situations, i.e., the seronegative recipient of a heart lung/lung transplant recipient from a seropositive donor, or a seropositive heart lung/lung transplant recipient, as severe CMV disease is much more prevalent in these patients than in heart transplant recipients.

Active Immunization. Plotkin has reported the interim results of a randomized, controlled trial of live human CMV (Towne strain) vaccine in 172 renal transplant recipients. The incidence of CMV infection and disease was not altered but the frequency of severe disease was markedly decreased in vaccinated vs. placebo-treated seropositive recipients of seropositive donor kidneys (P < .05).

Both groups received similar regimens to prevent and treat rejection and had the same average number of rejection episodes. One- and five-year actuarial survival rates for cadaver renal allografts were 73% and 62%, respectively, for vaccinees, vs. 40% and 25%, respectively, for control placebo patients.[34]

Acyclovir. Meyers et al. reported a significant decrease in CMV infection and serious disease with concomitant improvement in overall survival in seropositive bone marrow transplant recipients receiving intravenous acyclovir prophylaxis (500 mg/m^2 every 8 hours) for 5 days before and 30 days after transplant.[35] Dummer et al., however, noted no benefit from 90 days of post-heart-transplant high-dose acyclovir, and 3 of 10 patients succumbed to CMV pneumonia after the drug was discontinued.[36]

Balfour et al. have reported the results of a randomized placebo-controlled study of prophylaxis with acyclovir in renal transplant recipients using maximum doses of 800 mg q.i.d. for 3 months post transplant. The incidence of CMV infection/disease was significantly decreased and, in particular, primary infection in seronegative recipients was averted.[37]

Ganciclovir. This highly active nucleoside analogue is more toxic than acyclovir and therefore is less appropriate for prophylaxis. A trial of combined ganciclovir and CMVIG prophylaxis in allogenic bone marrow transplantation is under way (C. Jordan, personal communication). Clearly trials of combinations of active and passive immunization and antiviral prophylaxis need to be undertaken.

EPSTEIN-BARR VIRUS

Viral Pathogenesis

The Epstein-Barr virus (EBV) binds to the complement receptor C3d (other terminology: CR2) found on B-1 lymphocytes, developing T-lymphocytes, non-T, non-B lymphocytes, and epithelial cells. The infection of B-lymphocytes has been the most extensively studied. In primary infection two types of processes occur: productive, cytolytic infection, which results in linear DNA replication and new viral progeny; and non-productive, latent infection, which does not lyse the host cell but, rather, results in the polyclonal or monoclonal transformation of cells into lymphoblastoid cell lines (LCL) containing episomal viral genomes replaced in constant balance with host cell DNA. These LCL produce their own B-cell growth factor and grow indefinitely (immortalization); they not only perpetually produce viral antigens but also secrete immunoglobulins and may facilitate augmented transcription of cellular oncogenes. In normal hosts, nonproductive infection predominates and a latent carrier state ensues.[1-3]

Because the lymphomas seen in transplantation are of recipient cell origin,[4] the sequence of events in the development of lymphoproliferative syndromes (LPS) as a result of primary infection in recipients would seem to be as follows: donor LCL are transplanted as passenger cells; reactivation occurs due to recipient immunosuppression; and new viral progeny establish primary infection in the recipient. Uncontrolled outgrowth of resultant recipient LCL can culminate in lymphoproliferative syndromes of recipient cell origin. Proliferating B-cells of donor origin have also been reported,[6,20] and would presumably represent reactivated infection in passenger LCL.

Viral expression in transformed cells is dependent upon intracellular and extracellular host regulatory phenomena. The immune response to EBV-induced polyclonal activation of B-lymphocytes is characterized by an increase in suppressor/cytotoxic (T8) lymphocytes, which suppress outgrowth of LCL and virus-associated immunoglobulin synthesis.

Cyclosporine A (CSA) spares suppressor cell populations but interferes with interleukin 1 and 2 production, thereby blocking the formation of specific cytotoxic effector cells that would normally limit the outgrowth of EBV virus LCL.[5]

OKT3 abrogates cytotoxic T-cell effector functions by modulating the T3-Ti complex on all mature T-lymphocytes until the receptor complex reappears, thereby blocking the killing of LCL and preventing the long-term elimination of virally-transformed lymphocytes.[6]

Azathioprine and prednisone have nonspecific suppressive effects on many immune cell types.

Clinical Syndromes

Investigators at the University of Minnesota[7,8] and the University of Pittsburgh,[9,10] among others, have clearly linked post-transplant lymphoma to EBV.

The incidence of lymphoma in renal transplant recipients is 30–50 times that of the general population,[11] and 26% of malignancies in 1600 transplant recipients recorded at the Cincinnati Transplant Tumor Registry are lymphomas, predominantly pleomorphic large-cell tumors resembling immunoblastic sarcoma.[3] Lymphoid neoplasms occurred in 7% of patients surviving more than 3 months after cardiac transplantation with conventional immunosuppression at Stanford University.[12] In the early CSA era the same center reported a 13% incidence of lymphoma.[13] More recent studies using lower doses of CSA without other immunosuppressive agents have shown reduction in both the frequency of serologic reactivation and the incidence of lymphoma.[3]

Because more than 90% of adults have serologic evidence of EBV infection, primary infection in adult transplant recipients is unusual; in children, however, 50% of EBV infections are primary. Ho et al. cite an incidence of primary infection in approximately 80% of seronegatives and reactivation in 40% of seropositives. The overall incidence of lymphoproliferative syndromes in Pittsburgh in 1981–1985 was 1.4% (adults 0.8%, children 4%). Primary infection caused 70% of LPS overall, and 10 of 11 children with LPS had primary infection. Therefore, primary infection was much more likely than reactivation to result in LPS. The frequency of EBV-associated LPS in children had not changed between 1983 and 1986 but had declined in adults. This was attributed to the ability to monitor CSA levels and adjust doses.[10] Hanto et al. have devised a clinical and pathologic classification of EBV-associated LPS in renal transplant recipients (Table 1).[16]

Group I patients (mean age 23 years[3]) present within the first year of transplantation, may have "acyclovir-responsive" disease (see comments under Treatment), and may not require reduction in immunosuppression.

Group II patients are similar to those in Group I but pathologically show evidence of malignant transformation. The B-cell proliferation is still considered to be acyclovir-responsive but concomitant reduction in immunosuppression is needed and subsequent serial biopsies are indicated to monitor for monoclonal transformation. The patients often succumb to aggressive disseminated disease characterized by refractory lactic acidosis and disseminated intravascular coagulation.

TABLE 1. Clinicopathologic Grouping of EBV-LPS (Hanto et al.[16])

	Clinical	Histology	Immunologic Cell Typing	Cytogenetics
Group I (benign)	Infectious mononucleosis-like illness	Polymorphic diffuse B-cell hyperplasia	Polyclonal B-cell proliferation	Normal karyotype
Group II (early malignant transformation)	Infectious mononucleosis-like illness	Polymorphic B-cell lymphoma	Polyclonal B-cell proliferation	Clonal cytogenetic abnormalities
Group III (monoclonal lymphoma)	Localized solid tumor masses	Polymorphic B-cell lymphoma	Monoclonal B-cell proliferation	Clonal cytogenetic abnormalities

Recently, EBV genomes have been demonstrated in three T-cell lymphomas in patients with chronic EBV infection.[14] A T-cell lymphoma was reported in a renal transplant recipient but EBV genomes were not specifically sought. This association bears further study.[15]

Group III patients tend to be older (mean age 48 years[3]) and present longer after transplantation (average 6 years[3]) with acyclovir-insensitive solid tumors, presumably composed of latently-infected B-cells of monoclonal origin. The prognosis is poor, with a mortality rate of $> 80\%$.

Patients in all groups may be asymptomatic at presentation. Ho et al. found no difference in the clinical course according to age, time of onset, or clonality;[9] however, their patients fit well into Hanto's clinicopathologic groups.[10]

Diagnosis

Serology. The normal host generates high levels of IgG and IgM antibody to viral capsid antigen (VCA-IgG, VCA-IgM) during acute infection along with transient levels of antibody to the diffuse component of early antigen (EA-d). Weeks to months later antibody to EBV nuclear antigen (EBNA) develops. In some patients with protracted illness EA-r (restricted component) antibody may emerge when EA-d lapses. The only reliable marker of infection in transplant recipients is seroconversion or a four-fold rise in VCA IgG. Some patients may generate an IgM response and some may also develop persistent EA-r antibody. None manifests heterophile antibodies.

Other Studies. Lymphoproliferative lesions should be examined histologically and surface markers of lymphoid cells studied to determine clonality. EBNA staining of touch imprints and frozen sections using appropriate controls, and DNA hybridization studies on fresh tissue frozen at $-70°C$ to detect EBV genomes, help to establish EBV causality.[17] Karyotypic analysis also helps to detect the presence of cytogenetic abnormalities such as oncogenic translocations.

Treatment

Altering Immunosuppression. In 1984 Starzl et al. described 17 recipients of various organs who subsequently developed LPS while on regimens containing CSA. In patients in whom LPS was diagnosed premortem, immunosuppression was decreased in all but one. Eight patients had combinations of surgical excision, irradiation, chemotherapy, and acyclovir.[18] Overall, tumor-free survival occurred in 11, 6 of whom had reduction of immunosuppression as the only treatment.

In Pittsburgh, the usual approach to patients with EBV-LPS is to decrease CSA to a dose that provides serum levels of 50–100 ng/ml by high-density liquid chromatography (HDLC). If an organ is expendable, immunosuppression may be stopped altogether. Acyclovir is reserved for unresponsive lesions.

Acyclovir. The group at the University of Minnesota has been the main proponent of acyclovir therapy (500 mg/m^2 every 8 hours) for patients with Group I or Group II LPS (vide supra). However, although acyclovir inhibits EBV replication, reduces numbers of VCA-positive cells, decreases the number of viral genomes per cell *in vitro,* and suppresses oral EBV shedding *in vivo*, the effects persist only during the course of therapy. Return of viral replication and clinical LPS occurs when acyclovir is stopped. Of particular concern is the possibility that acyclovir therapy may facilitate the transition from polyclonal to monoclonal B-cell lymphoma; such tumors contain latently infected LCL which are acyclovir-insensitive because there is no active production of DNA polymerase for acyclovir to inhibit.[19]

Ganciclovir. Ganciclovir is more potent *in vitro* than acyclovir against EBV. A recent report details two patients with severe polyclonal LPS unresponsive to reduction of immunosuppression and acyclovir who were treated with ganciclovir at a dose of 3 mg/kg every 12 hours. One patient survived and is free of evidence of LPS 6 months after transplant nephrectomy. More data are clearly needed.

Monoclonal Antibodies. Blanche et al. reported success with the treatment of two children with EBV polyclonal LPS following HLA-mismatched bone marrow transplantation with T-cell depletion. Two antibodies were used: CD24, which binds B cells at all steps of differentiation; and CD21, an anti-C3d (anti-CR2) receptor antibody. Both patients had failed cessation of CSA but had complete resolution of abnormalities over 2–3 weeks after antibody infusions and remain well after 1 year of follow-up.[20]

Prevention

The population at risk is the seronegative recipient of a seropositive organ; this is almost exclusively a young patient for whom no practical means of prevention exists. Because there is some evidence that OKT3 may potentiate EBV-induced lymphoproliferation,[6,21] it might be advisable to forego OKT3 prophylaxis in young patients (S. Dummer, personal communication) and to consider this risk when using OKT3 or any antilymphocyte preparation to treat rejection in this population.

HUMAN IMMUNE DEFICIENCY VIRUS (HIV)

Exogenous infection of SNR has now been reported in transplantation of kidney, heart, liver, pancreas, and bone marrow, and in bone and skin grafting. Overt acquired immune deficiency syndrome (AIDS) can be seen as early as 4 months post transplant. Bowen et al.[1] described the serologic events following transplantation of a kidney from an unsuspected seropositive donor into a seronegative recipient; at 4 days postoperatively, p24 antigen could be measured and antibody production started on day 51.

This case was also instructive in that donor's family and friends denied any high-risk activities and the HIV antibody was negative; however, a second antibody test, the result of which was known only postoperatively, was positive. In retrospect the first test was probably falsely negative through dilution by massive blood transfusion of the donor, a motor vehicle accident victim. Repeated questioning of friends revealed that the donor had been homosexual.

Another pitfall in HIV antibody testing has been identified by Wittwer et al.,[2] who found a 25% incidence of false-positive HIV antibody tests by ELISA in renal transplant candidates with $> 50\%$ reactivity in lymphocyte panels, compared with the incidence in the general blood donor pool of $< 1\%$. Western blot was negative in these patients but with its overall false-positive rate of 8% (exclusive of ELISA results), false positives for both tests could be predicted to occur in this subpopulation. The authors recommend testing with the ELISA based on viral antigens produced in the LAV cell line CEM-F (Genetic Systems), which yielded no false-positive results in their patients.

Carbone et al.[3] stated that the diagnosis of AIDS in a transplant recipient is difficult, as many of the infections and malignancies can be common to both types of immunodeficiencies. He suggested that the type of infection, timing of onset, humoral response to the organism, T-cell lymphocyte subset characteristics, and type of immunosuppression can help to distinguish between complications of immunosuppression and AIDS. The Centers for Disease Control (CDC) changed the surveillance case definition of AIDS in 1987, however, to include "indicator diseases" in patients with other causes of immunodeficiency as long as serologic evidence of HIV infection is present.[4] Therefore, it is no longer difficult to make the diagnosis of AIDS in a transplant patient, but Carbone's observations help to differentiate between contributing immunodeficient states.

The following recommendations are adapted from Rubin et al.:[5]

1. All potential donors and recipients should be screened for HIV antibody as close to the time of transplant as possible and before multiple blood transfusions in the donor.

2. Careful histories should be obtained from donor and recipient to ascertain exposure to high-risk activities, including male homosexual/bisexual experience, intravenous drug abuse, hemophilia, imprisonment, immigration from endemic areas, and sexual intercourse with high-risk persons. Strong consideration should be given to excluding donors with such histories regardless of serostatus.

3. The inadvertently transplanted seronegative recipient of a seropositive donor, or the recipient who seroconverts postoperatively, should be treated with azidothymidine (AZT), although at the lower doses suggested by Erice et al.[6] to avoid synergistic bone marrow toxicity between azathioprine and AZT. This would entail starting with 100 mg every 8 hours and increasing gradually after 3-4 weeks (if no side effects occur) to the usual dose of 200 mg every 4 hours.

Two other retroviruses (HIV-2 and HTLV-1) hold potential for transmission in the transplant setting. The first is a cause of AIDS in West Africa and, by extension, in Western Europe. The second virus causes T-cell leukemias and lymphomas and a spastic paraparesis in Japan, the Caribbean, and the southeastern United States. Routine screening is not yet available.

TOXOPLASMA GONDII

Pathogenesis

The life cycle of the protozoan *Toxoplasma gondii* is completed in the cat, the only animal known to excrete the infectious oocyst,[1] which is ingested by a variety of intermediate hosts, including domestic animals whose meat and organs contain encysted parasites.[2] Humans acquire toxoplasma by ingesting soil contaminated with oocysts while farming, gardening, or changing cat litter, or by eating uncooked or undercooked meat such as steak tartare, or possibly by drinking unpasteurized milk.[3]

Less commonly, the organism can be transmitted transplacentally to cause congenital toxoplasma, or via blood transfusion, especially leukocyte transfusions. *Toxoplasma gondii* remains viable in banked blood for 50 days at 5°C and can be isolated from buffy coat cells of the blood over long periods of time in asymptomatic patients.[4] Because cysts persist in muscle, heart, brain, leukocytes, and lymph nodes for years, the organism can also be transmitted by transplantation.[5] Heart transplant recipients have a higher incidence of toxoplasmosis than do renal or liver transplant recipients.[6]

Clinical Syndromes

Prevalence of antibody to *Toxoplasma gondii* varies with age and geographical location. In the usual thoracic organ donor population in the United States, approximately 15–30% will have had toxoplasmic infection (data adapted from Feldman[7]), and the transplantation of a heart from a seropositive donor into a seronegative recipient has been estimated to occur 10% of the time.[8]

Clinical disease in thoracic transplant recipients occurs in the context of primary infection and is rare as a consequence of reactivation.[9] Experience with allogeneic BMTR may differ.[10] Disease can coincide with seroconversion between 4–6 weeks post transplantation or can follow by as much as 10 months.[9]

Acquired toxoplasmosis in the immunodeficient host is a disseminated disease with frequent involvement of the central nervous system with encephalitis, meningoencephalitis, or mass lesions and cerebrospinal fluid mononuclear pleocytosis with high protein concentration. In heart transplant recipients, myocarditis simulating graft rejection is a more common mode of presentation. Pneumonitis can occur concomitantly.[11]

Diagnosis

Strict pathologic and serologic criteria for the diagnosis of active infection and disease have been advocated by Remington[9,11] and as applied to thoracic transplantation include:

- compatible clinical manifestations
- histologic demonstration of toxoplasma tachyzoites in body fluid tissue or in association with numerous cysts in a localized area of tissue
- isolation of *Toxoplasma gondii* from blood or body fluids
- conversion from negative to positive on toxoplasma IgG antibody
- high toxoplasma IgM titers with a single high-titer IgG antibody test

Tests in common usage include the indirect fluorescent antibody test (IFA), which measures IgG antibodies and the IgM immunofluorescent antibody test (IgM-IFA). Significant ($\geq$ 4 fold) rises in antibody titer can occur without symptoms in transplant patients and many will not generate an IgM-IFA response.

Treatment

Pyrimethamine and sulfadiazine or triple-sulfa constitute successful therapy in most cases. Patients with significant organ involvement should receive a loading dose of pyrimethamine, 50 mg PO twice a day for two days followed by a maintenance dose of 25 mg every other day or 25–50 mg daily for the first 2 weeks if the patient is severely ill. Complete blood and platelet counts must be followed closely; hematologic side effects can be countered with oral folinic acid (leukovorin) 5–10 mg per day.

Sulfadiazine, 75 mg/kg (up to 4 gm total) loading dose, followed by 100 mg/kg/day (up to 8 gm/day) in two divided doses, is added for synergy.

The regimen is given for 4–6 weeks after the resolution of symptoms and signs, often resulting in therapy for 6 months or more. Approximately 80% of patients improve.[11]

Prevention

Donor and recipient should be tested and seronegative recipients of organs from seropositive donors be periodicially retested post transplant. As there is a high likelihood of developing significant disease, asymptomatic seronegative donors who seroconvert are usually treated. Seronegative recipients of seronegative organs should be taught to avoid activities that would expose them to Toxoplasma: (1) use gloves when handling raw meat, (2) eat well-cooked meat, (3) delegate litter-box care to another, and (4) avoid cat feces while gardening or in children's sandboxes. There is good direct evidence that sulfonamide or sulfa/trimethoprim prophylaxis prevents toxoplasmosis,[6,12] and this may constitute another benefit of *Pneumocystis carinii*/Nocardia pneumonia prevention.

REFERENCES

Cytomegalovirus

1. Ho M: Cytomegalovirus: Biology and infection. In Greenough WB, Merigan TC (eds): Current Topics in Infectious Disease. New York, Plenum, 1982, p 20.
2. Andreone PA, Olivari MT, Elick B, et al: Reduction of infectious complications following heart transplantation with triple drug immunotherapy. J heart Transplant 5:13–19, 1986.
3. Pterson PK, Balfour HH Jr, Marker SC, et al: Cytomegalovirus disease in renal allograft recipients: A prospective study of the clinical features, risk factors and impact of renal transplantation. Medicine (Baltimore) 59:283–300, 1980.
4. Singh N, Drummer JS, Kusne S, et al: Infections with cytomegalovirus and other herpesviruses in 121 liver transplant recipients: Transmission by donated organ and the effect of OKT3 antibodies. J Infect Dis 158:124–131, 1988.
5. Alexander JA, Cuellar RE, Fadden RJ, et al: Cytomegalovirus infection of the upper gastrointestinal tract before and after liver transplantation. Transplantation 46:378–382, 1988.
6. van der Bij W, Forensma R, van Son WJ, et al: Rapid immunodiagnosis of active cytomegalovirus infection by monoclonal antibody staining of blood leucocytes. J Med Virol 25:179–188, 1988.
7. van der Bij W, van Dyk RB, van Son WJ, et al: Antigen test for early diagnosis of active cytomegalovirus infection in heart transplant recipients. J Heart Transplant 7:106–110, 1988.
8. Crawford SW, Bowden RA, Hackman RC, et al: Rapid detection of cytomegalovirus infection by bronchoalveolar lavage and centrifugation culture. Ann Intern Med 108:180–185, 1984.
9. Stockel E, Popow-Kraupp T, Heinz FX, et al: Potential of in situ hybridization for early diagnosis of productive cytomegalovirus infection. J Clin Microbiol 26:2536–2540, 1988.
10. Demmler GJ, Buffone GJ, Schimbor CM, et al: Detection of cytomegalovirus in urine from newborns by using polymerase chain reaction DNA amplification. J Infect Dis 158:1177–1184, 1988.
11. Shibata D, Martin WJ, Appleman MD, et al: Detection of cytomegalovirus DNA in peripheral blood of patients infected with human immunodeficiency virus. J Infect Dis 158:1185–1192, 1988.
12. Ho M: Cytomegalovirus: Biology and infection. In Greenough WB, Merigan TC (eds): Current Topics in Infectious Disease. New York, Plenum, 1982, p 53.
13. Erice A, Chou S, Biron KK, et al: Progressive disease due to ganciclovir-resistant cytomegalovirus in immunocompromised patients. N Engl J Med 320:289–292, 1989.
14. Ludwin D, White N, Tsai S, et al: Results of prospective matching for cytomegalovirus status in renal transplant recipients. Transplant Proc 19:3433–3434, 1987.

15. Bowden RA, Ayers M, Flournoy N, et al: Cytomegalovirus immunoglobulin and seronegative blood products to prevent primary cytomegalovirus infection after bone marrow transplant. N Engl J Med 314:1006–1010, 1986.

16. Meyers JD, Leszczynski J, Zaia JA, et al: Prevention of cytomegalovirus infection by cytomegalovirus immune globulin after bone marrow transplantation. Ann Intern Med 98:442–446, 1983.

17. Winston DJ, Pollard RB, Ho WG, et al: Cytomegalovirus immune plasma in bone marrow transplant recipients. Ann Intern Med 97:11–18, 1982.

18. Winston DJ, Ho WG, Cheng-Hsien L, et al: Intravenous immune globulin for prevention of cytomegalovirus infection and interstitital pneumonia after bone marrow transplantation. Ann Intern Med 106:12–18, 1987.

19. Snydman DR, Werner BG, Heinze-Lacey B, et al: Use of cytomegalovirus immune globulin to prevent cytomegalovirus disease in renal transplant recipients. N Engl J Med 317:1049–1054, 1987.

20. Snydman DR, Werner BG, Tilney NL, et al: A further analysis of primary cytomegalovirus disease prevention in renal transplant recipients with a cytomegalovirus immune globulin: Interim comparison of a randomized and an open-label trial. Transplant Proc 20:24–30, 1988.

21. Elfenbein G, Krischer J, Rand K, et al: Preliminary results of a multicenter trial to prevent death from cytomegalovirus pneumonia with intravenous immunoglobulin after allogenic bone marrow transplantation. Transplant Proc 19(Suppl 7):138–143, 1987.

22. Gibert R, Habib R, Allard JP, et al: Prevalence of CMV ELISA antibody: Titer and neutralizing activity in intramuscular immune globulin of placental origin. Transplant Proc 19:4083–4086, 1987.

23. Emanuel D: Issues concerning the use of intravenous immunoglobulin for the immunoprophylaxis of cytomegalovirus infections in allogenic bone marrow transplant recipients. Monogr Allergy (Karger, Basel) 23:216–224, 1988.

24. Emanuel D, Peppard J, Chehimi J, et al: The diagnostic, prophylactic, and therapeutic uses of monoclonal antibodies to human cytomegalovirus. Transplant Proc 19(Suppl 7):132–137, 1987.

25. Love KR: Nonbacterial infections in thoracic transplantation. In Emery RW, Pritzker MR (eds): Cardiothoracic Transplantation. Cardiac Surgery: State of the Art Reviews, vol. 2, no. 4. Philadelphia, Hanley & Belfus, Inc., 1988, pp 647–657 (75 references).

26. Harbison MA, DeGirolami PC, Jenkins RL, et al: Ganciclovir therapy of several cytomegalovirus infections in solid-organ transplant recipients. Transplantation 46:82–88, 1988.

27. de Hemptinne B, Lamy ME, Salizzoni M, et al: Successful treatment of cytomegalovirus disease with 9-(1,3-dihydroxy-2 propoxymethyl) guanine). Transplant Proc 20(Suppl 1):652–655, 1988.

28. Paya CV, Hermans PE, Smith TF, et al: Efficacy of ganciclovir in liver and kidney transplant recipients with severe cytomegalovirus infection. Transplantation 46:229–234, 1988.

29. Watson FS, O'Connell JB, Amber IJ, et al: Treatment of cytomegalovirus pneumonia in heart transplant recipients with 9-(1,3-dihydroxy-2-propoxymethyl) guanine (DHPG). J Heart Transpl 7:102–105, 1988.

30. Reed EC, Bowden RA, Dandliker PS, et al: Efficacy of cytomegalovirus immunoglobulin in marrow transplant recipients with cytomegalovirus pneumonia. J Infect Dis 156:641–644, 1987.

31. Reed EC, Bowden RA, Dandliker PS, et al: Treatment of cytomegalovirus pneumonia with ganciclovir and intravenous cytomegalovirus immunoglobulin in patients with bone marrow transplants. Ann Intern Med 15:783–788, 1988.

32. Emanuel D, Cunningham I, Jules-Elysee K, et al: Cytomegalovirus pneumonia after bone marrow transplantation successfully treated with the combination of ganciclovir and high-dose intravenous immunoglobulin. Ann Intern Med 15:777–782, 1988.

33. Locke TJ, Odom NS, Tapson JS, et al: Successful treatment with trisodium phosphonoformate for primary cytomegalovirus infection after heart transplantation. J Heart Transplant 6:120–122, 1987.

34. Brayman KL, Dafoe DC, Smythe WR, et al: Prophylaxis of serious cytomegalovirus infection in renal transplant candidates using live human cytomegalovirus vaccine. Arch Surg 123:1502–1508, 1988.

35. Meyers JD, Reed EC, Shepp DH, et al: Acyclovir for prevention of cytomegalovirus infection and disease after allogeneic marrow transplantation. N Engl J Med 318:70–75, 1988.

36. Dummer JS, White LT, Ho M, et al: Morbidity of cytomegalovirus infection in recipients of heart or heart-lung transplants who received cyclosporine. J Infect Dis 152:1182–1190, 1985.

37. Balfour HH, Chace BA, Stapleton JT, et al: A randomized, placebo-controlled trial of oral acyclovir for the prevention of cytomegalovirus disease in recipients of renal allografts. N Engl J Med 320:1381–1387, 1989.

Epstein-Barr Virus

1. Schooley RT, Dolin R: Epstein: Barr virus (infectious mononucleosis). In Mandell G, Douglas RG Jr, Bennett JE (eds): Principles and Practice of Infectious Diseases, 2nd ed. New York, John Wiley & Sons, 1985, pp 971–982.
2. Dillner J, Kallin B: The Epstein-Barr virus proteins. Adv Cancer Res 50:95–158, 1988.
3. List AF, Greco FA, Vogler LB: Lymphoproliferative disease in immunocompromised hosts: The role of Epstein-Barr virus. J Clin Oncol 5:1673–1689, 1987.
4. Sullivan JL: Epstein-Barr virus and lymphoproliferative disorders. Sem Hematol 25:269–279, 1988.
5. Hanto DW, Gajl Peczalska KJ, Frizzera G, et al: Epstein-Barr virus (EBV)-induced polyclonal and monoclonal B-cell lymphoproliferative diseases occurring after renal transplantation: Clinical, pathologic, and virological findings and implications for therapy. Ann Surg 198:356–369, 1983.
6. Ren EC, Chan SH: Possible enhancement of Epstein-Barr virus infections by the use of OKT3 in transplant recipients. Transplantation 45:988–989, 1988.
7. Hanto DW, Frizzera G, Purtilo D: A clinical spectrum of lymphoproliferative disorders in renal transplant recipients and evidence for the role of Epstein-Barr virus. Cancer Res 41:4253–4261, 1981.
8. Saemundsen AK, Purtilo DT, Sakamoto K: Documentation of Epstein-Barr virus infection in immunodeficient patients with life threatening lymphoproliferative diseases by Epstein-Barr virus complementary RNA/DNA and viral DNA/DNA hybridization. Cancer Res 41:4237–4242, 1981.
9. Ho M, Miller G, Atchison RW: Epstein-Barr virus infections and DNA hybridization studies in post transplantation lymphoma and lymphoproliferative lesions: The role of primary infection. J Infect Dis 152:876–886, 1985.
10. Ho M, Jaffe R, Miller G: The frequency of Epstein-Barr virus infection and associated lymphoproliferative syndrome after transplantation and its manifestation in children. Transplantation 45:719–727, 1988.
11. Penn I: Lymphomas complicating organ transplantation. Transplant Proc 15(Suppl 1):2790–2797, 1983.
12. Weintraub J, Warnke RA: Lymphoma in cardiac allotransplant recipients: Clinical and histological features and immunologic phenotype. Transplantation 33:347–351, 1982.
13. Bieber CP, Hebersling RL, Jamieson SW: Lymphoma in cardiac transplant recipients: Association with the use of cyclosporin A, prednisone, and antithymocyte globulin. In Purtilo DT (ed): Immune Deficiency and Cancer: Epstein-Barr Virus and Lymphoproliferative Malignancies. New York, Plenum, 1984, pp 309–320.
14. Jones JF, Shurin S, Abramowsky C, et al: T cell lymphomas containing Epstein-Barr viral DNA in patients with chronic Epstein-Barr virus infections. N Engl J Med 318:733–741, 1988.
15. Lippman SM, Grogan TM, Carry P, et al: Post transplantation T cell lymphoblastic lymphoma. Am J Med 82:814–816, 1987.
16. Hanto DW, Frizzera G, Gajl-Peczalska KJ: Acyclovir therapy of Epstein-Barr virus-induced post-transplant lymphoproliferative diseases. Transplant Proc 17:89–92, 1985.
17. Purtilo DT, Sakamoto K, Saemundsen AK: Documentation of Epstein-Barr virus infection in immunodeficient patients with life-threatening lymphoproliferative diseases by clinical, virological, and immunopathological studies. Cancer Res 41:4226–4236, 1981.
18. Starzl TE, Porter KA, Iwatsuki S, et al: Reversibility of lymphomas and lymphoproliferative lesions developing under cyclosporin-steroid therapy. Lancet 17:583–587, 1984.
19. Hanto DW, Frizzera G, Gajl-Peczalska KJ: Epstein-Barr virus-induced B-cell lymphoma after renal transplantation: Acyclovir therapy and transition from polyclonal to monoclonal B-cell proliferation. N Engl J Med 306:913–918, 1982.
20. Blanche S, LeDiest F, Veber F, et al: Treatment of severe Epstein-Barr virus-induced polyclonal B-lymphocyte proliferation by anti-B cell monoclonal antibodies: Two cases after HLA-mismatched bone marrow transplantation. Ann Intern Med 108:199–203, 1988.
21. Martin PJ, Shulman HM, Schubach WH, et al: Fatal Epstein-Barr virus-associated proliferation of donor B cells after treatment of acute graft-versus-host disease with a murine anti-T-cell antibody. Ann Intern Med 101:301–305, 1984.

Human Immunodeficiency Virus (HIV)

1. Bowen PA II, Lobel SA, Caruana RJ, et al: Transmission of human immunodeficiency virus (HIV) by transplantation: Clinical aspects and time course analysis of viral antigenemia and antibody production. Ann Intern Med 108:1046–1048, 1988.

2. Wittiwer CT, Smith AM, Ash KO, et al: False-positive antibody tests for human immunodeficiency virus in transplant patients with antilymphocyte antibodies. Transplantation 44:843–844, 1987.
3. Carbone LG, Cohen DJ, Hardy MA, et al: Determination of acquired immunodeficiency syndrome (AIDS) after renal transplantation. Am J Kidney Dis 10:387–392, 1988.
4. Centers for Disease Control: Revision of the CDC Surveillance case definition for acquired immunodeficiency syndrome. MMWR 3s–15s, 1987.
5. Rubin RH, Jenkins RL, Byers WS Jr, et al: The acquired immune deficiency syndrome and transplantation. Transplantation 44:1–4, 1987.
6. Erice A, Rhame FS, Dunn DL, et al: Neutropenia in an HIV-1 infected renal transplant recipient treated with ziodovudine. JAMA 259:3407–3408, 1988.
7. Licensure of screening tests for antibody to human T-lymphotropic virus type I. MMWR 37:736–747, 1988.
8. Cohen ND, Munoz, Reitz BA, et al: Transmission of retroviruses by transfusion of screened blood in patients undergoing cardiac surgery. N Engl J Med 320:1172–1176, 1989.

Toxoplasma gondii

1. Frankel JK: Microbiology of *Toxoplasma gondii*. In Hammond DH, Long PL (eds): Parasite Life Cycle and Immunology. Baltimore, University Park Press, 1973, p 343.
2. Shafer N: Toxoplasmosis. New York State J Med 1049–1061, 1975.
3. Riemann HP, Meyer ME, Theiss JH, et al: Toxoplasmosis in an infant fed unpasteurized goat's milk. J Pediatr 87:573–576, 1975.
4. Miller MJ, Aronson WJ, Remington JS: Late parasitemia in asymptomatic cases of acquired toxoplasmosis. Ann Intern Med 71:139–145, 1969.
5. Ruskin J, Remington JS: Toxoplasmosis in the compromised host. Ann Intern Med 84:193–199, 1976.
6. Rubin RH, Tolkoff-Rubin NE: Opportunistic infections in renal allograft recipients. Transplant Proc 20(Suppl 8):12–18, 1988.
7. Feldman H: Toxoplasmosis: An overview. Bull NY Acad Med 50:110–127, 1974.
8. Luft BJ, Naot Y, Araujo FG, et al: Primary and reactivation toxoplasma infection in patients with cardiac transplants: Clinical spectrum and problems in diagnosis in a defined population. Ann Intern Med 99:27–31, 1983.
9. Shepp DH, Hackman RC, Conley FK, et al: Toxoplasma gondii reactivation identified by detection of parasitemia in tissue culture. Ann Intern Med 103:218–221, 1985.
10. Hofflin JM, Potasman I, Baldwin JC, et al: Infectious complications in heart transplant recipients receiving cyclosporine and corticosteroids. Ann Intern Med 106:209–216, 1987.
11. McCabe RE, Remington JS: *Toxoplasma gondii*. In Mandell GL, Douglas RG, Bennett JE (eds): Infectious Diseases, 2nd ed. New York, John Wiley & Sons, 1979, pp 1540–1549.
12. Andreone PA, Olivari MT, Elick B, et al: Reduction of infectious complications following heart transplantation with triple-drug immunotherapy. J Heart Transplant 5:13–19, 1986.

DANIEL H. DUNN, MD
FRANCES M. HOFFMAN, RN, MS

GENERAL SURGICAL DISEASES AFTER CARDIOPULMONARY TRANSPLANTATION

Daniel H. Dunn, MD
General Surgeon
Abbott Northwestern Hospital
Clinical Assistant Professor
   of Surgery
Department of Surgery
University of Minnesota
Minneapolis, Minnesota

Frances M. Hoffman, RN, MS
Transplant Clinic Coordinator
Division of Cardiothoracic
   Transplantation
Abbott Northwestern Hospital
Minneapolis, Minnesota

Reprint requests to:
Daniel H. Dunn, MD
General Surgery
Abbott Northwestern Hospital
800 East 28th St.
Minneapolis, MN 55407

Case Report. A 40-year-old woman awoke with fever, nausea, and vomiting. Three days later, because of intractable cardiogenic shock from acute viral myocarditis, placement of a Jarvik-7-70 was required. After 44 days of support, a donor heart became available. Following orthotopic cardiac transplantation, she developed acute renal failure and required hemodialysis. Ongoing pulmonary failure required long-term ventilatory support and tracheostomy. The first of many gastrointestinal complications was esophagitis, which was treated medically. She complained of abdominal pain and was found to have pancreatitis, which persisted with frequent exacerbations and remissions. Treated nonoperatively for 2 months, she was kept NPO, making nutritional support a particularly challenging aspect of her care. A feeding jejunostomy was placed on the 32nd postoperative day, and a period of prolonged ileus followed. Recurrent episodes of pancreatitis eventually led to formation of multiple pancreatic pseudocysts localized to the body and tail of the pancreas. Because the pseudocysts did not resolve over a prolonged period, a distal pancreatectomy and splenectomy were performed 5 months after transplantation. During her recovery from this operation, she developed duodenal ulceration despite antacid therapy. Gastric outlet obstruction secondary to persistent peptic ulcer disease required operative intervention eight months following transplantation. A vagotomy and pyloroplasty were followed by a wound abscess.

Recurrent infections, including cytomegalovirus, Candida, Pseuodomonas, and a variety of enteric pathogens involving the lungs, blood, gastrointestinal tract, and central nervous system, eventually led to this patient's death from multiple organ failure and sepsis 10 months following heart transplantation.

INTRODUCTION

This patient's hospital course illustrates the multitude of general surgical problems that thoracic transplant patients may develop. Fortunately, this case is the exception. Most thoracic transplant patients have uncomplicated recoveries and do not require general surgical evaluation. Still others have symptoms that require surgical assessment but do not require intervention. Finally, there are those patients who, following transplantation, develop general surgical diseases that occur frequently in the normal population. Surgical intervention is required but the presence of the disease process is not a direct result of the transplant procedure and/or immunosuppressive therapy. The therapeutic options are unavoidably influenced by the fact that the patient has a heart transplant.

To designate any general surgical disease that occurs after transplantation as a general surgical complication is misleading, since not all are complications of heart transplantation. Villar et al.[8] included patients with cholelithiasis requiring elective cholecystectomy in a series of patients with gastrointestinal complications after heart transplantation. Likewise Colon et al.[4] included biliary colic requiring cholecystectomy as a "complication." In the cardiac transplant group. Steed et al.[8] included inguinal or ventral hernia and perirectal abscess as "general surgical complications" following heart transplantation. If the incidence of true general surgical complications following thoracic transplantation was calculated in these series, it would be quite low. Transplant centers that take a conservative approach to treatment of asymptomatic biliary tract disease will have a lower incidence of general surgical "complications." It is clear that a more accurate method is needed in the classification of general surgical complications in order to distinguish true general surgical complications from general surgical diseases that are not directly related to the transplant procedure.

REVIEW OF GENERAL SURGICAL DISEASES FOLLOWING THORACIC TRANSPLANTATION AT THE MINNEAPOLIS HEART INSTITUTE

From January 1985 to January 1989, 78 cardiac and cardiopulmonary transplants were performed in 75 patients. Sixty-nine patients had heart transplants, three had heart-lung transplants, and three patients had double lung transplants. Twenty-four patients were evaluated postoperatively by the general surgical service and form the basis of this review.

In order to more accurately define the actual incidence of general surgical complications related to transplantation and to distinguish these complications from general surgical diseases experienced by the recipient population, patients are divided into three categories:

    I. General surgical complications related to thoracic transplantation
    II. General surgical diseases occurring after transplantation not directly related to the transplant procedure
    III. Nonsurgical diseases following transplantation which require surgical evaluation

General Surgical Complications in Thoracic Transplant Patients

Eight patients (11%) had general surgical complications following thoracic transplantation (Table 1). A 52-year-old man began to complain of abdominal pain on the first post-transplant day. Persistent hypotension ensued and for 3

TABLE 1.   General Surgical Complications Related to Thoracic Transplantation

Age/Sex	Transplant	Complication	Onset (Postop day)	Surgical Procedure
53 M	heart	small bowel infarction	1	—
40 F	heart	pancreatitis, multiple pseudocysts	29	feeding jejunostomy, distal pancreatectomy, splenectomy
		duodenal ulcer, pyloric channel ulcer	103	—
		pyloric channel obstruction	192	vagotomy, pyloroplasty
39 F	heart-lung	gastric atony	5	pyloroplasty
49 M	heart	bleeding gastric ulcer	13	—
57 M	heart	pancreatitis	5	ERCP and sphincterotomy, cholecystectomy
50 M	heart	pancreatitis	10	—
49 M	heart	acute cholecystitis with common bile duct obstruction	15	cholecystectomy
		subhepatic abscess	32	drainage of perihepatic space
59 M	heart	thrombocytopenia	60	splenectomy

days following transplantation he required supportive measures including vasopressor and ventilatory support. His abdomen became distended and his WBC was 30,000. While he was undergoing further evaluation, he had a cardiac arrest and died. Autopsy showed massive small bowel infarction along with gastric and pancreatic necrosis. No portal vein thrombi were seen and the mesenteric vessels were not occluded. His disease process was possibly secondary to persistent severe hypotension, or, perhaps a large thrombus in the portal vein lysed prior to his death. This patients represents the only death due to a general surgical complication following transplantation.

The 40-year-old woman described in the case report had several general surgical complications, including peptic ulcer disease and pancreatitis. She also eventually died of multiple organ system failure.

A 39-year-old woman developed gastric atony following heart-lung transplantation. She was unable to tolerate any oral intake and her x-rays showed a distended stomach. Pyloroplasty was performed 1 month postoperatively and she recovered without incident.

Following heart transplantation, a 49-year-old man developed gastrointestinal bleeding. Upper gastrointestinal endoscopy showed two gastric ulcers. He had been receiving antacid therapy in the immediate postoperative period and, therefore, the dosages were increased and the interval shortened. He responded well and has had no further evidence of bleeding.

Three patients had postoperative pancreatitis. One patient's clinical course has already been discussed. The second patient was a 57-year-old man who developed abdominal pain and an elevated level of amylase on the fifth postoperative day. This episode rapidly resolved only to recur several times over the next 6 months. He was hospitalized many times for abdominal pain and had an extensive workup. The ultrasound of the gallbladder on occasion showed "sludge." His course was then complicated by non-A–non-B hepatitis. Because of his multiple admissions for mild pancreatitis and the questionable ultrasound, he underwent endoscopic retrograde cholangiopancreatography (ERCP). He continued to have exacerbations of pancreatitis. Repeat ultrasound did not show stones but, because of the recurrent episodes of pancreatitis, thought to be unrelated to medications, he underwent cholecystectomy. The gallbladder did not contain stones but the bile culture showed 4+ *Klebsiella pneumoniae,* which was treated with a course of antibiotics. The patient continued to have periodic admissions for abdominal pain but gradually improved.

The third patient was a 50-year-old man who developed pancreatitis on the 10th post-transplant day. Resolution occurred by the third postoperative week, with no subsequent episodes. Ultrasound showed gallstones and, because of right upper quadrant abdominal pain, he underwent an uneventful cholecystectomy 1 year following transplant.

Postoperative cholecystitis occurred in only one patient. On the 14th postoperative day, a 49-year-old man developed obstructive jaundice and abdominal pain. Cholecystectomy and common bile duct exploration showed acute cholecystitis and common duct stones. The patient was discharged 2 weeks later. Six days after discharge, he was readmitted with a common bile duct leak and subhepatic abscess. Reexploration of the perihepatic space was performed, with drainage of subhepatic space. The postoperative course was prolonged.

Another patient developed thrombocytopenia in the second postoperative month. He required periodic gamma globulin injections which were followed by a rise in the platelet count to 50,000 to 60,000, but these increases were short-lived. Ten months after transplantation a splenectomy was performed. Platelet counts dramatically increased and have remained in the normal range 1 year after splenectomy.

In summary, 8 of 75 patients had nine complications that were directly related to their transplant (11%). There were two deaths in this group, only one of which was related to the general surgical complication.

General Surgical Disease After Thoracic Transplantation

Eight patients (11%) developed general surgical disease following their transplants (Table 2). Three had signs and symptoms of cholecystitis from 10 months to 1 year following transplantation. All had biliary colic but they did not have an acute illness, and all underwent elective cholecystectomy without complication.

A 49-year-old man had a heart transplant in May 1987. Almost 2 years later the patient began to experience difficulty in swallowing. Upper gastrointestinal endoscopy showed a stricture at the gastroesophageal junction, which was biopsied. The pathology was signet ring cell adenocarcinoma. An esophagogastrectomy through a combined abdominal and thoracic approach was performed. His postoperative course was uncomplicated. Two of seven lymph nodes were involved with metastatic adenocarcinoma. Seven months postoperative, the patient shows no evidence of recurrent disease.

Four patients had minor general surgical problems. A 60-year-old woman had microcalcifications on a mammography and had a benign breast biopsy. A 46-year-old man had a perirectal abscess drained without complication. A 51-year-old

TABLE 2.   General Surgical Diseases Occurring After Thoracic Transplantation

Age/Sex	Transplant	Diagnosis	Onset (Postop day)	Procedure
50 M	heart	chronic cholecystitis, cholelithiasis	365	cholecystectomy
59 F	heart	gallstone, pancreatitis, cholelithiasis	306	ERCP, cholecystectomy
50 F	heart	cholecystitis, cholelithiasis	365	cholecystectomy
60 F	heart	breast fibroadenoma	*	breast biopsy
46 M	heart	rectal abscess	252	flexible sigmoidoscopy
51 M	heart	bilateral inguinal hernia	*	bilateral inguinal hernia repair
59 M	heart	adenomatous polyp	*	colonoscopy and polypectomy
49 M	heart	cancer of gastro-esophageal junction	526	esophagogastrectomy, pyloroplasty, feeding jejunostomy

* Denotes a pre-transplant condition.

man had bilateral inguinal hernia repair without complications 6 months after transplantation. A 51-year-old man had a benign colonic polyp removed endoscopically. No further treatment was recommended.

Nonsurgical Diseases Requiring Surgical Evaluation

A special category of patients requiring general surgical evaluation are those who have cytomegalovirus (CMV) infection involving the gastrointestinal tract (Table 3). Nine patients presented with symptoms of abdominal pain, fever, chills, and general malaise. Most of the patients were evaluated by the general surgical service because of crampy mid-abdominal pain. The onset of symptoms was 19 to 62 days (average 42 days) following transplantation. They did not show signs of an acute surgical abdomen. Evaluation included endoscopy of either the upper (8 patients) or lower gastrointestinal tract (1 patient). Confirmation of CMV infection was made through identified viral inclusions on tissue biopsy (8 patients) or positive CMV culture (1 patient).

TABLE 3.   Nonsurgical Diseases Requiring General Surgical Evaluation: CMV Disease of the Gastrointestinal Tract

Age/Sex	Transplant	CMV location	Onset (Postop day)	Duration of Glanciclovir (days)
59 M	heart	stomach	50	3
59 M	heart	stomach, duodenum	45	4
51 M	heart	stomach, duodenum	46	28
54 M	heart	stomach, blood	19	14
61 M	heart	stomach	62	35
29 M	heart	stomach, duodenum	42	14
41 M	heart	stomach	45	14
47 M	double lung	stomach	27	14
61 F	heart	stomach, colon	45	28

Seven patients received ganciclovir (DHPG) for 14 days and three patients received additional therapy for failure to improve after the first treatment. Ganciclovir was discontinued when signs of bone marrow toxicity occurred after 4 days of therapy in one patient, and after 3 days in another. There were no long-term complications related to ganciclovir therapy for CMV infection in this group.

DISCUSSION

The true incidence of post-transplant general surgical complications directly related to transplantation in this series is 11%. The incidence of general surgical diseases in patients after transplantation not directly related to the transplant is 11%. Patients who require general surgical evaluation but have nonsurgical complications of transplantation have CMV gastrointestinal ulceration for the most part (12%). It is important that the general surgeon be consulted in these latter cases, because complications may occur which require surgical intervention.[1,2,3,6]

Villar[8] reported seven patients (4%) requiring emergency operations for general surgical complications following transplantation. The mortality of the group was 71%. Other series have reported a high mortality with emergency operations performed in the early post-transplant period.[4,5,7] We had no postoperative deaths following general surgical procedures, either emergency or elective. However, we did not in turn see the type of complications for which a higher mortality would be expected, i.e., perforated peptic ulcer, perforated diverticulitis, hemorrhagic pancreatitis.

The operative mortality for elective general surgical cases following transplantation is low and may eventually approach the operative mortality in normal age-matched groups. The use of cyclosporine and the rapid reduction in dosages of corticosteroids used following transplant has had a major impact on the incidence and mortality of complications that were heretofore commonplace.

The classification of patients into three groups requiring general surgical evaluation is useful. The 11% incidence of actual transplant-related general surgical complications in our series was relatively low. If the same classification were used for other similarly reported series, the incidence of general surgical complications would also be low, thus giving a true post-transplant complication rate. The incidence of other general surgical diseases in the transplant population is worth noting, because this knowledge could potentially change the manner in which we treat these patients. For example, patients with symptomatic cholelithiasis are usually encouraged to have cholecystectomy to prevent the complications of calculous biliary tract disease. Should asymptomatic patients be treated in the same manner? Thus far, it would seem reasonable to treat transplant patients with asymptomatic cholelithiasis in the same manner as the normal population without symptoms. The incidence of late complications has not been reported to be any higher in the transplant patient population.

The question of pre-transplant cholecystectomy arises with the symptomatic patient undergoing evaluation for transplant. The degree of symptomatology and the cardiac condition of the patient must be considered together to arrive at an appropriate decision. We have performed cholecystectomy in a patient who had daily biliary colic for 2 weeks and who was otherwise an acceptable cardiac transplant candidate. He underwent cholecystectomy without incident. Three days postoperatively his cardiac status worsened and he required intra-aortic balloon assistance for 2 weeks before cardiac transplantation. However, other patients who did not have current symptoms but had been symptomatic in the past did not have pre-transplant cholecystectomy. They later had an elective cholecystectomy without complication.

Another option now available for treating patients with gallstone pancreatitis is ERCP and sphincterotomy. We used this procedure in the early post-transplant period in two patients, the advantage being that pancreatitis usually resolves and the common bile duct stone is removed. Later, an elective cholecystectomy may be performed. This procedure has recently been suggested as treatment for any cause of pancreatitis, resulting in a more rapid resolution of pancreatitis.

SUMMARY

In general, surgical complications and diseases after thoracic transplantation are common. The operative mortality for emergent operations has been reported to be high, whereas the elective operative mortality is close to zero. Biliary tract and pancreas are the most common organ systems involved. An aggressive diagnostic and therapeutic approach should be taken in this group of patients to ensure an early rather than late resolution of complications.

REFERENCES

1. Alexander JA, Cuellar RE, Fadden RJ, et al: Cytomegalovirus infection of the upper gastrointestinal tract before and after liver transplantation. Transplantation 46:378, 1988.
2. Branwell NH, Davies RA, Koshal A, et al: Fatal gastrointestinal hemorrhage caused by cytomegalovirus duodenitis and ulceration after heart transplantation. J Heart Transplant 6:303, 1987.
3. Cohen EB, Komorowski RA, Kauffman HM Jr, Adams M: Unexpectedly high incidence of cytomegalovirus infection in apparent peptic ulcers in renal transplant recipients. Surgery 97:606, 1985.
4. Colon R, Frazier OH, Kahan BD, et al: Complications in cardiac transplant patients requiring general surgery. Surgery 103:32, 1988.
5. Jones MT, Menkis AH, Kostuk WJ, McKenzie FN: Management of general surgical problems after cardiac transplantation. Can J Surg 31(4):259, 1988.
6. Spender GD, Shulman HM, Myerson D, et al: Diffuse intestinal ulceration after marrow transplantation: a clinicopathologic study of 13 patients. Hum Pathol 17:621, 1986.
7. Steed DL, Brown B, Reilly JJ, et al: General surgical complications in heart and heart-lung transplantation. Surgery 98:739, 1985.
8. Villar HV, Neal DD, Levinson M, et al: Gastrointestinal complications after human transplantation and mechanical heart replacement. Am J Surg 157:168, 1989.

D.K.C. COOPER, MA, MD, PhD, FRCS

PRESENT STATUS OF CARDIAC XENOTRANSPLANTATION

Cardiothoracic Surgeon
Director of Research
  and Education
Oklahoma Transplantation
  Institute
Baptist Medical Center
Oklahoma City, Oklahoma
Formerly, Associate Professor
  of Cardiothoracic Surgery
University of Cape Town
  Medical School
Cape Town, South Africa

Reprint requests to:
D.K.C. Cooper, MD
Oklahoma Transplantation
  Institute
Baptist Medical Center
3300 N.W. Expressway
Oklahoma City, OK 73112

There are insufficient numbers of donor organs for the needs of transplant programs. Although a mechanical device might conceivably solve the problem of heart transplantation in this respect, it is unlikely that an implantable device will be developed within the foreseeable future to take the place of such organs as the liver and kidney. An obvious answer to the donor shortage is the use of animal organs. With regard to the heart, there are several animals that would be anatomically suitable. An animal heart would have many advantages over a mechanical device. The need for anticoagulation and the risk of either hemorrhage or thromboemboli would be avoided, there would be no risk of microorganisms causing infection by entering the body via percutaneous power lines, and there would, of course, be no risk of mechanical failure.

The immune response, however, to a xenograft is known to be more aggressive than that to an allograft, and this has proved to be a formidable problem to overcome. The introduction of cyclosporine, by improving the results of allografting and thus accentuating the need for a markedly increased donor supply, has stimulated surgeons to look anew at the possibilities of xenotransplantation.

ARE XENOGRAFTS LIKELY TO WORK?

At the present time, the answer to this question would seem to be largely dependent on what animal is chosen as the donor for man. Calne has suggested that xenografts can be

CARDIAC SURGERY: State of the Art Reviews—Vol. 3, No. 3, October 1989
Philadelphia, Hanley & Belfus, Inc.

661

divided into two major groups: those that are *concordant* (where rejection will be by a cellular mechanism similar to that seen after allografting), and those that are *discordant* (where rejection will be by a vascular, or hyperacute, mechanism similar to that seen when allografting is carried out in a sensitized host.[4] Transplantation between two closely related animal species, e.g., chimpanzee to man, would be expected to be concordant, although this is not always so, and that between distantly related animals, e.g., pig to man, to be discordant. The present evidence is that concordant xenotransplants might well function satisfactorily with the currently available pharmacologic immunosuppressive agents, but that discordant xenografts would certainly fail within minutes or hours of transplantation.

CLINICAL EXPERIENCE WITH XENOTRANSPLANTATION OF SOLID ORGANS

Even before cyclosporine was introduced, there was a small experience with the use of primate organs in man. Reemtsma and colleagues carried out a series of xenograft kidney transplants using the chimpanzee as a donor, with graft survival in one patient for 9 months.[19,20] Maintenance immunosuppressive therapy was with azathioprine and corticosteroids only. This clinical trial was performed at a time before cadaver kidney transplants had been introduced, when there was little alternative for the patient in end-stage renal disease. Starzl had a rather less successful experience using the baboon as donor,[28] and also carried out a small number of liver transplants using the chimpanzee;[10,27] function was obtained for short periods of time.

A chimpanzee heart was transplanted by Hardy but proved too small to support the circulation,[12] and chimpanzee and baboon hearts were transplanted in the heterotopic position by Barnard without long-term success.[13] More recently, Bailey and colleagues transplanted a baboon heart into a neonate with survival for 21 days.[2]

Clinical experience with discordant xenografts has been extremely limited in recent years (although there were several attempts in the early part of this century), but a sheep heart transplanted by Cooley in 1968 was rejected hyperacutely (i.e., by vascular, humoral, or antibody-mediated rejection rather than by cellular rejection),[5] as were pig hearts transplanted by Ross and Longmore in 1968 (D.B. Longmore, personal communication).

From this small clinical experience it would seem that if the chimpanzee is used as a donor for man, and immunosuppression is with the currently available drugs, there is a reasonable chance that transplantation would be successful for some weeks or months. This would at least allow the chimpanzee heart to be used in the heterotopic position as a bridge to allotransplantation. Such a clinical policy was considered by the Columbia University group (E.A. Rose, personal communication), but was not implemented due to the extreme shortage of chimpanzees as experimental animals; the likely controversy that such a policy would arouse in sections of the general public opposed to the use of animals in this way was also considered.

If a lower primate such as the baboon were to be used as donor, the chances of success would seem less likely, confirming the wider phylogenetic distance between this species and man.[26] The use of an animal other than a primate would almost certainly be doomed to immediate failure, unless some new method of preventing hyperacute rejection were introduced.

TABLE 1. Selected Results of Cardiac Transplantation from Cynomolgus Monkey to Baboon (Columbia University, New York)*

Group	n	Graft Survival (Days)
		(Mean +/- SD)
1. No IS (control)	9	7 (+/- 3)
2. CYA, MP	6	77 (+/- 67)
3. CYA, AZA, MP	7	61 (+/- 48)
4. CYA, AZA	6	77 (+/- 68)
5. CYA, AZA, MP, ATG	5	81 (+/- 22)
6. Transfusion, CYA	10	42 (+/- 61)

* Modified from Reemtsma et al.[21]
SD = standard deviation; IS = immunosuppressive therapy; CYA = cyclosporine; MP = methylprednisolone; AZA = azathioprine; ATG = rabbit anti-baboon thymocyte globulin; Transfusion = pretransplant blood transfusion.

RECENT EXPERIMENTAL EXPERIENCE

Cardiac Xenotransplantation Between Closely Related Animal Species

In recent years there have been two extensive studies of cardiac xenotransplantation between closely related primates (Tables 1 and 2). In the first, at Columbia University in New York, the baboon was used as recipient and the cynomolgus monkey as donor, a concordant relationship (Table 1).[3,21,24,25] These studies showed almost uniform, greatly prolonged survival of the grafted hearts when transplanted in the heterotopic position (in the neck) and with immunosuppression of the host by a combination of currently available drugs. Of great interest, but of some disappointment, was the observation that when the hearts were transplanted into the orthotopic position, survival times were significantly reduced.[25] The explanation for this fact is not clear, but possibly the need for the heart to perform a significant amount of work in the orthotopic position contributed to early failure when rejection intervened; in contrast, the nonworking heart in the neck could continue functioning for prolonged periods.

TABLE 2. Selected Results of Cardiac Transplantation from African Green (Vervet) Monkey to Baboon (University of Cape Town Medical School, Cape Town, South Africa)

Group		n	Graft Survival (Days)
			(Mean +/- SD)
1. No IS (control)		9	10 (+/- 5)
2. ABO-incomp.; no IS		9	7 (+/- 6)
3. CYA, AZA, MP		6	13 (+/- 8)
4. ABO-incomp.; CYA AZA, MP		5	11 (+/- 11)
5. CYA, AZA, MP	IV MP	5	19 (+/- 22)
6. CYA, AZA, MP, RATG	therapy for	6	43 (+/- 19)
7. 15-DS, CYA, AZA, MP	rejection	7	20 (+/- 12)
8. 15-DS, CYA, MP	episodes	5	36 (+/- 14)
9. TLI, CYA, AZA, MP		5	16 (+/- 10)
10. ABO-incomp.; TLI, CYA, AZA, MP		5	18 (+/- 11)

ABO-incomp. = donor and recipient incompatible for ABO blood group; RATG = rabbit anti-human thymocyte globulin; 15-DS = 15-deoxyspergualin; TLI = total lymphoid irradiation; other abbreviations as in Table 1.

The fact that vascular (hyperacute) rejection was never seen in this model was also of interest, as the cynomolgus monkey is phylogenetically rather more distantly related to the baboon than is the African green (vervet) monkey that was used in the other extensive study, performed at the University of Cape Town Medical School; in this latter study histopathologic features of vascular rejection were seen in 50–80% of the transplants.[7-9,22,23]

In the vervet to baboon model, the results of xenotransplantation were less successful (Table 2). Despite maintenance immunosuppressive therapy, a significant number of hearts failed in the early days following transplantation.[8,9] Intensive immunsuppression, with treatment of acute rejection episodes by bolus methylprednisolone, extended graft survival further, but was associated with high morbidity and mortality.[22,23] Similarly, the addition of pre-transplant total lymphoid irradiation extended graft survival, but was again related to an unacceptable mortality.[7] The Cape Town study would act as a warning that, following xenografting, even between closely related animal species, the risk of vascular or mixed (vascular and cellular) rejection remains significant.

In the "Baby Fae" (baboon to infant) case referred to earlier,[2] there was some evidence that ABO-blood group antibodies played a significant role in the rejection process, but the Cape Town study would indicate that the anti-species antibodies (e.g., anti-African green monkey) play a more significant role in inducing rejection than do the anti-ABO blood group antibodies.[8,9]

Cardiac Xenotransplantation Between Distantly Related Animal Species

Recent laboratory experience with discordant xenografts is more limited, although several studies were reported in the early 1970s. In this model, hyperacute vascular rejection occurs inevitably, and, to date, no totally successful preventive method has been developed. The most likely methods of blocking hyperacute rejection would appear to be by pre- and post-transplant plasmapheresis or antibody adsorption.[6,11,14,16,18,31] Plasma exchange was investigated extensively in the 1970s, with prolongation of graft function from a few minutes to several hours, but the period of graft survival remained too short to be of clinical value. Studies investigating the efficacy of antibody adsorption have shown similar short-term prolongation of function.

Of interest in this respect is the experience of Alexandre and his group with clinical kidney *allo*transplantation across the ABO-blood group barrier.[1] They have achieved success by combining pre-transplant splenectomy with pre- and post-transplant plasmapheresis to remove anti-A and/or anti-B antibodies. The exact role of splenectomy remains uncertain but would appear to be an important part of this therapy. At present, several groups are exploring the role of plasmapheresis with and without splenectomy as a means of removing species-specific antibodies. Alexandre and colleagues have shown that, even if anti-A or anti-B antibodies return after transplantation, their presence is not always associated with the development of vascular or cellular rejection. Several renal grafts have functioned satisfactorily for some years in the presence of high antibody titers. It is hoped that this technique, or some modification of it, might bring success with xenotransplants.

A sophistication would be to remove only those antibodies that are essential in inducing vascular rejection, although it is still not absolutely certain that an antigen-antibody reaction is essential for hyperacute rejection to occur, as there are some data that in discordant species hyperacute rejection develops from primary activation of the alternative complement pathway.[15] Plasmapheresis removes all antibodies from the circulating blood, but a refinement would be to remove only the anti-species antibodies, possibly by passing the plasma through a column of tissue presenting the species antigen (e.g., pig myocardium), in order to adsorb the species-specific antibody (anti-pig) out of the blood. This result has been achieved by passing the blood through another donor-specific organ (e.g., the kidney) before performing heart transplantation. In the pig-to-baboon model,[6] survival of a pig heart has been prolonged from 3 hours (control) to 4 days when prior antibody adsorption had been carried out using the same pig's kidneys. Further antibodies are produced, however, and repeated adsorption by this method results in sensitization.

Both plasmapheresis[29] and extracorporeal immunoadsorption with staphylococcus protein A[17] have been used successfully to remove HLA antibodies from the blood of highly sensitized patients needing renal allotransplantation. When coupled with pre- or post-transplant immunosuppressive therapy, resynthesis of the antibodies can be successfully prevented, allowing long-term survival of renal allografts. A modification of this technique may result in successful xenotransplantation.

If suppression of anti-species antibody production does not provide the entire answer to the problem of xenografting, then the answer almost certainly lies somewhere within the complement system, which clearly plays an important role in the destruction of xenogeneic tissues. A means of inhibiting the complement cascade is clearly needed, and one possible method by which this might be achieved is by the use of monoclonal antibodies directed toward certain key receptor sites in the cascade.

Even if hyperacute rejection could be overcome following xenografting, it would seem likely that acute rejection would subsequently intervene, but it is hoped that the presently available pharmacologic agents might be successful in preventing or reversing such episodes. Graft atherosclerosis (chronic rejection) might prove to be a limiting factor more difficult to overcome.[21]

COMMENTS

Several problems remain unexplored or unresolved. Among them is the problem of cross-species antibodies. If a chimpanzee or pig heart is transplanted into man as a bridge to maintain life until an allograft is found, will antibodies develop against the donor cells that will cross-react with man and prevent a suitable human donor from being found? The present evidence is that such antibodies will not cross-react (E.A. Rose, personal communication).

It is known that primates can harbor viruses that might cause serious symptomatic disease in man, especially in an immunosuppressed individual. In particular, the lymphotropic retroviruses, which include viruses associated with immunodeficiency syndromes, are known to be carried by certain primates in the wild. Studies by the Cape Town group have shown that there is a lower incidence of such viruses in colony-bred animals than in wild-caught animals,[30] and therefore it is anticipated that this problem could be overcome by breeding programs. Pigs and other more domesticated animals would appear to be less likely to carry organisms that might prove fatal to man.

REFERENCES

1. Alexandre GPJ, Squifflet JP, De Bruyere M, et al: Present experiences in a series of 26 ABO-incompatible living donor renal allografts. Transplant Proc 19:4538, 1987.
2. Bailey LL, Nehlsen-Cannarella SL, Concepcion W, Jolley WB: Baboon-to-human cardiac xenotransplantation in a neonate. JAMA 254:3321, 1985.
3. Barnard CN, Wolpowitz A, Losman JG: Heterotopic cardiac transplantation with a xenograft for assistance of the left heart in cardiogenic shock after cardiopulmonary bypass. S Afr Med J 52:1035, 1977.
4. Calne RY: Organ transplantation between widely disparate species. Transplant Proc 2:550, 1970.
5. Cooley DA, Hallman GL, Bloodwell RD et al: Human heart transplantation: Experience with 12 cases. Am J Cardiol 22:804, 1968.
6. Cooper DKC, Human PA, Lexer G, et al: The effects of cyclosporine and antibody adsorption on pig cardiac xenograft survival in the baboon. J Heart Transplant 7:238, 1988.
7. Cooper DKC, Human PA, Reichart B: Prolongation of cardiac xenograft (vervet monkey to baboon) function by a combination of total lymphoid irradiation and immunosuppressive drug therapy. Transplant Proc 19:4441, 1987.
8. Cooper DKC, Human PA, Rose AG, et al: Can cardiac allografts and xenografts be transplanted across the ABO blood group barrier? Transplant Proc 21:549, 1989.
9. Cooper DKC, Human PA, Rose AG, et al: The role of ABO blood group compatibility in heart transplantation between closely related animal species: An experimental study using the vervet monkey to baboon cardiac xenograft model. J Thorac Cardiovasc Surg 97:447, 1989.
10. Giles GR, Boehmig HJ, Amemiya H, et al: Clinical heterotransplantation of the liver. Transplant Proc 2:506, 1970.
11. Giles GR, Boehmig HJ, Lilley J, et al: Mechanism and modification of rejection of heterografts between divergent species. Transplant Proc 2:522, 1970.
12. Hardy JD, Chavez CM, Kurrus FD, et al: Heart transplantation in man: Developmental studies and report of a case. JAMA 188:1132, 1964.
13. Kurlansky PA, Sadeghi AM, Michler RE, et al: Comparable survival of intra-species and cross-species primate cardiac transplants. Transplant Proc 19:1067, 1987.
14. Merkel FK, Bier M, Beavers CD, et al: Modification of xenograft response by selective plasmapheresis. Transplant Proc 3:534, 1971.
15. Miyagama S, Hirose H, Sirakura R, et al: The mechanism of discordant xenograft rejection. Transplant Proc 21:520, 1989.
16. Mozes MF, Gewurz H, Gunnarson A, et al: Xenograft rejection by dog and man: Isolated kidney perfusion with blood and plasma. Transplant Proc 3:531, 1971.
17. Palmer A, Taube DH, Welsh KI, et al: Removal of anti-HLA antibodies by extracorporeal immunoadsorption to enable renal transplantation. Lancet 1:10, 1989.
18. Perper RJ, Najarian JS: Experimental renal heterotransplantation. I. In widely divergent species. Transplantation 4:377, 1966.
19. Reemtsma K: Renal heterotransplantation from non-human primates to man. Ann NY Acad Sci 162:412, 1969.
20. Reemtsma K, McKracken BH, Schlegel JU, et al: Renal heterotransplantation in man. Ann Surg 160:384, 1964.
21. Reemtsma K, Pierson RN, Marboe CC, et al: Will atherosclerosis limit clinical xenografting? Transplant Proc 19:108, 1987.
22. Reichenspurner H, Human PA, Boehm DM, et al: Optimalization of immunosuppression after xenogeneic heart transplantation in primates. J Heart Transplant In press.
23. Rose AG, Cooper DKC, Human PA, et al: Histopathology of hyperacute rejection of the heart: Experimental and clinical observations in allografts and xenografts. J Heart Transplant, in press.
24. Sadeghi AM, Robbins RC, Smith CR, et al: Cardiac xenograft survival in baboons treated with cyclosporine in combination with conventional immunosuppression. Transplant Proc 19:1149, 1987.
25. Sadeghi AM, Robbins RC, Smith CR, et al: Cardiac xenotransplantation in primates. J Thorac Cardiovasc Surg 93:809, 1987.
26. Sarich VM: The origin of the hominids: An immunological approach. In Washburn SL, Jay PC (eds): Perspectives on Human Evolution. New York, Holt, Rhinehart and Winston, 1968, p. 94.
27. Starzl TE, Ishikawa M, Putnam CW, et al: Progress in and deterrents to orthotopic liver transplantation, with special reference to survival, resistance to hyperacute rejection, and biliary duct reconstruction. Transplant Proc 6:129, 1974.

28. Starzl TE, Marchioro TL, Peters GN, et al: Renal heterotransplantation from baboon to man: Experience with six cases. Transplantation 2:752, 1964.
29. Taube DH, Welsh KI, Kennedy LA, et al: Successful removal and prevention of resynthesis of anti-HLA antibody. Transplantation 37:254, 1984.
30. Van Der Reit F. de St J, Human PA, Cooper DKC, et al: Virological implications of the use of primates in xenotransplantation. Transplant Proc 19:4068, 1987.
31. Yashikova H, McCalmon RT, Putnam CW, et al: Attenuation of hyperacute xenograft rejection in unmodified hosts by extracorporeal plasma perfusion. Transplantation 24:78, 1977.

INDEX

Page numbers in **boldface** type indicate complete chapters.